THEORIES OF TRANSLATION

T0385957

THEORIES OF TRANSLATION

An Anthology of Essays
from Dryden to Derrida

Edited by
RAINER SCHULTE
and
JOHN BIGUENET

THE UNIVERSITY OF CHICAGO PRESS
CHICAGO AND LONDON

The University of Chicago Press, Chicago 60637
The University of Chicago Press, Ltd., London
© 1992 by The University of Chicago
All rights reserved. Published 1992
Printed and bound by CPI Group (UK) Ltd, Croydon, CR0 4YY

19 18 17 16 15 14 13 12 11   6 7 8 9 10

ISBN (cloth): 978-0-226-0 4870-3
ISBN (paper): 978-0-226-0 4871-0

Library of Congress Cataloging-in-Publication Data

Theories of translation : an anthology of essays from Dryden
  to Derrida / edited by Rainer Schulte and John Biguenet.
    p.   cm.
  Companion vol. to: The craft of translation.
  Includes bibliographical references.
  ISBN 978-0-226-04870-3 —ISBN 978-0-226-04871-0
  (pbk.)
  1. Translating and interpreting—History.   I. Schulte,
  Rainer, 1937–   .   II. Biguenet. John.
  P306.T453   1992
  418'.02'09—dc20   91-22882
                                                 CIP

⊗ The paper used in this publication meets the minimum
requirements of the American National Standard for
Information Sciences—Permanence of Paper for Printed
Library Materials, ANSI Z39.48-1992.

CONTENTS

INTRODUCTION

The act of translation and the reflection upon its function and usefulness for literary studies in general are an important, and often controversial, aspect of the tradition of Western literature. Many writers and scholars of the past and present have practiced the art of translation, and their practice prompted them to give expression to their insights into the translation process. While most of these writers left a legacy of considerable distinction as translators, they have held differing views on the possibilities and impossibilities of literary translation. However, a study of the various theoretical concepts either drawn from or brought to the practice of translation can provide entrance into the mechanisms that, through the art of translation, make crosscultural communication and understanding possible.

The only texts included in this collection that, chronologically speaking, fall outside the nineteenth and twentieth centuries are the excerpts from John Dryden. Already in his time, he mapped the diverse streams of translational thinking, streams that forged the guidelines for the discussions of more recent times. Some of his formulations have become all too familiar to those who have launched themselves, successfully or unsuccessfully, into the practice of translation. Dryden refers to his translation activities as "the disease of translation." He knows "that a man should be a nice critic in his mother-tongue before he attempts to translate a foreign language." He summarizes the translator's qualifications in the following manner: "The qualification of a translator worth reading must be a mastery of the language he translates out of, and that he translates into; but if a deficiency be to be allowed in either, it is in the original, since if he be but master enough of the tongue of his author as to be master of his sense, it is possible for him to express that sense with eloquence in his own, if he have a thorough command of that."

Naturally, translation theories of the last two hundred years need to be seen in a historical context. They were not born ex nihilo. After all, they bring together the dynamics of thought dialogues, and of the heated discussions concerning the impact and usefulness of translation practices. In order to give the reader a sense of translation history, this anthology opens with Hugo Friedrich's outline of the major translation attitudes from the Romans to the present. His essay entitled "On the Art of Translation," originally delivered as a speech in 1965, crystallizes some of the major

1

ideas that have shaped translation thinking throughout the centuries. His remarks are valuable not only for their clear assessment of historical perspectives that have modified theories of translation in the past, but also for summarizing early in his essay all those questions that have become the major concerns of translators and scholars working in the field of translation studies.

Friedrich begins his historical overview of translation theories with the Roman Empire. During that time translation meant incorporating subject matters of the foreign culture into the language of one's own culture without paying particular attention to lexical or stylistic characteristics of the original source-language texts. For the Romans, translating literary and philosophical works meant looting those elements from Greek culture that would enhance the aesthetic dimensions of their own culture. Whether a translation accurately transmitted the linguistic and semantic meanings of the original did not appear to be a primary concern of the translator. Cicero proclaimed that he was translating ideas and their forms and was therefore less interested in a word-for-word rendering of the original-language text.

Saint Jerome, the famous translator of the Greek bible into Latin, strongly favors Cicero's view. In Saint Jerome's eyes, the translator conquers the concepts of another language without necessarily transferring the words that expressed these concepts in the original language. Once again, translation meant expropriating ideas and insights from another culture to enrich one's own language. Saint Jerome also saw himself in competition with the original text, and the goal was to supersede the foreign text, since the translator had the ability and the freedom to make the translation better than the original.

If the appropriation of content appeared to be the major concern of translators during the Roman Empire, translators during the Renaissance period explored the possibilities of how linguistic structures from another language could enrich their own. Translators saw no necessity to move toward the original, but rather assessed the foreignness of the source-language text in terms of its revitalizing power for their own language. Thus, the translators in both the Roman Empire and the Renaissance considered the act of translation a rigorous exploitation of the original in order to enhance the linguistic and aesthetic dimensions of their own language. Whether a translation distorted the meanings inherent in the original text was of minor concern to the translator.

That attitude toward translation—translation seen as the exploitation of the original source-language text—underwent a dramatic change in the middle of the eighteenth century. Translators and writers began to see other languages as equals and not as inferior forms of expression in comparison to their own languages. Writers like Denis Diderot and D'Alembert, among others, are responsible for initiating these changes. Respect for the foreign in the original source-language text emerges as a guiding principle, and with that change of perspective, a desire to adjust and adapt to the foreign.

This sense of responsibility toward the foreign in the original text continues as a strong undercurrent of nineteenth- and twentieth-century theoretical outlooks on the art and craft of translation. The present anthology covers some of the major documents of that development from the early nineteenth century to contemporary theories of translation. A steady expansion of writings on the theory of translation has taken place from the nineteenth into the twentieth century. Wilhelm von Humboldt, Friedrich Nietzsche, Johann Wolfgang von Goethe, Matthew Arnold, and Arthur Schopenhauer, among others, intensified the dialogue about the art and craft of translation in the nineteenth century. Walter Benjamin and José Ortega y Gasset carried their heritage into the twentieth century. Some of them formulated their ideas in the form of complete essays (e.g., Friedrich Schleiermacher in "On the Different Methods of Translating" and Walter Benjamin in "The Task of the Translator"); others chose the forum of the introduction to their own translations to expand on their theoretical views (e.g., Wilhelm von Humboldt's introduction to "Agamemnon," Dante Gabriel Rossetti's preface to *The Early Italian Poets,* and Paul Valéry's "Variations on the Eclogues").

Even though these writers accept the basic premise of moving the translation toward the original text, their theoretical comments refine different aspects of the translation process in the transferral of texts from one language to another.

Wilhelm von Humboldt emphasizes fidelity to the whole of the text rather than its parts and details. Fidelity cannot be found in literalness, but rather in adequate equivalencies from one language to another. Humboldt's outlook finds reaffirmation in Arthur Schopenhauer's comments on equivalencies: "Not every word in one language has an exact equivalent in another. Thus, not all concepts that are expressed through the words of one language are exactly the same as the ones that are expressed through the words of another." The problem of equivalencies is even more delicate and problematic in the realm of poetic expressions. Here, according to Schopenhauer, equivalents are not possible: "Poems cannot be translated, they can only be rewritten, which is always quite an ambiguous undertaking."

However, that recognition leads to another important insight. Since exact equivalents cannot be established for the transferral of poetic texts, the reader/translator can get closer to the original source-language text through the existence of multiple translations. Humboldt welcomed the idea of multiple translations. The various perspectives created by different translators of the same text offer readers the opportunity to enter deeper into the essence of a given poem or prose piece. Humboldt writes: "Furthermore, readers of a national language who cannot read the classics in the original will get to know them better through multiple translations rather than just one translation." The importance of multiple translations as a form of seeing and understanding was to become a major concern of nineteenth- and twentieth-century theoretical thinking in the field of translation studies.

Clearly, these ways of thinking emphasize the necessity to take the translator toward the foreign text. The foreignness of the text should be maintained as completely as possible in the transferral from the original language into the translated language. August Wilhelm Schlegel writes: "I have tried to render the nature of the original according to the impression it made on me. To try to smooth it over or to embellish it would be to destroy it."

Matthew Arnold, whose essay "On Translating Homer" could not be included in the present collection because of its excessive length, represents a continuation and intensification of the ideas and aesthetic views promoted by Humboldt and Schlegel. Because of Arnold's important contribution to the field of translation theory, it is necessary to highlight the major points of his essay. Arnold thinks through the intricate relationships that exist between translator and original text. He elaborates on his own translation theories by discussing various translations of Homer's work. The nature of the impact of Homer's work cannot be reconstructed by the contemporary reader/translator. Thus, to expect the contemporary reader to react to Homer's work the way Homer's audience did in his time would be futile. Translators have to interact with Homer from their own frame of mind; it is their response to the

Homeric texts that gives shape to the perspectives of their translations.

> No one can tell him [the translator] how Homer affected the Greeks; but there are those who can tell him how Homer affects *them*. Those are scholars, who possess, at the same time with knowledge of Greek, adequate poetical taste and feeling. No translation will seem to them of much worth compared with the original; but they alone can say whether the translation produces more or less the same effect upon them as the original. . . . Let not the translator, then, trust to his notions of what the ancient Greeks would have thought of him; he will lose himself in the vague. Let him not trust to what the ordinary English reader thinks of him; he will be taking the blind for his guide. Let him not trust to his own judgment of his own work; he may be misled by individual caprices. Let him ask how his work affects those who both know Greek and can appreciate poetry.

Arnold's inclusion of scholarship as a major component in the act of translation coincides with Schlegel's desire to establish a union of translator and literary scholar, of recreative artist and universally educated savant. It is the scholar who can guarantee a certain precision and accuracy with respect to the translation and, therefore, one should study the effect that the Greek text has on the scholar and how the scholar approaches the text in order to gain a fuller understanding of it. Arnold continues:

> [The translator] is to try to satisfy *scholars*, because scholars alone have the means of really judging him. A scholar may be a pedant, it is true, and then his judgment will be worthless; but a scholar may also have poetical feeling, and then he can judge him truly; whereas all the poetical feeling in the world will not enable a man who is not a scholar to judge him truly. For the translator is to reproduce Homer, and the scholar alone has the means of knowing that Homer who is to be reproduced. He knows him but imperfectly, for he is separated from him by time, race, and language; but he alone knows him at all.

This notion of the necessary relationship between scholar and translator has become an important issue for the theory and practice of translation in the twentieth century.

Arnold also reaffirms Schopenhauer's views of equivalencies. Arnold thinks that the process of translation must recreate the manner and movement of a poet or a text rather than looking for exact equivalencies for each word. And, like Humboldt, he con-

ceived of the text as a whole rather than just the individual details. Arnold writes:

> To suppose that it is *fidelity* to an original to give its matter, unless you at the same time give its manner; or, rather, to suppose that you can really give its matter at all, unless you can give its manner, is just the mistake of our pre-Raphaelite school of painters, who do not understand that the peculiar effect of nature resides in the whole and not in the parts. So the peculiar effect of a poet resides in his manner and movement, not in his words taken separately.

The idea that the translator should try to reproduce the totality of the original source-language text in the translated language has shaped the theory and practice of translation from the nineteenth century into the twentieth. Perhaps the only major exception to that practice is Nabokov, who maintains that only a literal translation, a word-for-word translation, is a valid one.

While writers like Humboldt, Schlegel, and Arnold were particularly interested in illuminating the nature of the translation process, it was natural that questions concerning the methodologies of translation needed to be addressed as well. Schleiermacher went so far as to entitle his essay "On the Different Methods of Translating." Goethe crystallized his views on the different kinds of translation at the end of the *East-West Divan*. Goethe defined three kinds of translations: the simple prosaic translation, the parodistic translation in which the translator tries to appropriate only the foreign content, and the translation in which the translator tries to make the translation identical with the original.

Schleiermacher incorporated Goethe's insight into the translation process and added his now-famous comments on the relationship between reader-translator-author. "Either the translator leaves the writer alone as much as possible and moves the reader toward the writer, or he leaves the reader alone as much as possible and moves the writer toward the reader." These ideas and attitudes are later taken up by Walter Benjamin and José Ortega y Gasset.

The boundaries around the field of translation studies continue to expand. Concerns about the immediate reality of transplanting a text from one language into another lead to considerations about methods and perhaps even systems that could categorize the translation process. However, it has become clear that translational thinking is fundamental to all acts of human communication and that indeed all acts of communication are acts of translation. Thus,

it is quite natural that investigations into the nature of language, its origin and function, should constitute an integral part of translational thinking. A direct line of associations can be established between Arthur Schopenhauer, Roman Jakobson, Jacques Derrida, and Michael Riffaterre. Schopenhauer writes: "This confirms that one thinks differently in every language, that our thinking is modified and newly tinged through the learning of each foreign language, and that polyglotism is, apart from its many immediate advantages, a direct means of educating the mind by correcting and perfecting our perceptions through the emerging diversity and refinement of concepts. At the same time, polyglotism increases the flexibility of thinking since, through the learning of many languages, the concept increasingly separates itself from the word."

Jakobson insists that "languages differ essentially in what they *must* convey and not in what they *may* convey." He also continues Goethe's and Schleiermacher's traditions by classifying translation into three kinds: intralingual translation or *rewording,* interlingual translation or *translation proper,* and intersemiotic translation or *transmutation.* The latter is an interpretation of verbal signs by means of signs of nonverbal systems, e.g., from verbal art into music, dance, cinema, or painting.

Octavio Paz opens his extremely insightful essay with these words: "When we learn to speak, we are learning to translate; the child who asks his mother the meaning of a word is really asking her to translate the unfamiliar term into the simple words he already knows. In this sense, translation within the same language is not essentially different from translation between two tongues." Paz carries this idea one step further. Translation takes place between languages and within the same language, but the very medium that makes translation possible—namely language itself—is essentially a translation. "No text can be completely original because language itself, in its very essence, is already a translation: first from the nonverbal world and then because each sign and each phrase is a translation of another sign, another phrase."

In the realm of verbal expressions, Paz delineates the function of words both in a poetic and prose text. Whereas in the prose piece words tend to be "univocal," they generally retain their multiplicity of meanings in a poetic context. Here again, the emphasis is on the recognition of the plurality of meanings inherent in poetic texts. Words, their specific placement within a text, create connotations that reflect multiple ways of looking at and interpreting the

world. Thus, Paz concludes: "A plurality of languages and societies: each language is a view of the world, each civilization is a world."

Paz's concepts reverberate in Hans Erich Nossack's comments on the relationship of writing and translation. For Nossack, the act of writing a literary piece is already an act of translation: "Because writing itself is already translating." Paz sees language as the translation medium for nonverbal signs. Furthermore, through the translation process one reaches a deeper understanding of one's own language. The interaction with the words of the foreign language expands one's native language. To produce equivalencies for certain metaphors in the source language, the translator may have to find words in English that are normally not part of general usage. Thus, writers who are involved in translating enrich their own language. In the larger context then, one could say, with Nossack, that translating authors from other cultures can prevent a literature from becoming too nationalistic or too provincial.

In his effort to clarify the translatability of texts and to "come to terms with the otherness of languages," Walter Benjamin finds the impetus for his theoretical considerations on translation in Rudolf Pannwitz's study on *Die Krise der europäischen Kultur*. Pannwitz's two major concerns are the necessity to enrich one's own language through the act of translation and to move the translation toward the original source-language text. He writes:

> Our translations, even the best, proceed from a false premise. They want to germanize Hindi, Greek, English, instead of hindi-izing, grecizing, anglicizing German. They have a much greater respect for the little ways of their own language than for the spirit of the foreign work. The fundamental error of the translator is that he maintains the accidental state of his own language, instead of letting it suffer the shock of the foreign language. He must, particularly if he translates a language very remote from his own, penetrate to the ultimate elements of language itself, where word, image, tone become one; he must widen and deepen his language through the foreign one.

Yves Bonnefoy in his essay "Translating Poetry" transfers that idea also to the poetic act. The immersion of the poet as translator into the foreign work—and let us not ignore Bonnefoy's admonition: "if a work does not compel us, it is untranslatable"—refines the poet's sensibility and at the same time recreates his own poetic energy.

As language itself is a translation, the act of recreating language through the reading process constitutes another form of translation. The German philosopher Hans Georg Gadamer succinctly summarizes the essence of the act of reading in relation to the translation process. "Reading is already translation, and translation is translation for the second time. . . . The process of translating comprises in its essence the whole secret of human understanding of the world and of social communication." The notion of reading as yet another act of translation develops into a major undercurrent of translation theories in the twentieth century, culminating in the so-called reception theory, and in the statement that all acts of communication are acts of translation.

Communication can take place on several levels: the communication through the artistic creation, the communication through the reading and interpretation of texts, and the communication of texts from one language to another by transforming them through the act of translation. At all times, translation involves an act of transformation. The authors of this anthology have focused in one way or another on the delicate changes and challenges that are inherent in the transformational process of translation. They have given translation and translation studies a new importance in an age where methods of interpretation have caused a great deal of confusion and dissatisfaction in colleges and universities, where communication has become more and more fragmentary.

Two distinct impressions can be drawn from these essays: (1) the transferral of the foreign from other languages into our own allows us to explore and formulate emotions and concepts that otherwise we would not have experienced; and (2) the act of translation continuously stretches the linguistic boundaries of one's own language. In that sense, translation functions as a revitalizing force of language. Translation can foster the creation of new words in the receptor language and influence the grammatical and semantic structures of that language. In short, translation should be seen as a form of linguistic and conceptual enrichment.

Moreover, translation not only revitalizes the expressive possibilities of a language, but also the research methods by which we study the art of interpretation. The methodologies employed by the translator can become a model by which we interpret literary texts in general. Translation thinking is always concerned with the reconstruction of processes, and therefore constitutes a form of dynamic rather than static interpretation.

Thus, translation and translation research function as an organizing principle that refocuses the interpretation of a text from a content-oriented to a process-oriented way of seeing texts and situations. Disciplines have had a tendency to separate subject matters that by their very nature are intricately connected. The reconstruction of the translation process reaffirms that interconnectedness, since the problem-solving character of translation forces the translator to include a variety of disciplines and interdisciplines to respond to the specific needs of a text which make a translation possible. In that sense, translation activities are always interdisciplinary and present themselves today as an integrating force in a fragmentary and discontinuous world.

ONE

HUGO FRIEDRICH
On the Art of Translation
Translated by Rainer Schulte and John Biguenet

In a rather disturbing way, literary translations continue to be
threatened by the boundaries that exist between languages. Thus,
the art of translation will always have to cope with the reality of
untranslatability from one language to another. Actually, one could
say that, in a poetic sense, the art of translation is affected by language boundaries in proportion to the shades of subtlety of the
original and the demands translators place on themselves. Naturally, translators want to do justice to their own art by accommo-
dating the literary demands on language of the original text. Translators find themselves constantly restricted by those language
boundaries and by the pressing necessity to remain, as closely as
possible, faithful to the original text.

Even though the scope of my subject is rather limited, I would
like to outline the larger framework within which questions concerning the art of translation should be discussed: Is translation
something that concerns the cultural interaction of an entire nation
with another? Is translation just the reaction of one writer to another? Does translation resurrect and revitalize a forgotten work,
or does it just keep a work alive to satisfy tradition? Does translation distort the foreign in an old work under the pressure of specific contemporary aesthetic views? Do translators pay close attention to the differences inherent in languages or do they ignore
them? Does the translation create levels of meaning that were not
necessarily visible in the original text so that the translated text
reaches a higher level of aesthetic existence? What is the relation-

From "Zur Frage der Übersetzungskunst," delivered as a speech on July 24, 1965,
in Heidelberg and reprinted by Carl Winter Universitätsverlag, Heidelberg, 1965.

ship between translation and interpretation: when do the two meet
and when does translation follow its own laws? These are some of
the questions that fall within the larger context of literary translation.

In Europe, literary translation has been known since the age of
the Romans; translation shows how the literature and philosophy
of the Romans gained strength from their Greek models. Ennius'
attempts to transplant Greek texts into Latin were at that time still
acts of submission that caused awkward lexical Graecisms to enter
into the translations. Later, however, translation from the Greek
came to mean something else for the Romans: The appropriation
of the original without any real concern for the stylistic and linguistic idiosyncracies of the original; translation meant transformation in order to mold the foreign into the linguistic structures
of one's own culture. Latin was not violated in any form, not even
when the original text violated the structure of its own language
by deviating from normally accepted conventions through the invention of neologisms, new word associations, and unusual stylistic and syntactical creations. The theoretical underpinning of this
attitude can be found in the writings of Cicero, who, with respect
to his own translation of Demosthenes, wrote:

> I translate the ideas, their forms, or as one might say, their shapes;
> however, I translate them into a language that is in tune with our
> conventions of usage *(verbis ad nostram consuetudinem aptis)*. There-
> fore, I did not have to make a word-for-word translation but rather a
> translation that reflects the general stylistic features *(genus)* and the
> meaning *(vis)* of the foreign words." [*De optimo genere oratorum*]

During the early Christian period, Saint Jerome adopted these
sentences almost verbatim. On the occasion of his Latin translation
of the Greek Septuagint, he formulated his views on the art of
translation in a treatise (in the form of a letter addressed to Pam-
machius) entitled *De optimo genere interpretandi*. Once again it is
the target language, Latin, that dictates the rules. It "reproduces
the peculiar features of a foreign language with those features of
one's own language" *(proprietates alterius linguae suis proprietatibus
explicaret)*. A few lines later, we find the following statement by
Saint Jerome, which sounds even in his words like a declaration of
power by a Roman emperor: "The translator considers thought
content a prisoner *(quasi captivos sensus)* which he transplants into

his own language with the prerogative of a conqueror *(iure victo-ris)*." This is one of the most rigorous manifestations of Latin cultural and linguistic imperialism, which despises the foreign word as something alien but appropriates the foreign meaning in order to dominate it through the translator's own language.

Furthermore, the Romans developed another concept concerning the theory and practice of translation that can easily be seen as an extension of the one mentioned above. Translation is seen as a contest with the original text *(certamen atque aemulatio*—Quintilian). The goal is to surpass the original and, in doing so, to consider the original as a source of inspiration for the creation of new expressions in one's own language—yet, never to the degree of exaggerated deviation from common usage that might occur in the original text.

From this second type of translation—enrichment of language by surpassing the original—logically follows a third approach. This approach is based on the premise that the purpose of translation is to go beyond the appropriation of content to a releasing of those linguistic and aesthetic energies that heretofore had existed only as pure possibility in one's own language and had never been materialized before. The beginning of this premise can be traced back to Quintilian and Pliny; it was to become the dominant characteristic of European translation theories of the Renaissance. Its most striking hallmark is its effort to "enrich" *(enrichir, arricchire, aumentar)*. Again, one does not move toward the original in this case. The original is brought over in order to reveal the latent stylistic possibilities in one's own language that are different from the original.

Perhaps the most striking example of this way of thinking about translation theory is the rendering into French by Malherbe of the Lucilius letters of Seneca at the turn of the seventeenth century. Hardly anything remains of Seneca's stylistic features. His short unconnected sentences with their somewhat idealistic laconicisms are dissolved and transformed into a totally different style that until then had been unknown or little known in French literature. Thus, we are confronted with the rather astounding phenomenon that, through a translation totally opposed to the spirit and the stylistic characteristics of Seneca's language, a new type of prose is introduced into modern French. Where Seneca writes short sentences that border on obscurity, where he juxtaposes his formulations almost like blocks of stone, Malherbe creates chains of sentences, conversational connections and interactions, logical sequences, and explanations of meaning. He ranks ideas according to their major and minor importance, and he repeats the same content each time in a different form. The uncertain, often chaotic, yet always colorful richness of previous French prose characteristic of writers like Rabelais, Bonaventure des Périers, and Montaigne begins to disappear and the beauty, precision, and politeness of classical French writing begins to emerge. This form of writing took root as the result of a translation in which the translator felt free not only to appropriate the content of the original texts but also to create a style in opposition to that in the source language. Thus a new style of writing emerged, of which La Bruyère was later to say that its well-balanced forms and transparency sufficed to lead to the natural creation of ideas.

The above-outlined variations on the conception of translation as an act of "carrying over" support the theory that translation is an interaction between two literatures and their respective cultures in which the source language continuously appears in opposition to the target language. Nietzsche continued to affirm—or perhaps better said, Nietzsche once again affirmed—translation as an act of transformation when he wrote, in *The Gay Science,* "Indeed, at that time translation meant to conquer."

Yet, in the meantime, beginning with the second half of the eighteenth century, a totally new type of translation and of translation theory emerged that ran parallel to the increasing tolerance of cultural differences. This tolerance manifested itself as a sense of history, which meant the recognition that a diversity of European languages existed, that each one of these languages had its own laws, and that it was necessary to reduce the artistic, intellectual, or any other rivalry between languages and give equal standing to all languages. These insights are most particularly applicable to lexical, semantic, and syntactical incongruities between languages. This incongruity generally surfaces most conspicuously in those moments when the creative forces of language begin to be employed. Indeed, the problem of untranslatability has always been present. An example taken at random is the comment made by Dante *(Convivio)* that, of necessity, the poetic glimmer of the original is lost in translation. The theoreticians of the Renaissance were also familiar with this problem; they considered it a lesser problem, however, which could not be separated from the creative ambition of the translator and which at the same time did not interfere with the envisioned creation in one's own language. But it is only in the eighteenth century that the problem begins to be discussed in a systematic manner and placed in the larger context of historical and linguistic thinking: in France by Diderot and d'Alembert and in Germany by Schleiermacher and Wilhelm von Humboldt.

The immediate reaction was a sense of resignation: there is no such thing as an adequate translation; at best, one can hope for some tentative approximation. Respect for the spirit of the original source-language text seemed to make all attempts at translation illusory. Yet this sense of resignation did not last very long. It was recognized that, despite the lexical and syntactical differences between languages, an affinity existed among their internal structures. This affinity surfaces more conspicuously in literary translation than in simultaneous and consecutive translation or even in the erroneous equivalents of dictionaries. Thus, the respect for the foreign was followed by the courage to move toward the foreign—yet obviously not with the argument of *iure victoris*.

The affinity between the internal structures of languages indeed makes it possible to adapt linguistic subtleties of the target language to its foreign original. This kind of adaptation happens in the area of style, whereby style must be understood, in the context of rhetoric, as the total art of language *(elocutio)*, but even more as the heights and depths of language *(genera)*. The attitude that the translator displays toward the individual stylistic characteristics of a work indicates whether the translator will yield to the original text or conquer it, whether he will stop at acknowledging the differences between languages or whether he will move toward a possible rapprochement of styles between languages.

The latter was established as the norm for the art of translation with the works of Schleiermacher and Humboldt: a movement toward the original, perhaps even a changing into the foreign for the sake of its foreignness.

Schleiermacher expressed that idea in the following way: whenever an original text demonstrates great strength of style, it not only is nourished by the inherent possibilities of that language but also surpasses that language as "an act that can only be created and explained by the very nature of the original language." This theory of translation also acknowledges a difference between languages. More importantly, however, it establishes a distinction between language as reality *(Gegebenheit)* and language as act *(Tat)*, that is, style. The latter has to be understood—in a totally nonclassical sense—as the disparity between the actual national language

and the individual creation of language. Thus, the translator is en-
joined "not to leave the reader in peace and to move the writer
toward him, but to leave the writer in peace (i.e., untouched) and
move the reader toward the writer." The translator should write in
a language "that not only avoids common daily usage (just as the
original source language avoids it) but gives the impression of lean-
ing toward the foreign sensibility." In other words, all the power is
generated by the original. This power becomes the creative impulse
of the translation, which escapes from the daily usage of language
in the same measure as the original has done. The creative stylistic
power of the original has to become visible in the translation; it
even has to regenerate itself as the creative force of style in the
target language. Similarly, Humboldt claims that a stylistic transplantation of the source language into the target language must
take place, and he points to the danger of underestimating the level
of style. "Ambiguities of the original that are part of the essential
character of a work have to be maintained. . . . One can't afford to
change something that is elevated, exaggerated and unusual in the
original to something light and easily accessible in the translation."

The demands that Schleiermacher and Humboldt make can no
longer be omitted from any subsequent theories of the art of translation. Yet current practitioners of translation rarely follow these
theories. This is especially true for translators who are themselves
distinguished writers. Often writer-translators practice the opposite mistake: instead of maintaining the style of the original, they
elevate it. And if we follow the premise that all power comes from
the original, then we must also accept the notion that the stylistic
features of the translation should conform to those of the original,
even when the original text is written in an ordinary or lower-class
style. Starting with the middle of the eighteenth century, Greek and
Roman rhetorical devices became an integral part of the theory of
translation, devices that classical antiquity had never applied to
translation theories. This practice signals the apex of translation
theories in the time after classical antiquity. Can one afford to ignore these theories? . . .

*

[We omit the second part of the speech, in which Friedrich
discusses Rainer Maria Rilke's translation of the fourth sonnet of
Louise Labé into German.]

T W O

JOHN DRYDEN
On Translation

I

. . . It remains that I should say somewhat of Poetical Translations in general, and give my opinion (with submission to better judgments), which way of version seems to be the most proper.

All translation, I suppose, may be reduced to these three heads.

First, that of metaphrase, or turning an author word by word, and line by line, from one language into another. Thus, or near this manner, was Horace his *Art of Poetry* translated by Ben Johnson. The second way is that of paraphrase, or translation with latitude, where the author is kept in view by the translator, so as never to be lost, but his words are not so strictly followed as his sense; and that too is admitted to be amplified, but not altered. Such is Mr. Waller's translation of Virgil's Fourth *Æneid.* The third way is that of imitation, where the translator (if now he has not lost that name) assumes the liberty, not only to vary from the words and sense, but to forsake them both as he sees occasion; and taking only some general hints from the original, to run division on the groundwork, as he pleases. Such is Mr. Cowley's practice in turning two Odes of Pindar, and one of Horace, into English.

Concerning the first of these methods, our master Horace has given us this caution:

> Nec verbum verbo curabis reddere, fidus
> Interpres . . .
>
> Nor word for word too faithfully translate;

From the preface to Dryden's translation of *Ovid's Epistles* (1680).

With one exception identified below, excerpts in this chapter are reproduced from *Essays of John Dryden*, vols. 1 and 2, ed. W. P. Ker (New York: Russell, 1961).

as the Earl of Roscommon has excellently rendered it. Too faithfully is, indeed, pedantically: 'tis a faith like that which proceeds
from superstition, blind and zealous. . . .

*

Take it in the expression of Sir John Denham to Sir Richard
Fanshaw, on his version of the *Pastor Fido:*

That servile path thou nobly dost decline,
Of tracing word by word, and line by line:
A new and nobler way thou dost pursue,
To make translations and translators too:
They but preserve the ashes, thou the flame,
True to his sense, but truer to his fame.

'Tis almost impossible to translate verbally, and well, at the
same time; for the Latin (a most severe and compendious language) often expresses that in one word, which either the barbarity
or the narrowness of modern tongues cannot supply in more. 'Tis
frequent, also, that the conceit is couched in some expression,
which will be lost in English:

Atque iidem venti vela fidemque ferent.

What poet of our nation is so happy as to express this thought
literally in English, and to strike wit, or almost sense, out of it?
     In short, the verbal copier is encumbered with so many diffi-
culties at once, that he can never disentangle himself from all. He
is to consider, at the same time, the thought of his author, and his
words, and to find out the counterpart to each in another language;
and, besides this, he is to confine himself to the compass of numbers, and the slavery of rhyme. 'Tis much like dancing on ropes
with fettered legs: a man may shun a fall by using caution; but the
gracefulness of motion is not to be expected: and when we have
said the best of it, 'tis but a foolish task; for no sober man would
put himself into a danger for the applause of escaping without
breaking his neck. We see Ben Johnson could not avoid obscurity
in his literal translation of Horace, attempted in the same compass
of lines: nay, Horace himself could scarce have done it to a Greek
poet:

Brevis esse laboro, obscurus fio:

either perspicuity or gracefulness will frequently be wanting. Horace has indeed avoided both these rocks in his translation of the three first lines of Homer's *Odysseis,* which he has contracted into two:

Dic mihi musa virum captae post tempora Trojae,
Qui mores hominum multorum vidit, et urbes.

Muse, speak the man, who, since the siege of Troy,
So many towns, such change of manners saw.
EARL OF ROSCOMMON.

But then the sufferings of Ulysses, which are a considerable part of that sentence, are omitted:

Ὅς μάλα πολλὰ πλάγχθη.

The consideration of these difficulties, in a servile, literal translation, not long since made two of our famous wits, Sir John Denham and Mr. Cowley, to contrive another way of turning authors into our tongue, called, by the latter of them, imitation. As they were friends, I suppose they communicated their thoughts on this subject to each other; and therefore their reasons for it are little different, though the practice of one is much more moderate. I take imitation of an author, in their sense, to be an endeavour of a later poet to write like one who has written before him, on the same subject; that is, not to translate his words, or to be confined to his sense, but only to set him as a pattern, and to write, as he supposes that author would have done, had he lived in our age, and in our country. Yet I dare not say, that either of them have carried this libertine way of rendering authors (as Mr. Cowley calls it) so far as my definition reaches; for in the *Pindaric Odes,* the customs and ceremonies of ancient Greece are still preserved. But I know not what mischief may arise hereafter from the example of such an innovation, when writers of unequal parts to him shall imitate so bold an undertaking. To add and to diminish what we please, which is the way avowed by him, ought only to be granted to Mr. Cowley, and that too only in his translation of Pindar; because he alone was able to make him amends, by giving him better of his

own, whenever he refused his author's thoughts. Pindar is generally known to be a dark writer, to want connection, (I mean as to
our understanding,) to soar out of sight, and leave his reader at a
gaze. So wild and ungovernable a poet cannot be translated literally; his genius is too strong to bear a chain, and Samson-like he
shakes it off. A genius so elevated and unconfined as Mr. Cowley's,
was but necessary to make Pindar speak English, and that was to
be performed by no other way than imitation. But if Virgil, or
Ovid, or any regular intelligible authors, be thus used, 'tis no
longer to be called their work, when neither the thoughts nor
words are drawn from the original; but instead of them there is
something new produced, which is almost the creation of another
hand. By this way, 'tis true, somewhat that is excellent may be invented, perhaps more excellent than the first design; though Virgil
must be still excepted, when that *perhaps* takes place. Yet he who is
inquisitive to know an author's thoughts will be disappointed in
his expectation; and 'tis not always that a man will be contented to
have a present made him, when he expects the payment of a debt.
To state it fairly; imitation of an author is the most advantageous
way for a translator to show himself, but the greatest wrong which
can be done to the memory and reputation of the dead. Sir John
Denham (who advised more liberty than he took himself) gives his
reason for his innovation, in his admirable Preface before the translation of the Second *Æneid:* "Poetry is of so subtile a spirit, that, in
pouring out of one language into another, it will all evaporate; and,
if a new spirit be not added in the transfusion, there will remain
nothing but a *caput mortuum*." I confess this argument holds good
against a literal translation; but who defends it? Imitation and verbal version are, in my opinion, the two extremes which ought to
be avoided; and therefore, when I have proposed the mean betwixt
them, it will be seen how far his argument will reach.
    No man is capable of translating poetry, who, besides a genius
to that art, is not a master both of his author's language, and of his
own; nor must we understand the language only of the poet, but
his particular turn of thoughts and expression, which are the characters that distinguish, and as it were individuate him from all other
writers. When we are come thus far, 'tis time to look into ourselves,
to conform our genius to his, to give his thought either the same
turn, if our tongue will bear it, or, if not, to vary but the dress, not
to alter or destroy the substance. The like care must be taken of the
more outward ornaments, the words. When they appear (which is

but seldom) literally graceful, it were an injury to the author that
they should be changed. But since every language is so full of its
own proprieties, that what is beautiful in one, is often barbarous,
nay sometimes nonsense, in another, it would be unreasonable to
limit a translator to the narrow compass of his author's words: 'tis
enough if he choose out some expression which does not vitiate
the sense. I suppose he may stretch his chain to such a latitude; but
by innovation of thoughts, methinks he breaks it. By this means
the spirit of an author may be transfused, and yet not lost: and thus
'tis plain, that the reason alleged by Sir John Denham has no farther
force than to expression; for thought, if it be translated truly, cannot be lost in another language; but the words that convey it to
our apprehension (which are the image and ornament of that
thought), may be so ill chosen, as to make it appear in an unhand-
some dress, and rob it of its native lustre. There is, therefore, a
liberty to be allowed for the expression; neither is it necessary that
words and lines should be confined to the measure of their original.
The sense of an author, generally speaking, is to be sacred and in-
violable. If the fancy of Ovid be luxuriant, 'tis his character to be
so; and if I retrench it, he is no longer Ovid. It will be replied, that
he receives advantage by this lopping of his superfluous branches;
but I rejoin, that a translator has no such right. When a painter
copies from the life, I suppose he has no privilege to alter features
and lineaments, under pretence that his picture will look better:
perhaps the face which he has drawn would be more exact, if the
eyes or nose were altered; but 'tis his business to make it resemble
the original. In two cases only there may a seeming difficulty arise;
that is, if the thought be notoriously trivial or dishonest; but the
same answer will serve for both, that then they ought not to be
translated:

> . . . Et quae
> Desperes tractata nitescere posse, relinquas.

Thus I have ventured to give my opinion on this subject
against the authority of two great men, but I hope without offence
to either of their memories; for I both loved them living, and rev-
erence them now they are dead. But if, after what I have urged, it
be thought by better judges that the praise of a translation consists
in adding new beauties to the piece, thereby to recompense the loss
which it sustains by change of language, I shall be willing to be

taught better, and to recant. In the meantime it seems to me that the true reason why we have so few versions which are tolerable, is not from the too close pursuing of the author's sense, but because there are so few who have all the talents which are requisite for translation, and that there is so little praise and so small encouragement for so considerable a part of learning. . . .

II

For this last half year I have been troubled with the disease (as I may call it) of translation; the cold prose fits of it, which are always the most tedious with me, were spent in the *History of the League:* the hot, which succeeded them, in this volume of Verse Miscellanies. The truth is, I fancied to myself a kind of ease in the change of the paroxysm; never suspecting but that the humour would have wasted itself in two or three *Pastorals* of Theocritus, and as many *Odes* of Horace. But finding, or at least thinking I found, something that was more pleasing in them than my ordinary productions, I encouraged myself to renew my old acquaintance with Lucretius and Virgil; and immediately fixed upon some parts of them, which had most affected me in the reading. These were my natural impulses for the undertaking. But there was an accidental motive which was full as forcible, and God forgive him who was the occasion of it. It was my Lord Roscommon's *Essay on Translated Verse,* which made me uneasy till I tried whether or no I was capable of following his rules, and of reducing the speculation into practice. For many a fair precept in poetry is, like a seeming demonstration in the mathematics, very specious in the diagram, but failing in the mechanic operation. I think I have generally observed his instructions; I am sure my reason is sufficiently convinced both of their truth and usefulness; which, in other words, is to confess no less a vanity, than to pretend that I have at least in some places made examples to his rules. Yet withal, I must acknowledge, that I have many times exceeded my commission; for I have both added and omitted, and even sometimes very boldly made such expositions of my authors, as no Dutch commentator will forgive me. Perhaps, in such particular passages, I have thought that I discovered some beauty yet undiscovered by those pedants, which none but a poet could have found. Where I have

From the preface to *Sylvae: Or, the Second Part of Poetical Miscellanies* (1685).

taken away some of their expressions, and cut them shorter, it may possibly be on this consideration, that what was beautiful in the Greek or Latin, would not appear so shining in the English: and where I have enlarged them, I desire the false critics would not always think, that those thoughts are wholly mine, but that either they are secretly in the poet, or may be fairly deduced from him; or at least, if both those considerations should fail, that my own is of a piece with his, and that if he were living, and an Englishman, they are such as he would probably have written.

For, after all, a translator is to make his author appear as charming as possibly he can, provided he maintains his character, and makes him not unlike himself. Translation is a kind of drawing after the life; where every one will acknowledge there is a double sort of likeness, a good one and a bad. 'Tis one thing to draw the outlines true, the features like, the proportions exact, the colouring itself perhaps tolerable; and another thing to make all these graceful, by the posture, the shadowings, and, chiefly, by the spirit which animates the whole. I cannot, without some indignation, look on an ill copy of an excellent original; much less can I behold with patience Virgil, Homer, and some others, whose beauties I have been endeavouring all my life to imitate, so abused, as I may say, to their faces, by a botching interpreter. What English readers, unacquainted with Greek or Latin, will believe me, or any other man, when we commend those authors, and confess we derive all that is pardonable in us from their fountains, if they take those to be the same poets whom our Oglebys have translated? But I dare assure them, that a good poet is no more like himself in a dull translation, than his carcass would be to his living body. There are many who understand Greek and Latin, and yet are ignorant of their mother-tongue. The proprieties and delicacies of the English are known to few; 'tis impossible even for a good wit to understand and practise them, without the help of a liberal education, long reading, and digesting of those few good authors we have amongst us, the knowledge of men and manners, the freedom of habitudes and conversation with the best company of both sexes; and, in short, without wearing off the rust which he contracted while he was laying in a stock of learning. Thus difficult it is to understand the purity of English, and critically to discern not only good writers from bad, and a proper style from a corrupt, but also to distinguish that which is pure in a good author, from that which is vicious and corrupt in him. And for want of all these requisites, or the greatest

part of them, most of our ingenious young men take up some
cried-up English poet for their model, adore him, and imitate him,
as they think, without knowing wherein he is defective, where he
is boyish and trifling, wherein either his thoughts are improper to
his subject, or his expressions unworthy of his thoughts, or the
turn of both is unharmonious. Thus it appears necessary, that a
man should be a nice critic in his mother-tongue before he attempts to translate a foreign language. Neither is it sufficient, that
he be able to judge of words and style; but he must be a master of
them too; he must perfectly understand his author's tongue, and
absolutely command his own. So that to be a thorough translator,
he must be a thorough poet. Neither is it enough to give his author's sense in good English, in poetical expressions, and in musical
numbers; for though all these are exceeding difficult to perform,
there yet remains an harder task; and 'tis a secret of which few
translators have sufficiently thought. I have already hinted a word
or two concerning it; that is, the maintaining the character of an
author, which distinguishes him from all others, and makes him
appear that individual poet whom you would interpret. For example, not only the thoughts, but the style and versification of
Virgil and Ovid are very different: yet I see, even in our best poets,
who have translated some parts of them, that they have confounded their several talents; and, by endeavouring only at the
sweetness and harmony of numbers, have made them both so much
alike, that, if I did not know the originals, I should never be able
to judge by the copies which was Virgil, and which was Ovid. It
was objected against a late noble painter, that he drew many graceful pictures, but few of them were like. And this happened to him,
because he always studied himself more than those who sat to him.
In such translators I can easily distinguish the hand which performed the work, but I cannot distinguish their poet from another.
Suppose two authors are equally sweet, yet there is a great distinction to be made in sweetness, as in that of sugar and that of honey.
. . .

III

. . . I had long since considered that the way to please the best
judges is not to translate a poet literally, and Virgil least of any

From the dedication of the *Aeneis* (1697).

other: for, his peculiar beauty lying in his choice of words, I am
excluded from it by the narrow compass of our heroic verse, unless
I would make use of monosyllables only, and those clogged with
consonants, which are the dead weight of our mother-tongue. 'Tis
possible, I confess, though it rarely happens, that a verse of monosyllables may sound harmoniously; and some examples of it I have
seen. My first line of the *Æneis* is not harsh—

Arms, and the Man I sing, who forc'd by Fate, &c.

But a much better instance may be given from the last line of
Manilius, made English by our learned and judicious Mr. Creech—

Nor could the World have borne so fierce a Flame—

where the many liquid consonants are placed so artfully, that they
give a pleasing sound to the words, though they are all of one
syllable.

'Tis true, I have been sometimes forced upon it in other places
of this work: but I never did it out of choice; I was either in haste,
or Virgil gave me no occasion for the ornament of words; for it
seldom happens but a monosyllable line turns verse to prose; and
even that prose is rugged and unharmonious. Philarchus, I remember, taxes Balzac for placing twenty monosyllables in file, without
one dissyllable betwixt them. The way I have taken is not so strait
as metaphrase, nor so loose as paraphrase: some things too I have
omitted, and sometimes have added of my own. Yet the omissions,
I hope, are but of circumstances, and such as would have no grace
in English; and the additions, I also hope, are easily deduced from
Virgil's sense. They will seem (at least I have the vanity to think
so), not stuck into him, but growing out of him. He studies brevity
more than any other poet: but he had the advantage of a language
wherein much may be comprehended in a little space. We, and all
the modern tongues, have more articles and pronouns, besides
signs of tenses and cases, and other barbarities on which our speech
is built by the faults of our forefathers. The Romans founded theirs
upon the Greek: and the Greeks, we know, were labouring many
hundred years upon their language, before they brought it to perfection. They rejected all those signs, and cut off as many articles
as they could spare; comprehending in one word what we are con-
strained to express in two; which is one reason why we cannot

write so concisely as they have done. The word *pater*, for example, signifies not only *a* father, but *your* father, *my* father, *his* or *her* father, all included in a word.

This inconvenience is common to all modern tongues; and this alone constrains us to employ more words than the ancients needed. But having before observed that Virgil endeavours to be short, and at the same time elegant, I pursue the excellence and forsake the brevity: for there he is like ambergris, a rich perfume, but of so close and glutinous a body, that it must be opened with inferior scents of musk or civet, or the sweetness will not be drawn out into another language.

On the whole matter, I thought fit to steer betwixt the two extremes of paraphrase and literal translation; to keep as near my author as I could, without losing all his graces, the most eminent of which are in the beauty of his words; and those words, I must add, are always figurative. Such of these as would retain their elegance in our tongue, I have endeavoured to graff on it; but most of them are of necessity to be lost, because they will not shine in any but their own. Virgil has sometimes two of them in a line; but the scantiness of our heroic verse is not capable of receiving more than one; and that too must expiate for many others which have none. Such is the difference of the languages, or such my want of skill in choosing words. Yet I may presume to say, and I hope with as much reason as the French translator, that, taking all the materials of this divine author, I have endeavoured to make Virgil speak such English as he would himself have spoken, if he had been born in England, and in this present age.

IV

. . . I have almost done with Chaucer, when I have answered some objections relating to my present work. I find some people are offended that I have turned these tales into modern English; because they think them unworthy of my pains, and look on Chaucer as a dry, old-fashioned wit, not worth reviving. I have often heard the late Earl of Leicester say, that Mr. Cowley himself was of that opinion; who, having read him over at my Lord's request, declared he had no taste of him. I dare not advance my opinion against the judgment of so great an author; but I think it fair, how-

From Preface to the *Fables* (1700).

ever, to leave the decision to the public. Mr. Cowley was too modest to set up for a dictator; and being shocked perhaps with his old
style, never examined into the depth of his good sense. Chaucer, I
confess, is a rough diamond, and must first be polished ere he
shines. I deny not likewise, that, living in our early days of poetry,
he writes not always of a piece; but sometimes mingles trivial
things with those of greater moment. Sometimes also, though not
often, he runs riot, like Ovid, and knows not when he has said
enough. But there are more great wits besides Chaucer, whose fault
is their excess of conceits, and those ill sorted. An author is not to
write all he can, but only all he ought. Having observed this redundancy in Chaucer, (as it is an easy matter for a man of ordinary
parts to find a fault in one of greater,) I have not tied myself to a
literal translation; but have often omitted what I judged unnecessary, or not of dignity enough to appear in the company of better
thoughts. I have presumed farther in some places, and added somewhat of my own where I thought my author was deficient, and had
not given his thoughts their true lustre, for want of words in the
beginning of our language. And to this I was the more embold-
ened, because (if I may be permitted to say it of myself) I found I
had a soul congenial to his, and that I had been conversant in the
same studies. Another poet, in another age, may take the same liberty with my writings; if at least they live long enough to deserve
correction. It was also necessary sometimes to restore the sense of
Chaucer, which was lost or mangled in the errors of the press. Let
this example suffice at present: in the story of *Palamon and Arcite,*
where the temple of Diana is described, you find these verses, in all
the editions of our author:

> There saw I *Danè* turned into a Tree,
> I mean not the Goddess *Diane,*
> But *Venus* Daughter, which that hight *Danè.*

Which after a little consideration I knew was to be reformed into
this sense, that Daphne the daughter of Peneus was turned into a
tree. I durst not make thus bold with Ovid, lest some future Mil-
bourne should arise, and say, I varied from my author, because I
understood him not.

But there are other judges, who think I ought not to have
translated Chaucer into English, out of a quite contrary notion:
they suppose there is a certain veneration due to his old language;

and that it is little less than profanation and sacrilege to alter it. They are farther of opinion, that somewhat of his good sense will suffer in this transfusion, and much of the beauty of his thoughts will infallibly be lost, which appear with more grace in their old habit. Of this opinion was that excellent person whom I mentioned, the late Earl of Leicester, who valued Chaucer as much as Mr. Cowley despised him. My Lord dissuaded me from this attempt, (for I was thinking of it some years before his death,) and his authority prevailed so far with me, as to defer my undertaking while he lived, in deference to him: yet my reason was not convinced with what he urged against it. If the first end of a writer be to be understood, then, as his language grows obsolete, his thoughts must grow obscure—

> Multa renascentur, quae nunc cecidere; cadentque
> Quae nunc sunt in honore vocabula, si volet usus,
> Quem penes arbitrium est et jus et norma loquendi.

When an ancient word for its sound and significancy deserves to be revived, I have that reasonable veneration for antiquity to restore it. All beyond this is superstition. Words are not like landmarks, so sacred as never to be removed; customs are changed, and even statutes are silently repealed, when the reason ceases for which they were enacted. As for the other part of the argument, that his thoughts will lose of their original beauty by the innovation of words; in the first place, not only their beauty, but their being is lost, where they are no longer understood, which is the present case. I grant that something must be lost in all transfusion, that is, in all translations; but the sense will remain, which would otherwise be lost, or at least be maimed, when it is scarce intelligible, and that but to a few. How few are there who can read Chaucer, so as to understand him perfectly? And if imperfectly, then with less profit, and no pleasure. 'Tis not for the use of some old Saxon friends, that I have taken these pains with him: let them neglect my version, because they have no need of it. I made it for their sakes who understand sense and poetry as well as they, when that poetry and sense is put into words which they understand. I will go farther, and dare to add, that what beauties I lose in some places, I give to others which had them not originally: but in this I may be partial to myself; let the reader judge, and I submit to his decision. Yet I think I have just occasion to complain of them, who because

they understand Chaucer, would deprive the greater part of their
countrymen of the same advantage, and hoard him up, as misers
do their grandam gold, only to look on it themselves, and hinder
others from making use of it. In sum, I seriously protest, that no
man ever had, or can have, a greater veneration for Chaucer than
myself. I have translated some part of his works, only that I might
perpetuate his memory, or at least refresh it, amongst my countrymen. If I have altered him anywhere for the better, I must at the
same time acknowledge, that I could have done nothing without
him. *Facile est inventis addere* is no great commendation; and I am
not so vain to think I have deserved a greater. I will conclude what
I have to say of him singly, with this one remark: A lady of my
acquaintance, who keeps a kind of correspondence with some authors of the fair sex in France, has been informed by them, that
Mademoiselle de Scudery, who is as old as Sibyl, and inspired like
her by the same God of Poetry, is at this time translating Chaucer
into modern French. From which I gather, that he has been formerly translated into the old Provençal; for how she should come
to understand old English, I know not. But the matter of fact being
true, it makes me think that there is something in it like fatality;
that, after certain periods of time, the fame and memory of great
Wits should be renewed, as Chaucer is both in France and England.
If this be wholly chance, 'tis extraordinary; and I dare not call it
more, for fear of being taxed with superstition. . . .

V

. . . This has brought me to say a word or two about translation in general: in which no nation might more excel than the English,[1] tho' as matters are now managed, we come so far short of
the French. There may, indeed, be a reason assigned, which bears
a very great probability; and that is that here the booksellers are
the undertakers of works of this nature, and they are persons more

---

From "The Life of Lucian" (1711). Reproduced from vol. 2 of John Dryden, *Of
Dramatic Poesy and Other Critical Essays*, ed. George Watson (London: J. M. Dent
and Sons, 1962). Footnotes are Watson's notes.
   1. Dryden makes his appeal at the threshold of the second great age of English
translation, which his own Virgil of 1697 inaugurated. It was followed by Pope's
Homer (1715–26), Rowe's Lucan (1718), Gilbert West's Pindar (1749), Elizabeth
Carter's Epictetus (1758), Thomas Twining's version of Aristotle's *Poetics* (1789),
and other translations that owe their vigor to Dryden's precept and example.

devoted to their own gain than the public honour. They are very
parsimonious in rewarding the wretched scribblers they employ;
and care not how the business is done, so that it be but done. They
live by selling titles, not books, and if that carry off one impression,
they have their ends, and value not the curses they and their authors
meet with from the bubbled chapmen.[2] While translations are thus
at the disposal of the booksellers, and have no better judges or
rewarders of the performance, it is impossible that we should make
any progress in an art so very useful to an enquiring people, and
for the improvement and spreading of knowledge, which is none
of the worst preservatives against slavery.

It must be confessed that when the bookseller has interest with
gentlemen of genius and quality above the mercenary prospects of
little writers, as in that of Plutarch's *Lives,* and this of Lucian, the
reader may satisfy himself that he shall have the author's spirit and
soul in the traduction. These gentlemen know very well that they
are not to creep after the words of their author in so servile a manner as some have done. For that must infallibly throw them on a
necessity of introducing a new mode of diction and phraseology
with which we are not at all acquainted, and would incur that cen-
sure which my Lord Dorset made formerly on those of Mr Spence,
viz. 'that he was so cunning a translator that a man must consult
the original to understand the version.' For every language has a
propriety and idiom peculiar to itself, which cannot be conveyed
to another without perpetual absurdities.

The qualification of a translator worth reading must be a mastery of the language he translates out of, and that he translates into;
but if a deficience be to be allowed in either, it is in the original,
since if he be but master enough of the tongue of his author as to
be master of his sense, it is possible for him to express that sense
with eloquence in his own, if he have a thorough command of that.
But without the latter he can never arrive at the useful and the
delightful, without which reading is a penance and fatigue.

'Tis true that there will be a great many beauties which in every
tongue depend on the diction, that will be left in the version of a
man not skilled in the original language of the author. But then,
on the other side: first, it is impossible to render all those little
ornaments of speech in any two languages; and if he have a mastery
in the sense and spirit of his author, and in his own language have

2. I.e., cheated salesmen in books.

a style and happiness of expression, he will easily supply all that is lost by that defect.

A translator that would write with any force or spirit of an original must never dwell on the words of his author. He ought to possess himself entirely and perfectly comprehend the genius and sense of his author, the nature of the subject, and the terms of the art or subject treated of. And then he will express himself as justly, and with as much life, as if he wrote an original: whereas he who copies word for word loses all the spirit in the tedious transfusion.

I would not be understood that he should be at liberty to give such a turn as Mr Spence has in some of his, where for the fine raillery and Attic salt of Lucian, we find the gross expressions of Billingsgate, or Moorfields and Bartholomew Fair. For I write not to such translators, but to men capacious of the soul and genius of their authors, without which all their labour will be of no use but to disgrace themselves, and injure the author that falls into their slaughter-house.

I believe I need give no other rules to the reader than the following version, where example will be stronger than precept, to which I now refer them. In which a man justly qualified for a translator will discover many rules extremely useful to that end. But [to] a man who wants these natural qualifications which are necessary for such an undertaking, all particular precepts are of no other use than to make him a more remarkable coxcomb.

THREE

ARTHUR SCHOPENHAUER

On Language and Words

Translated by Peter Mollenhauer

The word is the most enduring substance of the human race. Once a poet has properly embodied his most fleeting emotion in the most appropriate words, then this emotion will continue to live on through these words for millennia and will flourish anew in every sensitive reader. . . .

Not every word in one language has an exact equivalent in another. Thus, not all concepts that are expressed through the words of one language are exactly the same as the ones that are expressed through the words of another. . . .

Sometimes a language lacks the word for a certain concept even though it exists in most, perhaps all, other languages: a rather scandalous example is the absence of a word in French for "to stand." On the other hand, for certain concepts a word exists only in one language and is then adopted by other languages. . . . At times, a foreign language introduces a conceptual nuance for which there is no word in our own language. Then anyone who is concerned about the exact presentation of his or her thoughts will use the foreign word and ignore the barking of pedantic purists. In all cases where a certain word cannot render exactly the same concept in another language, the dictionary will offer several synonyms. They all hit the meaning of the concept, yet not in a concentric manner. They indicate the directions of meaning that delineate the boundaries within which the concept moves. . . . This causes unavoidable imperfection in all translations. Rarely can a characteris-

From "Über Sprache und Worte," in *Parerga und Paralipomena* (1800), as reprinted in *Sämmtliche Werke*, ed. Julius Frauenstädt, vol. 6, chapter 25, section 309 (Leipzig: Brockhaus, 1891), pp. 601–7.

tic, terse, and significant sentence be transplanted from one language to another so that it will produce exactly the same effect in the new language. Even in the realm of prose, the most nearly perfect translation will at best relate to the original in the same way that a musical piece relates to its transposition into another key. Musicians know what that means. Every translation either remains dead and its style appears forced, wooden, and unnatural, or it frees itself of the constraints of adherence to language, and therefore is satisfied with the notion of an *à peu près*, which rings false. A library of translations resembles a gallery with reproductions of paintings. Take translations of authors from antiquity: they are as obvious a surrogate as chicory for coffee. Poems cannot be translated; they can only be transposed, and that is always awkward.

Hence, when we learn a language, our main problem lies in understanding every concept for which the foreign language has a word, but for which our own language lacks an exact equivalent— as is often the case. Thus, in learning a foreign language one must map out several new spheres of concepts in one's own mind that did not exist before. Consequently, one does not only learn words but acquires concepts. This is particularly true for the learning of classical languages, since the ways in which the ancients expressed themselves differ considerably more from ours than modern languages vary from one another. This is most conspicuously evident with translation into Latin: expressions totally different from the original have to be used. Indeed, the ideas to be transplanted into Latin have to be totally reconstituted and remolded; the idea has to be dissolved into its most basic components and then reconstructed in the new language. It is precisely through this process that the mind benefits so much from the learning of ancient languages. One can only fathom the spirit of the language to be learned after one has correctly grasped the concepts that this language designates through individual words, and when one is capable of immediately associating each word with its corresponding concept in the foreign language. We will never grasp the spirit of the foreign language if we first translate each word into our mother tongue and then associate it with its conceptual affinity in that language—which does not always correspond to the concepts of the source language—and the same holds true for entire sentences. If one has properly grasped the spirit of a foreign language, one has also taken a large step toward understanding the nation that speaks that language for, as the style is related to the mind of the individual, so is the language to the mind of the nation. A complete mastery of another language has taken place when one is capable of translating not books but oneself into the other language, so that without losing one's own individuality one can immediately communicate in that language, and thereby please foreigners as well as one's countrymen in the same manner.

People of limited intellectual abilities will not easily master a foreign language. They actually learn the words; however, they always use the words only in the sense of the approximate equivalent in the mother tongue, and they always maintain those expressions and sentences peculiar to the mother tongue. They are incapable of acquiring the "spirit" of the foreign language. This can be explained by the fact that their thinking is not generated by its own substance but, for the most part, is borrowed from their mother tongue, whose current phrases and expressions substitute for their own thoughts. Therefore they use only worn-out patterns of speech (hackney'd phrases; *phrases banales*) in their own language, which they put together so awkwardly that one realizes how imperfectly they understand the meaning of what they are saying and how little their entire thinking goes beyond the mere use of words, so that it is not much more than mindless parrotry. Conversely, a person's originality of expression and the appropriateness of individual formulations used by such a person are an infallible indication of a superior mind.

From all this it becomes clear that new concepts are created during the process of learning a foreign language to give meaning to new signs. Moreover, it becomes clear that concepts that together made up a larger and vaguer one, since only one word existed for them, can be refined in their differentiation, and that relationships unknown until then are discovered because the foreign language expresses the concept through a trope or metaphor indigenous to that language. Therefore, an infinite number of nuances, similarities, differences, and relationships among objects rise to the level of consciousness as a result of learning the new language, and thus one perceives multiple perspectives of all phenomena. This confirms that one thinks differently in every language, that our thinking is modified and newly tinged through the learning of each foreign language, and that polyglotism is, apart from its many immediate advantages, a direct means of educating the mind by correcting and perfecting our perceptions through the emerging diversity and refinement of concepts. At the same time, polyglotism increases the flexibility of thinking since, through the learning of many languages, the concept increasingly separates itself from the word. The classical languages effect this to a much higher degree than the modern languages because they differ more from ours. This difference does not leave room for a word-for-word rendering but requires that we melt down our thoughts entirely and recast them into a different form. Or (if I may be permitted to bring in a comparison from chemistry), whereas translation of a modern language into another modern one requires only disassembly of the sentence to be translated into its obvious components and then the reassembly of them, the translation into Latin often requires a breakdown of a sentence into its most refined, elementary components (the pure thought content) from which the sentence is then regenerated in totally different forms. Thus it often happens that nouns in the text of one language can only be transplanted as verbs in another, or vice versa, and there are many other examples. The same process takes place when we translate classical languages into modern ones. Thus is revealed the distance of the relations that we can have with classical authors, by way of such translations. . . .

FOUR

FRIEDRICH SCHLEIERMACHER
From "On the Different Methods of Translating"

Translated by Waltraud Bartscht

The fact that speech is translated from one language into another confronts us everywhere in a variety of forms. On the one hand, this enables people who perhaps were originally separated from one another by the whole breadth of the earth to come into contact or perhaps to assimilate into one language the products of another language that has been extinct for many centuries. On the other hand, we need not even go outside the boundaries of one single language to find the same phenomenon. For the different tribal dialects of one nation and the different developments of the same language or dialect in different centuries are, in the strict sense of the word, different languages, which frequently require a complete translation. Even contemporaries who are not separated by dialects but who come from different social classes that have very little contact and who are far apart in their education can often communicate with each other only through a similar process of translation. Are we not often compelled, after all, to translate for ourselves the words of another person who is quite like us, but of a different temperament and mind? For when we feel that in our mouth the same words would have an entirely different meaning, or here a stronger or there a weaker weight than in his, and that we would use quite different words and phrases if we wanted to express in our way the same things he meant to say, then it seems, as we define

The treatise "Methoden des Übersetzens" was read by Schleiermacher on 24 June 1813, at the Royal Academy of Sciences in Berlin. Reprinted in *Friedrich Schleiermachers sämmtliche Werke, Dritte Abtheilung: Zur Philosophie*, vol. 2 (Berlin: Reimer, 1938), pp. 207–45.

this feeling for ourselves more closely, and as it becomes a thought in us, that we translate. Occasionally we must translate even our own words, when we want to make them our very own again. And this skill is practiced not only for the purpose of transplanting into foreign soil what a language has created in the fields of scholarship and the rhetorical arts, thereby expanding the horizon of the power of the mind, but it is also practiced in business transactions between individuals of different nations, and in diplomatic exchanges of independent governments, in which each is accustomed to speak in its own language to the other to ensure strict equality without making use of a dead language.

*

Of course, we do not mean to incorporate into our present discussion everything that falls within the large boundaries of this subject. That necessity to translate even within one's own language and dialect—which is more or less a temporary, emotional need— is just too much a thing of the moment in its impact to require any guidance other than that of the emotions; if rules were to be issued about this, they could only be rules that create a purely moral attitude for man in order to keep his mind open to things that are less closely related. If, however, we set this aside and deal with translations from a foreign language into our own, then we will be able to distinguish two different fields as well—not totally distinct, for this is seldom the case, but rather separated by boundaries that overlap—yet fields still distinctly different if one considers their final goals. The interpreter's job is in the business world and that of the true translator in the areas of scholarship and the arts. Those who find these definitions arbitrary—considering that interpreting is usually understood to mean oral transferral and translating the transplantation of written works—will forgive me for using them, since they respond quite well to the present need and since the two definitions are not particularly far removed from each other. Writing is appropriate for the fields of scholarship and the arts because writing gives their works permanence. To transfer scholarly and artistic works orally would be as useless as it seems impossible. For business transactions, on the other hand, writing is only a mechanical device. In this case, oral exchanges are the most appropriate ones, and written interpreting should basically be considered only a transcript of oral interpreting. . . .

*

The activity of translating is radically different from mere interpreting. Wherever the word is not totally bound by obvious objects or by external facts (which it is merely supposed to express), wherever the speaker is thinking more or less independently and therefore wants to express himself, he stands in an ambiguous relationship to language; and his speech will be understood correctly only insofar as this relationship is comprehended correctly. Every human being is, on the one hand, in the power of the language he speaks; he and his whole thinking are a product of it. He cannot, with complete certainty, think anything that lies outside the limits of language. The form of his concepts, the way and means of connecting them, is outlined for him through the language in which he is born and educated; intellect and imagination are bound by it. On the other hand, however, every freethinking and intellectually spontaneous human being also forms the language himself. For how else, but through these influences, would it have come to be and to grow from its first raw state to its more perfect formation in scholarship and art? In this sense, therefore, it is the living power of the individual that produces new forms in the malleable material of the language, originally only for the momentary purpose of communicating a transitory awareness; these forms, however, remain, now more, now less, in the language and taken up by others continue to spread. One can even say that only to the extent to which a person influences language does he deserve to be heard beyond his immediate environment.

By necessity, every utterance soon dies away, if, through a thousand voices, it can always be reproduced in the same way; only such an utterance that creates a new impulse in the life of the language itself can and may last longer. For this reason every free and higher discourse wants to be perceived in a twofold way: on the one hand, out of the spirit of the language of whose elements it is composed, a language that is bound and defined by that spirit and vividly conceived in the speaker; on the other hand, out of the speaker's emotions, as his own action, which can only be produced and explained by his nature. Indeed, every discourse of this kind is only understood, in the higher sense of the word, when both these aspects are perceived together in their true relationship to each other, so that one knows which of the two dominates in the whole or in individual parts. The spoken word can be understood as an act of the speaker only if it is felt, at the same time, where and how the power of language has taken hold of him, where thoughts have traveled down its lightning rod, where and how the roaming imagination has been captured in its forms. Also, speech as a product of language, and as an utterance of its spirit, can only be understood if, for example, the reader feels that only a Greek could think and speak in this way; that only this particular language could function in a human mind in this way; and that only this man could think and speak Greek in this way, that only he could comprehend and shape the language in this way, that only in this way is his living possession of the language's richness revealed: an alert sense for meter and euphony, the ability to think and create that belongs only to him. If understanding is already difficult within the same language, and presupposes a precise and profound penetration into the spirit of the language and into the characteristic traits of the writer, how much more will it not be a highly developed art when it deals with the products of a foreign and distant language!

Of course, whoever has acquired this art of understanding, through the most diligent treatment of language, through exact knowledge of the whole historical life of a nation, and through the most rigorous interpretation of individual works and their authors—he, of course, but only *he*—can desire to open up to his compatriots and contemporaries that same understanding of the masterworks of art and scholarship. However, doubts must arise when he comes closer to the task, when he wants to define his purposes more clearly and begins to assess his own means. Should he try to bring two people together who are so totally separated from each other—as his fellow man, who is completely ignorant of the author's language, and the author himself are—into such an immediate relationship as that of author and reader? Or, even if he wants to open up to his readers only the same relationship and the same pleasure that he enjoys, marked by traces of hard work and imbued with a sense of the foreign, how can he achieve all this with the means at his disposal? If his readers are supposed to understand, then they must comprehend the spirit of the language that was native to the writer, and they must be able to see his peculiar way of thinking and feeling. In order to reach these two goals, the translator can offer them nothing but his language, which nowhere quite corresponds to the other, and himself, whose interpretive understanding of his writer is now more and now less clear, and whose appreciation and admiration of the writer is now greater, now less. Does not translation, considered in this way, appear a foolish undertaking?

*

In despair, therefore, of ever reaching this goal or, rather, before one could get to the point of clearly realizing it, two other ways have been invented for establishing acquaintance with the works of foreign languages (not for the actual sense of art or of language, but for the intellectual necessity on the one hand and for the intellectual art on the other) whereby some of these difficulties are forcibly cleared away, others wisely circumvented, but the idea of translation, as it is specified here, is completely relinquished. These two inventions are paraphrase and imitation.

Paraphrase seeks to overcome the irrationality of languages, but only in a mechanical way. It says to itself, "Even if I do not find a word in my language that corresponds to that in the original language, I still want to retain its value by the addition of limiting or expanding definitions." Thus paraphrase labors its way through an accumulation of loosely defined details, vacillating between a cumbersome "too much" and a tormenting "too little." In this way it can perhaps render the content with limited precision, but it completely abandons the impression made by the original. Because the living speech has been irretrievably killed, everyone feels that it could not have come originally and in this way from the emotions of a human being. The paraphraser deals with the elements of both languages as if they were mathematical symbols that can be reduced to the same value by increasing or decreasing them, but neither the spirit of the transformed language nor that of the original can be revealed by such a procedure. If, moreover, paraphrase seeks to mark the traces of the connection of thoughts psychologically—where they are vague and tend to lose themselves—by means of subclauses, then it strives at the same time, especially in difficult works, to take the place of a commentary, and bears even less relationship to the concept of translation.

Imitation, on the other hand, submits to the irrationality of languages. It concedes that no replica of a verbal work of art can be produced in another language that would correspond exactly in

its individual parts to the individual parts of the original. Therefore, with the difference of languages (to which so many other
differences are essentially connected), there remains nothing else to
be done but to prepare an imitation, a whole composed from parts
noticeably different from the parts of the original, but which nevertheless comes as close in its effect to that original whole as the
difference in material permits. Such a recreation is no longer the
work itself. It is also by no means intended to represent and render
effectively the spirit of the original language; rather the foreignness
created in the original undergoes a substantial transformation. A
work of this kind, taking into account the difference of language,
morals, and education, is supposed to be, as much as possible, the
same thing for its readers as the original was for its own readers;
by trying to maintain this sameness of reaction, one sacrifices the
identity of the work. Thus, the imitator has not the slightest intention of bringing the two together—the writer of the original and
the reader of the imitation—because he does not believe that an
immediate relationship between them is possible; he only wants to
give to the latter an impression similar to that which the contemporaries of the original received from it.

Paraphrase is applied more in the field of scholarship, imitation
more in that of the arts; and just as everyone admits that a work of
art loses its tone, its splendor, its whole artistic content by para-
phrasing, so no one has probably ever been foolish enough to prepare an imitation of a scholarly masterpiece that treats its content
freely. Both procedures, however, cannot satisfy that person who,
inspired by the value of a foreign masterpiece, wants to communicate its power to those who speak his own language, and who has
the stricter concept of translation in mind. Paraphrase and imitation cannot therefore be more closely evaluated here, because they
deviate from this concept; they are mentioned only to outline the
boundaries of the field with which we are concerned.

*

But now the true translator, who really wants to bring together
these two entirely separate persons, his author and his reader, and
to assist the latter in obtaining the most correct and complete
understanding and enjoyment possible of the former without,
however, forcing him out of the sphere of his mother tongue—
what paths are open to the translator for that purpose? In my opin-

ion, there are only two. Either the translator leaves the writer alone as much as possible and moves the reader toward the writer, or he leaves the reader alone as much as possible and moves the writer toward the reader. Both paths are so completely different from one another that one of them must definitely be adhered to as strictly as possible, since a highly unreliable result would emerge from mixing them, and it is likely that author and reader would not come together at all. The difference between the two methods, and the fact that they are in this kind of relationship, must be immediately obvious. For in the first case, the translator takes pains, by means of his work, to compensate for the reader's lack of understanding of the original language. He seeks to communicate to his readers the same image, the same impression that he himself has gained— through his knowledge of the original language—of the work as it stands, and therefore to move the readers to his viewpoint, which is actually foreign to them. If, however, the translation seeks to let its Roman author, for example, speak as he would have spoken and written as a German to Germans, it does not move the author to where the translator stands because the author does not speak German to him but Latin; on the contrary, it moves the author immediately into the world of the German readers and transforms him into one of them—and that is precisely the other case. The first translation will be perfect in its way if one can say that had the author learned German as well as the translator Latin, he would not have translated his work, originally composed in Latin, any differently than the translator has done. But the second translation, which does not show the author how he would have translated himself but how he originally, as a German, would have written German, can have no other standard of perfection than the assurance that, if all the German readers could be transformed into experts and contemporaries of the author, then the original work would become for them exactly the same as the translation, since the author has transformed himself into a German.

This method, obviously, is on the mind of all those who use the formula that an author should be translated as if he himself had written in German. From this juxtaposition, it should become immediately evident how different the procedure must be in every detail, and how everything would turn out to be unintelligible and unsuccessful if one were to switch methods within the same project. Furthermore, I wish to assert that there could be, besides these two methods, no third one that would have a definite goal in mind.

Actually, no other methods are possible. The two separate parties must either meet in the middle at a certain point, which will always be that of the translator, or one party must completely link up with the other. Of these two possibilities, only one falls into the area of translation; the other would take place if, in our case, the German readers were to grasp the Latin language completely, or rather if the language were to take hold of the readers completely to the point of actually transforming them. Therefore, whatever has been said about translations that follow the letter and translations that follow the meaning, about faithful and free translations (and whatever other expressions may have been advanced), even if they claim to be different methods they must always be reduced to those two mentioned earlier. But if mistakes or virtues are to be discussed in this context, then the translation that faithfully reproduces the meaning, or the translation that is too literal or too free according to one method, must be different from the other. It is therefore my intention—setting aside all individual questions about this subject that have already been treated by the experts—to examine only the most general features of both these methods, and to do this in order to show what the disadvantages (as well as the limits of their applicability) of each are, and to what extent each best achieves the goals of translation. From the perspective of such a general survey, two things would remain to be done, to which this discussion is only the introduction. For each of the two methods, rules could be designed—taking into consideration the different genres of speech—and the best attempts that have been made according to either method could be compared and evaluated; in this way one could elucidate the matter even more. However, I must leave both projects to others, or at least for another occasion.

*

The method that aims, by means of translation, to give the reader the same impression that he as a German would receive from reading the work in the original language must of course first determine what kind of understanding of the original language it wants to imitate. For there is one kind it should not imitate, and one it cannot imitate.

The former is a schoolboy-like understanding that laboriously and almost repulsively stumbles through and botches the details, and yet nowhere attains to a clear view of the whole, to a vivid and firm comprehension of the context. So long as the educated part of a nation, as a whole, still has no experience of a more intimate penetration into foreign languages, then those who have progressed beyond this level should be prevented by their good judgment from undertaking this kind of translation. If they took their own understanding as a yardstick, they themselves would hardly be understood, and would accomplish little; but should their translation represent common understanding, then their clumsy work would rapidly disappear from the stage. In such a time, free imitations should first awaken and sharpen the delight in what is foreign, and paraphrases may prepare a more general understanding, in order to pave the way for future translations. . . .

*

Translating therefore refers to a situation that lies midway between the two, and the translator's goal must be to provide his reader with the same image and the same pleasure as reading the work in the original language offers to the man educated in this way, whom we usually call, in the better sense of the word, the amateur or the connoisseur. To him the foreign language is familiar, but yet always remains foreign; he no longer, like students, has to think of every detail in the native language before he can grasp the whole, but he always remains conscious of the differences of that language from his mother tongue, even where he most consistently enjoys the beauty of a work. To be sure, the activity and the definition of this way of translating still remain disturbing enough for us, even after we have ascertained these points. We see that, just as the inclination to translate can only come into being when a certain ability to use foreign languages is widespread among the educated of the public, so the art will increase in the same manner as well, and the goal will be set higher and higher; but this can occur only when a taste for and knowledge of foreign intellectual works spread and increase among those in the nation who have exercised and educated their ear without, however, making the knowledge of language their actual business. But at the same time, we cannot conceal the fact that the more readers are receptive to such translations, the more the difficulties of the venture also increase, especially if one looks at the most characteristic products of the arts and scholarship of a nation, which, after all, are the most important objects for the translator. That is, just as language is a historical fact, so there is no proper sense for it without a sense of its history. Languages are not invented, but they are gradually discovered, and all arbitrary work on them and in them is stupid; scholarship and art are the powers by means of which this discovery is promoted and accomplished.

Every excellent mind, in which a part of a nation's perceptions acquire a particular form by one of these two methods, becomes active in his language, and his works must therefore contain a part of its history as well. This causes great, indeed often insurmountable, difficulties for the translator of scholarly works because whoever endowed with sufficient knowledge reads an excellent work of this kind in the original language will not miss the influence of it on language. He notices which words, which combinations, appear to him in the first splendor of newness; he sees how they infiltrate the language through the special needs of the author's mind and his power of expression; and this observation essentially determines the impression he receives. It is therefore a part of the task of translation to communicate this very impression to the readers; otherwise an extremely significant part of that which is intended for them often gets lost.

But how can this be achieved? To be specific, how often will an old, worn-out word in our language be the only one to correspond to a new word in the original, so that the translator, if he wanted to show the quality of the work as something that forms language, would have to put a foreign content in its place, and would therefore have to escape into the field of imitation! Even when he can render something new with something new, the word that is closest in etymology and derivation will not reproduce the meaning completely, and he will have to create other word associations if he does not want to violate the immediate context! He will have to console himself with the fact that in other places, where the author has used old and well-known words, he makes up for his shortcomings, and therefore he will achieve results in the work as a whole that he is not able to attain in every individual case. But if one looks at a master's word formations in their totality, at his use of related words and word-roots in a multitude of interrelated writings, how can the translator succeed here, since the system of concepts and their signs in the translator's language is entirely different from that in the original language, and the word-roots, instead of being synchronically identical, cut across each other in the strangest directions. It is impossible, therefore, for the translator's use of language to be as coherent as that of his author. Here he will have to be content to attain in single parts what he cannot achieve in the total work. He will ask his readers to understand that they cannot think of the other writings as rigorously as the readers of the original could, but rather that they must consider each one on its own. His readers should even be willing to praise the translator, if he succeeds in maintaining similarity with respect to the more important objects in specific writings (or even in individual parts of them only), so that no single word gets a multiplicity of quite different replacements, or so that a colorful variety does not prevail in the translation where in the original a clear relationship of expressions is presented without discontinuities. . . .

*

Still other difficulties become apparent when the translator considers his relationship to the language in which he writes and the relationship of his translation to his other works. If we exclude those marvelous masters to whom several languages feel as one, or to whom an acquired language is even more natural than their mother tongue (for whom, as we said before, one simply cannot translate), then all other people, no matter how fluently they read a foreign language, still retain the feeling of foreignness. How should the translator go about transmitting this feeling of foreignness to his readers, to whom he is presenting a translation in their mother tongue?

Of course, one will say that the answer to this riddle was found long ago, and that the riddle has often been solved more than adequately, for the more closely the translation follows the phrases of the original, the more foreign it will strike the reader. This might be true, and it is easy enough to laugh at this in general. But if one does not want to attain this joy too cheaply, if one does not want to throw out the most masterful and the worst schoolboyish translation with the same bathwater, then one must concede that an essential requirement of this method of translation is an attitude toward language that is not only not trivial, but that also lets us know that it has not grown completely freely, but rather has been bent toward an alien likeness. One must admit that to do this skillfully and with moderation, without disadvantage to one's own language and to oneself, is perhaps the greatest difficulty a translator has to overcome. The attempt seems to be the most extraordinary form of humiliation that a writer, who is not a bad writer, could inflict upon himself. Who would not like to have his native tongue appear everywhere in its most enticing beauty, of which every literary genre is capable? Who would not rather beget children who are in their parent's image rather than bastards? Who would like to show himself in less attractive and less graceful movements than he is capable of, and at least sometimes appear harsh and stiff, and shock the reader as much as is necessary to keep him aware of what he is doing? Who would gladly consent to be considered inept by studiously keeping as close to the foreign language as his own language permits, and to be blamed, like those parents who place their children in the hands of acrobats, for putting his mother tongue through foreign and unnatural contortions instead of exercising it skillfully in the gymnastics of his own language? Who, finally, likes to be smiled at with pity by the greatest experts and masters, suggesting that they would not understand his laborious and hasty German if they were not to support it with their knowledge of Greek and Latin!

These are the sacrifices that every translator must make; these are the dangers to which he exposes himself, if he does not observe the finest line in the endeavor to keep the tone of the language foreign, dangers from which he cannot escape entirely since everyone draws this line in a slightly different way each time. Moreover, if he takes into consideration the unavoidable influence of habit, he has to worry that something new will creep into his own free and original production through the act of translation, and that his gentle sense for the native well-being of the language might be somewhat dulled. And should he think of the vast army of imitators, and of the lethargy and mediocrity that prevail in the literary-writing public, then he must be shocked to see that he is responsible for so much looseness and lawlessness, for so much true clumsiness and stiffness, so much corruption of language; for almost only the best and the worst will not strive to gain a false advantage from his endeavors.

Complaints have often been heard that such translation must necessarily be detrimental to the purity of the language and to its smooth, continuous internal growth. Even if we want to put them aside for the time being, consoling ourselves that advantages cannot be placed next to these disadvantages, and that, since everything good also contains something bad, wisdom consists in obtaining as much as possible of the former and removing as little as possible from the latter, this much can certainly be ascertained from the difficult task of having to represent what is foreign in one's native language. . . .

*

These are the difficulties that stand in the way of this method of translation and the imperfections that are essentially inherent in it. But, granted that they exist, one still must acknowledge the venture itself, and its merit cannot be denied. It rests upon two conditions: that the understanding of foreign works be a well-known and desirable situation, and that a certain flexibility be attributed to the native language. Where these conditions are met, this type of translation becomes a natural phenomenon; since it influences the entire intellectual evolution and contains a certain value, it also creates definite enjoyment.

*

But what needs to be said about the opposite method, which requires no effort and no exertion from its reader, which wants to conjure the foreign author into his immediate presence and to show the work as it would have been if the author himself had written it originally in the reader's language? This requirement has not seldom been expressed as one that the true translator had to fulfill and as one that is far higher and more nearly perfect when compared to the former; individual attempts have also been made, perhaps even masterpieces, which all aimed at reaching this goal. Let us now evaluate this matter, and see whether it would not perhaps be appropriate if this method, which until now has certainly been used less frequently, could be used more often and could replace the other, which is of a dubious nature and in many ways ineffective.

*

We see immediately that the language of the translator has absolutely nothing to fear from this method. It must be his first rule not to allow himself anything—with respect to the relationship that exists between his work and a foreign language—which is not also permissible in an original work of the same genre in his native language. Indeed, as much as anyone else, he has the duty to observe at least the same scrupulous attention to the purity and perfection of language, to strive for the same grace and naturalness of style, for which his writer is praised in the original language. It is also certain, if we want to demonstrate to our compatriots very vividly what a writer meant for his language, that we can establish no better formula than to introduce him speaking in such a way as we imagine he would have spoken in our own language; this approach is all the more appropriate if the level of development at which he found his language has some resemblance to the level that our language has presently reached. We can imagine in a certain sense how Tacitus would have spoken if he had been a German or, expressed more precisely, how a German would speak who was for our language what Tacitus was for his; and happy is he who imagines this so vividly that he can really let Tacitus speak! But whether this could happen now, by letting this German Tacitus say the same things that the Roman Tacitus said in the Latin language, is another question that cannot easily be answered in the affirmative. For it is an entirely different matter to comprehend correctly the influence that a man has exerted upon his language and somehow to represent it, and again quite another matter to guess how his thoughts and their expression would have emerged if originally he had been accustomed to think and express himself in another language!

Whoever is convinced that thoughts and their expressions have the same internal and essential quality—and, after all, the whole art of understanding a discourse (and therefore all translation as well) is based on that conviction—can such a person separate a man from his native language and believe that he, or even only his chain of thoughts, could be one and the same in two languages? And if the thoughts are different in certain ways, can this person presume to deconstruct the discourse to its very core, to exclude the part that language itself contributes and by a chemical process, as it were, to combine these innermost parts with the essence and the power of another language? Evidently, in order to solve this problem, it would be necessary to remove completely from a man's written work everything that is, even in the remotest way, the effect of anything that he has said and heard in his mother tongue from childhood on. After that, one would have to feed into this man's naked and peculiar way of thinking—as it is directed toward a certain subject—everything that would have been the effect of all that

which he said and heard in the foreign language, from the beginning of his life, or from his first acquaintance with the language,
until he had become capable of original thinking and writing in it.
This will only be possible the day organic products can successfully
be combined by means of an artificial chemical process. Indeed, the
goal of translating in such a way as the author would have written
originally in the language of the translation is not only unattainable
but is also futile and empty in itself. For whoever recognizes the
creative power of language, as it is one with the character of the
nation, must also concede that for each of the greatest authors his
whole knowledge, and also the possibility of expressing it, is
formed in and through language, and that therefore no one adheres
to his language only mechanically, as if it were something externally
attached to him. As one can easily exchange a team of horses,
everyone can likewise choose to harness another language for his
thoughts; but every writer can produce original work only in his
mother tongue, and therefore the question cannot even be raised
how he would have written his works in another language. . . .

*

To what extent the applicability of this method is limited—
indeed in the field of translation it is almost equal to zero—is best
perceived when we consider the insurmountable difficulties it has
to face in the individual branches of art and scholarship. It must be
said that even in everyday usage there are only a few words in one
language to which a word in another language corresponds completely, so that the word could be used in all instances in which the
other is used and always produce in the same context the same
effect; this is even more true for all concepts (the more they are
imbued with a philosophical content), and it is most true of the
entire field of philosophy. Here more than anywhere else, every
language—in spite of the diverse views held simultaneously and
successively—still contains within itself a system of concepts
which, because they touch, connect with, and complement each
other in the same language, are one whole whose individual parts,
however, do not correspond to any of the systems of other languages, perhaps not even with the exception of God and Being, the
primal noun and the primal verb. For even that which is universal,
although situated outside the sphere of specific characteristic traits,
is still illuminated and colored by language.

Everyone's wisdom must be realized in this system of language. Everyone draws from what is there. Everyone helps to bring to light what is not yet there but latently present. Only in this way is the wisdom of the individual alive and can really govern his existence, which, indeed, he integrates completely into his language. If, therefore, the translator of a philosophical writer hesitates to bend the language of the translation, as much as it can be done, toward the original language, in order to give an idea of the system of concepts that was developed in it, and if he would have his writer speak as if he had originally formed thoughts and speech in another language, what can he do in view of the dissimilarity of elements in both languages, except to paraphrase—whereby, however, he does not attain his purpose, because a paraphrase will not and can never look like something that was originally produced in the author's language—or to transform the whole wisdom and learning of his author into the conceptual system of the translator's language, and in that way alter all the individual parts? By doing so, the translator has no way of telling how the wildest arbitrariness can be kept within limits. Indeed we have to say that a person who has only the slightest respect for philosophical endeavors and developments cannot begin to engage in such a loose game.

May Plato forgive my going from the philosopher to the writer of comedies. This genre is, as far as language is concerned, closest to the field of social conversation. The entire representation lives in the morals of the time and of the people, which in turn are vividly and perfectly reflected in the language. Gracefulness and naturalness are its foremost virtues, and that is exactly the reason why the difficulties of translating according to the method mentioned above are so enormous. For any approximation of a foreign language does damage to those virtues of presentation. Now if the translation wants to let the author of a play speak as if he had originally written in the language of the translation, then there are many things it cannot make him say, because they are not native to its people and therefore have no symbol in their language. In this case, the translator must either cut some parts out completely and thereby destroy the form and the power of the whole, or he must put something else in their place. In this field, the formula that is faithfully followed evidently leads to mere imitation, or to a still more repulsively conspicuous and confusing mixture of translation and imitation that throws the reader mercilessly back and forth like a ball between his world and the foreign one, between the author's

and the translator's invention and wit, from which he can draw no
pleasure, but will in the end certainly suffer dizziness and frustra-
tion enough. On the other hand, the translator who adheres to the
other method has no incentive at all to implement such arbitrary
changes, since his reader should always keep in mind that the author has lived in another world and written in another language.
He is bound only by the admittedly difficult art of supplying the
awareness of this foreign world in the shortest and most suitable
way, and of letting the greater ease and naturalness of the original
shine through everywhere.

These two examples, taken from the opposite ends of art and
scholarship, show clearly how little the actual purpose of all translating—an enjoyment of foreign works as unadulterated as possible—can be attained by a method that wants to breathe into the
translated work the total spirit of a language that is alien to it.
Moreover, every language has its peculiarity of rhythm for prose as
well as for poetry, and, if for once the assumption were to be
adopted that the author could have written in the language of the
translator, one would have to let him appear in the rhythm of that
language. In that way his work is even more distorted, and the
insight into his characteristic style, which the translation provides,
will be even more limited.

*

Indeed, this fiction, on which alone rests the theory of the
translator discussed here, goes far beyond the purpose of this enterprise. Seen from the first point of view, translating is a matter of
necessity for a nation of which only a small part can acquire sufficient knowledge of foreign languages, and of which a larger part
has a disposition toward the enjoyment of foreign works. If the
latter could merge completely with the former, then this form of
translation would be useless, and hardly anyone would take on this
thankless task.

It is different with the second point of view, which has nothing
to do with necessity, but is rather the work of concupiscence and
wantonness. The knowledge of foreign languages could be as widespread as possible, and the access to their loftiest works could be
open to anyone who is competent, and translation would still remain a curious enterprise, which would gather around itself more

and more eager listeners if someone were to promise to represent to us a work of Cicero or Plato in the same way as these men would have written it directly in German today. And if someone were to go so far as to do this not only in his own native tongue, but even in another, foreign one, he would appear to us as the greatest master in the difficult and almost impossible art of merging the spirits of the languages into one another. One can see that this would, strictly speaking, not be translation, and the result would not be the truest possible enjoyment of the works themselves; it would become more and more an imitation, and only the person who already knows these writers from somewhere else could actually enjoy such an artifact or work of art. And the actual goal could only be, in particular, to illustrate a similar relationship between certain expressions and combinations, and specific features in different languages and, in general, to illuminate the language with the characteristic spirit of a foreign master, but one who is completely separated and detached from his own language. . . .

*

Where do we go from here? Should we share this view and follow this advice? The ancients evidently translated little in that sense, and most modern peoples, discouraged by the difficulties of true translation, are content with imitation or paraphrase. Who would claim that anything has ever been *translated* into French from either the classical or the Germanic languages? But as much as we Germans might like to listen to this advice, we still would not follow it. An inner necessity, in which a peculiar mission of our nation is expressed clearly enough, has driven us in large numbers to translation; we cannot go back, and must go on. Just as our soil itself has probably become richer and more fertile, and our climate more lovely and mild after much transplanting of foreign plants, so do we feel that our language, which we practice less because of our Nordic lethargy, can only flourish and develop its own perfect power through the most varied contacts with what is foreign. And at the same time our nation seems to be destined, because of its respect for things foreign, and because of its disposition toward mediation, to carry all the treasures of foreign art and scholarship, together with its own, in its language, to unite them into a great historical whole, as it were, which would be kept safe in the center and heart of Europe; so that now, with the help of our language, everyone can enjoy, as purely and perfectly as it is possible for the foreigner, that which the most varied ages have brought forth. This seems indeed the true historical goal of translation on a large scale, as it is now indigenous to us. . . .

*

FIVE

WILHELM VON HUMBOLDT
From the Introduction to His Translation of *Agamemnon*

Translated by Sharon Sloan

Because of the unique character of a work such as Aeschylus's *Agamemnon*, it is untranslatable; yet it is untranslatable in a way quite different from all other works of great originality. It has repeatedly been observed and verified by both experience and research that no word in one language is completely equivalent to a word in another, if one disregards those expressions that designate purely physical objects. In this respect, languages are synonymic; each language expresses a concept somewhat differently, placing the nuance in each instance one step higher or lower on the ladder of perceptions. Such a synonymy of the major languages, or even of only Greek, Latin, and German (which would be especially appreciated) has never been undertaken, although fragments of such attempts can be found in the works of many writers; yet such a work, if prepared with intelligence, would undoubtedly be a most fascinating study.

A word is more than just the sign of a concept, for the concept could not come into existence, let alone be grasped, without the word; the indeterminate force of a thought forms itself into a word just as soft clouds form out of a clear blue sky. It should not be forgotten that the word has its own individual nature with its own specific character and specific shape, with its own power to affect the spirit, and that it is not without the ability to recreate itself. The origin of a word would be analogous to the origin of an ideal form in the imagination of the artist, if one wanted to think it

From *Aeschylos Agamemnon metrisch übersetzt* (Leipzig: Gerhard Fleischer dem Jüngern, 1816), as reprinted in *Gesammelte Schriften,* vol. 8 (Berlin: B. Behrs Verlag, 1909), pp. 119–46 through in human terms. (Such a conception is, however, impossible because to pronounce a word already presupposes the certainty of its being understood; speech itself can only be conceived of as a product of simultaneous interaction in which each person must carry within himself not only his own equal share of the work but the other's share as well, rather than just being in a position to help.) Similarly, this ideal form cannot be derived from something in the physical world; it springs from a pure energy of the mind and, in a concrete sense, out of nothingness. From this moment on, however, it enters into life, becomes real, and assumes a lasting form. What human being has not—even outside the realm of inspired artistic creations—created his own forms of fantasy, often early in childhood, and then lived with them thereafter more intimately than with the forms of reality?

How, then, could a word, whose meaning is not transmitted directly through the senses, ever be the perfect equivalent of a word in another language? It must of necessity present differences, and if an exact comparison of the best, the most careful, the most faithful translations is made, it is surprising to see the extent of the differences where the translators sought only to preserve the identity and uniformity of the original text. It can even be argued that the more a translation strives toward fidelity, the more it ultimately deviates from the original, for in attempting to imitate refined nuances and avoid simple generalities it can, in fact, only provide new and different nuances. Yet this should not deter us from translating. On the contrary, translation, especially poetic translation, is one of the most necessary tasks of any literature, partly because it directs those who do not know another language to forms of art and human experience that would otherwise have remained totally unknown, but above all because it increases the expressivity and depth of meaning of one's own language. For it is the wonderful characteristic of languages that, first and foremost, each one accommodates the general needs of everyday life; yet, through the spirit of the nation that shapes and forms it, a language can be infinitely enriched. It is not too bold to contend that everything, from the most elevated to the most profound, from the most forceful to the most fragile, can be expressed in every language, even in the dialects of primitive cultures, with which we are simply not well enough acquainted. (This is not to say that one language is not originally better than another or that some languages will not remain forever inaccessible.) Nevertheless these undertones of language slumber, as do the sounds of an unplayed instrument, until a nation learns how to draw them out.

All forms of language are symbols, not the objects themselves, not prearranged signs, but sounds; they find themselves, together with the objects and ideas that they represent, filtered through the mind in which they originated and continue to originate in a real or, one might even say, a mystical relationship. These objects of reality are held suspended in a partially dissolved state as ideas that can define, separate, and recombine with one another in such a way as to defy all imaginable limitations. A nobler, more profound, more fragile sense may be read into these symbols only if one imagines, expresses, receives, and then repeats them in such a way. Thus, without any noticeable transformation, language is raised to a higher level of expression, is expanded into a greater representation of complexity.

To the same extent that a language is enriched, a nation is also enriched. Think how the German language, to cite only one example, has profited since it began imitating Greek meter. And think how our nation has progressed, not just the well-educated among us but the masses as well—even women and children—since the Greeks have been available to our nation's readers in an authentic and undistorted form. It is impossible to overstate the importance of the service Klopstock rendered to the German nation with his first successful treatment of ancient meter or the even greater service of Voss, who may be said to have introduced classical antiquity into the German language. It is difficult to imagine a more powerful and beneficial impact on an already highly cultivated national culture, and it can be attributed entirely to him. His combined talent and strength of character allowed him to keep working and reworking a problem until he found that form, which of course may still be improved upon, in which, now and for as long as German is spoken, the ancients will be rendered in our language. Whoever creates such a true form may rest assured that his labor will endure, whereas a work of even the highest genius, if it is an isolated occurrence lacking such a form, will remain without consequence for the development of the language. If, however, translation is to give the language and spirit of a nation that which it does not possess or possesses in another form, then the first requirement is always fidelity. This fidelity must direct itself to the true character of the original and not rely on the incidentals, just as in general every good translation should grow out of a simple

and modest love of the original and the study that this love implies—and to which the translation always returns.

A necessary corollary to this view is that a translation should
indeed have a foreign flavor to it, but only to a certain degree; the
line beyond which this clearly becomes an error can easily be
drawn. As long as one does not feel the foreignness *(Fremdheit)* yet
does feel the foreign *(Fremde)*, a translation has reached its highest
goal; but where foreignness appears as such, and more than likely
even obscures the foreign, the translator betrays his inadequacy.
The instinct of the unbiased reader is not likely to miss this fine
line of separation. If the translator, out of an extreme aversion to
what is unusual, goes even further and strives to avoid the foreign
altogether (one often hears it said of translation that the translator
should write the way the author of the original would have written
in the language of the translator), then all translation and whatever
benefits translation may bring to a language and a nation are destroyed. (This kind of thinking has not taken into consideration
that, apart from discussions of the sciences and actual facts, no
writer would have written the same thing in the same way in another language.) How else has it happened that none of the spirit
of the ancients has been assimilated by the French as a nation? Even
though all of the major Greeks and Romans have been translated
into the French language, and some have even been translated into
the French style quite well, neither the spirit of antiquity nor even
an understanding of that spirit has permeated the French nation
(we are not speaking here of individual scholars).

In my own work, I have tried to approach the simplicity and
fidelity just described. With each new revision, I have strived to
remove more of what was not plainly stated in the text. The inabil-
ity to attain the peculiar beauty of the original easily entices one to
embellish it with foreign decoration, which as a rule simply produces a false coloring and a different tone. I have tried to guard
against un-Germanness and obscurity, but in the latter respect one
should not make unjust requirements that might preclude gaining
other, higher assets. A translation cannot and should not be a commentary. It should not contain ambiguities caused by insufficient
understanding of the language and awkward formulations; however, where the original only intimates without clearly expressing,
where it allows itself metaphors whose correlation is hard to grasp,
where it leaves out intermediate ideas, the translator commits an
injustice if he arbitrarily introduces a clarity that misrepresents the

character of the text. The obscurity one often finds in the writings of the ancients—*Agamemnon* presents an excellent example of this—is a result of the brevity and the boldness with which thoughts, images, emotions, memories, atonements, as they come out of the impassioned soul, are linked together with a disdain for any mediating connective sentences. As one thinks oneself into the mood of the poet, into his time, into the characters he puts on the stage, the obscurity gradually fades and is replaced by an intense clarity. A part of this careful attention must also be given to the translation: never expect that what is sublime, immense, and extraordinary in the original language will be easily and immediately comprehensible in the translation. Ease and clarity always remain virtues that a translator attains only with the utmost difficulty, and never through mere hard work and revision: they are due for the most part to fortuitous inspiration, and I know only too well to what extent my own translation falls short of what I would wish it to be.

S I X

JOHANN WOLFGANG VON GOETHE
Translations

Translated by Sharon Sloan

There are three kinds of translation. The first acquaints us with the foreign country on our own terms; a plain prose translation is best for this purpose. Prose in and of itself serves as the best introduction: it completely neutralizes the formal characteristics of any sort of poetic art and reduces even the most exuberant waves of poetic enthusiasm to still water. The plain prose translation surprises us with foreign splendors in the midst of our national domestic sensibility; in our everyday lives, and without our realizing what is happening to us—by lending our lives a nobler air—it genuinely uplifts us. Luther's Bible translation will produce this kind of effect with each reading.

Much would have been gained, for instance, if the *Nibelungen* had been set in good, solid prose at the outset, and labeled as popular literature. Then the brutal, dark, solemn, and strange sense of chivalry would still have spoken to us in its full power. Whether this would still be feasible or even advisable now is best decided by those who have more rigorously dedicated themselves to these matters of antiquity.

A second epoch follows, in which the translator endeavors to transport himself into the foreign situation but actually only appropriates the foreign idea and represents it as his own. I would like to call such an epoch *parodistic,* in the purest sense of that word. It is most often men of wit who feel drawn to the parodistic. The French make use of this style in the translation of all poetic works:

From "Übersetzungen," *Noten und Abhandlungen zum bessern Verständnis des west-östlichen Divans* (Stuttgart, 1819). Footnotes are translator's notes.

Delille's translations provide hundreds of examples.[1] In the same way that the French adapt foreign words to their pronunciation, they adapt feelings, thoughts, even objects; for every foreign fruit there must be a substitute grown in their own soil.

Wieland's translations are of this kind;[2] he, too, had his own peculiar understanding and taste, which he adapted to antiquity and foreign countries only to the extent that he found it convenient. This superb man can be seen as the representative of his time; he exercised an inordinate amount of influence in that, no matter what appealed to him, no matter how he absorbed and passed it on to his contemporaries, it was received by them as something pleasant and enjoyable.

Because we cannot linger for very long in either a perfect or an imperfect state but must, after all, undergo one transformation after another, we experienced the third epoch of translation, which is the final and highest of the three. In such periods, the goal of the translation is to achieve perfect identity with the original, so that the one does not exist instead of the other but in the other's place.

This kind met with the most resistance in its early stages, because the translator identifies so strongly with the original that he more or less gives up the uniqueness of his own nation, creating this third kind of text for which the taste of the masses has to be developed.

At first the public was not at all satisfied with Voss[3] (who will never be fully appreciated) until gradually the public's ear accustomed itself to this new kind of translation and became comfortable with it. Now anyone who assesses the extent of what has happened, what versatility has come to the Germans, what rhythmical and metrical advantages are available to the spirited, talented beginner, how Ariosto and Tasso, Shakespeare and Calderon have been brought to us two and three times over as Germanized foreigners, may hope that literary history will openly acknowledge who was the first to choose this path in spite of so many and varied obstacles.

For the most part, the works of von Hammer indicate a similar treatment of oriental masterpieces;[4] he suggests that the translation

1. Abbé Jacques Delille, a well-known and prolific French translator of Goethe's time.
2. Christoph Martin Wieland translated twenty-two of Shakespeare's plays into German between 1762 and 1766.
3. Johann Heinrich Voss, the German translator of Homer into hexameters.
4. Joseph von Hammer-Purgstall, the Viennese orientalist.

approximate as closely as possible the external form of the original work. How much more convincing the passages of a translation of Firdusi prove to be when produced by our friend himself compared to those reworked by an adaptor whose examples can be read in the *Fundgruben*.[5] Disfiguring a poet in this way is, in our opinion, the saddest mistake a diligent and quite capable translator can make.

Since, however, in every literature all of these three epochs are found to repeat and reverse themselves, as well as coexist simultaneously, a prose translation of the *Shahmama*[6] and the works of Nizami would still be in order. It could be used for a quick reading, which would open up the essential meaning of the work: we could enjoy the historical, the legendary, the larger ethical issues, and we would gradually become familiar with the attitudes and ways of thinking, until we could at last feel a kinship with them.

Think only of the undisputed applause we Germans have attributed to such a translation of the *Sakuntala*,[7] whose success we can most definitely ascribe to its plain prose, into which the poem has been dissolved. Now would be the proper time for a new translation of the third type that would not only correspond to the various dialects, rhythms, meters, and prosaic idioms in the original but would also, in a pleasant and familiar manner, renew the poem in all of its distinctiveness for us. Since a manuscript of this eternal work is available in Paris, a German living there could earn undying gratitude for undertaking such a work.

Similarly, the English translator of *Messenger of the Clouds*[8] deserves every honor, simply because our first acquaintance with this kind of a work is always such a momentous occasion in our lives. But his translation really belongs to the second epoch; using paraphrase and supplementary words, the translation flatters the Northern ear and senses with its iambic pentameter. I owe a debt of thanks to our own Kosegarten[9] for translating a few lines directly from the original source language, which indeed give a totally different impression. The Englishman took certain liberties as well, transposing motifs, which the trained aesthetic eye immediately discovers and condemns.

5. *Fundgruben des Orients,* a review of Oriental studies edited by von Hammer.
6. *The Book of Kings,* the Persian poet Firdusi's long poem.
7. The *Sakuntala* was written by the Indian dramatist Kalidasa.
8. Kalidasa's *Meghaduta,* translated by Horace H. Wilson.
9. Ludwig Gotthard Kosegarten, a scholar-author of Goethe's time.

The reason why we also call the third epoch the final one can be explained in a few words. A translation that attempts to identify itself with the original ultimately comes close to an interlinear version and greatly facilitates our understanding of the original. We are led, yes, compelled as it were, back to the source text: the circle, within which the approximation of the foreign and the familiar, the known and the unknown constantly move, is finally complete.

SEVEN

Dante Gabriel Rossetti
Preface to *The Early Italian Poets*

I NEED not dilate here on the characteristics of the first epoch of Italian Poetry; since the extent of my translated selections is sufficient to afford a complete view of it. Its great beauties may often remain unapproached in the versions here attempted; but, at the same time, its imperfections are not all to be charged to the translator. Among these I may refer to its limited range of subject and continual obscurity, as well as to its monotony in the use of rhymes or frequent substitution of assonances. But to compensate for much that is incomplete and inexperienced, these poems possess, in their degree, beauties of a kind which can never again exist in art; and offer, besides, a treasure of grace and variety in the formation of their metres. Nothing but a strong impression, first of their poetic value, and next of the biographical interest of some of them (chiefly of those in my second division), would have inclined me to bestow the time and trouble which have resulted in this collection.

Much has been said, and in many respects justly, against the value of metrical translation. But I think it would be admitted that the tributary art might find a not illegitimate use in the case of poems which come down to us in such a form as do these early Italian ones. Struggling originally with corrupt dialect and imperfect expression, and hardly kept alive through centuries of neglect, they have reached that last and worst state in which the coup de grâce has almost been dealt them by clumsy transcription and pedantic superstructure. At this stage the task of talking much more about them in any language is hardly to be entered upon; and a

This essay was first published in 1861.

translation (involving as it does the necessity of settling many points without discussion) remains perhaps the most direct form of commentary.

The life-blood of rhymed translation is this,—that a good poem shall not be turned into a bad one. The only true motive for putting poetry into a fresh language must be to endow a fresh nation, as far as possible, with one more possession of beauty. Poetry not being an exact science, literality of rendering is altogether secondary to this chief aim. I say *literality,*—not fidelity, which is by no means the same thing. When literality can be combined with what is thus the primary condition of success, the translator is fortunate, and must strive his utmost to unite them; when such object can only be attained by paraphrase, that is his only path.

Any merit possessed by these translations is derived from an effort to follow this principle; and, in some degree, from the fact that such painstaking in arrangement and descriptive heading as is often indispensable to old and especially to "occasional" poetry, has here been bestowed on these poets for the first time.

That there are many defects in these translations, or that the above merit is their defect, or that they have no merits but only defects, are discoveries so sure to be made if necessary (or perhaps here and there in any case), that I may safely leave them in other hands. The collection has probably a wider scope than some readers might look for, and includes now and then (though I believe in rare instances) matter which may not meet with universal approval; and whose introduction, needed as it is by the literary aim of my work, is I know inconsistent with the principles of pretty bookmaking. My wish has been to give a full and truthful view of early Italian poetry; not to make it appear to consist only of certain elements to the exclusion of others equally belonging to it.

Of the difficulties I have had to encounter,—the causes of imperfections for which I have no other excuse,—it is the reader's best privilege to remain ignorant; but I may perhaps be pardoned for briefly referring to such among these as concern the exigencies of translation. The task of the translator (and with all humility be it spoken) is one of some self-denial. Often would he avail himself of any special grace of his own idiom and epoch, if only his will belonged to him; often would some cadence serve him but for his author's structure—some structure but for his author's cadence; often the beautiful turn of a stanza must be weakened to adopt some rhyme which will tally, and he sees the poet revelling in abundance of language where himself is scantily supplied. Now he would slight the matter for the music, and now the music for the matter; but no, he must deal to each alike. Sometimes, too, a flaw in the work galls him, and he would fain remove it, doing for the poet that which his age denied him; but no,—it is not in the bond. His path is like that of Aladdin through the enchanted vaults: many are the precious fruits and flowers which he must pass by unheeded in search for the lamp alone; happy if at last, when brought to light, it does not prove that his old lamp has been exchanged for a new one,—glittering indeed to the eye, but scarcely of the same virtue nor with the same genius at its summons.

In relinquishing this work (which, small as it is, is the only contribution I expect to make to our English knowledge of old Italy), I feel, as it were, divided from my youth. The first associations I have are connected with my father's devoted studies, which, from his own point of view, have done so much towards the general investigation of Dante's writings. Thus, in those early days, all around me partook of the influence of the great Florentine; till, from viewing it as a natural element, I also, growing older, was drawn within the circle. I trust that from this the reader may place more confidence in a work not carelessly undertaken, though produced in the spare time of other pursuits more closely followed. He should perhaps be told that it has occupied the leisure moments of not a few years; thus affording, often at long intervals, every opportunity for consideration and revision; and that on the score of care, at least, he has no need to mistrust it.

Nevertheless, I know there is no great stir to be made by launching afresh, on high seas busy with new traffic, the ships which have been long outstripped and the ensigns which are grown strange. The feeling of self-doubt inseparable from such an attempt has been admirably expressed by a great living poet, in words which may be applied exactly to my humbler position, though relating in his case to a work all his own.

> Still, what if I approach the august sphere
> Named now with only one name,—disentwine
> That under current soft and argentine
> From its fierce mate in the majestic mass
> Leaven'd as the sea whose fire was mix'd with glass
> In John's transcendent vision,—launch once more

That lustre? Dante, pacer of the shore
Where glutted Hell disgorges filthiest gloom,
Unbitten by its whirring sulphur-spume—
Or whence the grieved and obscure waters slope
Into a darkness quieted by hope—
Plucker of amaranths grown beneath God's eye
In gracious twilights where His chosen lie,—
I would do this! If I should falter now! . . .
          (*Sordello,* by ROBERT BROWNING, Bk. 1)

*

EIGHT
FRIEDRICH NIETZSCHE
On the Problem of Translation

Translated by Peter Mollenhauer

I

One can gauge the degree of the historical sense an age possesses by the manner in which it translates texts and by the manner in which it seeks to incorporate past epochs and books into its own being. Corneille's Frenchmen—and even those of the Revolution—took hold of Roman antiquity in a manner that we—thanks to our more refined sense of history—would no longer have the courage to employ. And then Roman antiquity itself: how violently, and at the same time how naively, it pressed its hand upon everything good and sublime in the older periods of ancient Greece! Consider how the Romans translated this material to suit their own age and how intentionally as well as heedlessly they wiped away the wing-dust of the butterfly moment! Horace, off and on, translated Alcaeus or Archilochus; Propertius translated Callimachus and Philetas (poets who were in the same rank with Theocritus, if we be permitted to make such a judgment). How little concern these translators had for this or that experience by the actual creator who had imbued his poem with symbols of such experiences! As poets, they were averse to the antiquarian inquisitive spirit that precedes the historical sense. As poets they did not recognize the existence of the purely personal images and names of anything that served as the national costume or mask of a city, a coastal area, or a century, and therefore immediately replaced all this by present realities and by things Roman. They seemed to ask us: "Should we

From *Die fröhliche Wissenschaft* (1882), as reprinted in *Werke in drei Bänden,* vol.2, section 83 (Munich: Hanser, 1962), p. 91f.

not make antiquity to suit our own purposes and make *ourselves* comfortable in it? Why can't we breathe our soul into this dead body?—for it is dead, no doubt, and how ugly all dead things are!" These poet-translators did not know the pleasure of the historical sense; anything past and alien was an irritant to them, and as Romans they considered it to be nothing but a stimulus for yet another Roman conquest. In those days, indeed, to translate meant to conquer—not merely in the sense that one would omit the historical dimension but also in the sense that one would add a hint of contemporaneousness to the material translated and, above all, in the sense that one would delete the name of the poet and insert the translator's name in its place. And all this was done with the very best conscience as a member of the Roman Empire, without realizing that such actions constituted theft.

II

What is most difficult to translate from one language into another is the tempo of its style: that which is grounded in the character of the race or, to speak in a physiological manner, in the average tempo of its "metabolism." There are some well-meaning translations that are nothing but involuntary generalizations of the original and as such can almost be considered forgeries. This is so because they failed also to translate the original's courageous and cheerful tempo which helps us to be consoled for, if not to skip over, all that is dangerous in words and things. The German speaker is almost incapable of expressing this *presto* quality in his language and, as is fair to conclude, is incapable of many of the most delightful and daring *nuances* of unfettered, freethinking thought. Just as buffo and satyr are strangers to the corporeal and oral sense of the German, so will Aristophanes and Petronius be untranslatable to him. Everything that is pompous, viscous, or solemnly plump, all those tedious and boring turns of style are developed in the German in a superabundant variety. I hope I will be forgiven if I mention the fact that even Goethe's prose, with its mixture of stiffness and daintiness, is no exception. Reflecting "the good old times" of which it was a part, Goethe's prose was an

From *Jenseits von Gut und Böse* (Leipzig: C. G. Naumann, 1886), as reprinted in *Werke in drei Bänden*, vol. 2, section 28 (Munich: Hanser, 1962), p. 593f.

expression of German taste at a time when a "German taste" was still in existence—albeit a taste that was a rococo taste *in moribus et artibus,* in morals and arts. Lessing was an exception. He had the temperament of an actor who knows how to do as well as how to comprehend many things. Not without good reason did he translate Bayle, and take pleasure in seeking the intellectual company of a Diderot and a Voltaire, and even more so that of the Roman writers of comedy; he loved the tempo of freethinking, the flight away from Germany. But even if the German language were to speak with Lessing's prose, how could it possibly imitate the tempo of Machiavelli, who, in *The Prince,* lets us breathe the dry, fine air of Florence, and who cannot help but express the most serious matter in a refractory *allegrissimo:* perhaps he does this not without a malicious artistic inkling of the contrast he is daring to expose. His thoughts: long, difficult, hard, and dangerous! His tempo: gallop, accompanied by the very best and most mischievous mood! Finally, who could possibly dare to write a German translation of Petronius, who, more than any great musician to date, was the real maestro of the *presto* tempo in his inventions, his ideas, his words. What does the whole morass of a sick and evil world, even the "old world," matter if, as Petronius did, one possesses the wind's feet, its pulling strength and breath, and its liberating disdain—this wind that heals everything because it makes everything flow! And then consider Aristophanes, that illumining, complementary spirit for whose sake one can forgive all of ancient Greece for having existed at all, provided one grasps deep inside what exactly is in need of forgiveness, of transfiguration. I don't know of anything that caused me to dream more about Plato's obscurity and his Sphinx-like nature than the *petit fait* that I was lucky enough to receive: the fact that under the pillow on one's deathbed one would find no Bible, nothing Egyptian, nothing Pythagorean or Platonic—no, but only the writings of Aristophanes. Without Aristophanes, how would Plato have been able to bear life—a Greek life whose essence he negated?

NINE
WALTER BENJAMIN
The Task of the Translator
Translated by Harry Zohn

In the appreciation of a work of art or an art form, consideration of the receiver never proves fruitful. Not only is any reference to a certain public or its representatives misleading, but even the concept of an "ideal" receiver is detrimental in the theoretical consideration of art, since all it posits is the existence and nature of man as such. Art, in the same way, posits man's physical and spiritual existence, but in none of its works is it concerned with his response. No poem is intended for the reader, no picture for the beholder, no symphony for the listener.

Is a translation meant for readers who do not understand the original? This would seem to explain adequately the divergence of their standing in the realm of art. Moreover, it seems to be the only conceivable reason for saying "the same thing" repeatedly. For what does a literary work "say"? What does it communicate? It "tells" very little to those who understand it. Its essential quality is not statement or the imparting of information. Yet any translation which intends to perform a transmitting function cannot transmit anything but information—hence, something inessential. This is the hallmark of bad translations. But do we not generally regard as the essential substance of a literary work what it contains in addition to information—as even a poor translator will admit—the unfathomable, the mysterious, the "poetic," something that a transla-

This translation of the 1923 essay "Die Aufgabe des Übersetzers" appeared in Walter Benjamin, *Illuminations,* edited and with an Introduction by Hannah Arendt (New York: Harcourt, Brace and World, 1968); © 1955 by Suhrkamp Verlag, Frankfurt a.M., English translation © 1968 by Harcourt Brace Jovanovich, Inc., reprinted by permission of Harcourt Brace Jovanovich, Inc. See chapter 16, note 5, for additional information on the 1923 publication.

tor can reproduce only if he is also a poet? This, actually, is the cause of another characteristic of inferior translation, which consequently we may define as the inaccurate transmission of an inessential content. This will be true whenever a translation undertakes to serve the reader. However, if it were intended for the reader, the same would have to apply to the original. If the original does not exist for the reader's sake, how could the translation be understood on the basis of this premise?

Translation is a mode. To comprehend it as mode one must go back to the original, for that contains the law governing the translation: its translatability. The question of whether a work is translatable has a dual meaning. Either: Will an adequate translator ever be found among the totality of its readers? Or, more pertinently: Does its nature lend itself to translation and, therefore, in view of the significance of the mode, call for it? In principle, the first question can be decided only contingently; the second, however, apodictically. Only superficial thinking will deny the independent meaning of the latter and declare both questions to be of equal significance. . . . It should be pointed out that certain correlative concepts retain their meaning, and possibly their foremost significance, if they are referred exclusively to man. One might, for example, speak of an unforgettable life or moment even if all men had forgotten it. If the nature of such a life or moment required that it be unforgotten, that predicate would not imply a falsehood but merely a claim not fulfilled by men, and probably also a reference to a realm in which it *is* fulfilled: God's remembrance. Analogously, the translatability of linguistic creations ought to be considered even if men should prove unable to translate them. Given a strict concept of translation, would they not really be translatable to some degree? The question as to whether the translation of certain linguistic creations is called for ought to be posed in this sense. For this thought is valid here: If translation is a mode, translatability must be an essential feature of certain works.

Translatability is an essential quality of certain works, which is not to say that it is essential that they be translated; it means rather that a specific significance inherent in the original manifests itself in its translatability. It is plausible that no translation, however good it may be, can have any significance as regards the original. Yet, by virtue of its translatability the original is closely connected with the translation; in fact, this connection is all the closer since it is no longer of importance to the original. We may call this con-

nection a natural one, or, more specifically, a vital connection. Just
as the manifestations of life are intimately connected with the phenomenon of life without being of importance to it, a translation
issues from the original—not so much from its life as from its afterlife. For a translation comes later than the original, and since the
important works of world literature never find their chosen translators at the time of their origin, their translation marks their stage
of continued life. The idea of life and afterlife in works of art
should be regarded with an entirely unmetaphorical objectivity.
Even in times of narrowly prejudiced thought there was an inkling
that life was not limited to organic corporeality. But it cannot be a
matter of extending its dominion under the feeble scepter of the
soul, as Fechner tried to do, or, conversely, of basing its definition
on the even less conclusive factors of animality, such as sensation,
which characterize life only occasionally. The concept of life is
given its due only if everything that has a history of its own, and is
not merely the setting for history, is credited with life. In the final
analysis, the range of life must be determined by history rather than
by nature, least of all by such tenuous factors as sensation and soul.
The philosopher's task consists in comprehending all of natural life
through the more encompassing life of history. And indeed, is not
the continued life of works of art far easier to recognize than the
continual life of animal species? The history of the great works of
art tells us about their antecedents, their realization in the age of
the artist, their potentially eternal afterlife in succeeding generations. Where this last manifests itself, it is called fame. Translations
that are more than transmissions of subject matter come into being
when in the course of its survival a work has reached the age of its
fame. Contrary, therefore, to the claims of bad translators, such
translations do not so much serve the work as owe their existence
to it. The life of the originals attains in them to its ever-renewed
latest and most abundant flowering.

  Being a special and high form of life, this flowering is governed
by a special, high purposiveness. The relationship between life and
purposefulness, seemingly obvious yet almost beyond the grasp of
the intellect, reveals itself only if the ultimate purpose toward
which all single functions tend is sought not in its own sphere but
in a higher one. All purposeful manifestations of life, including
their very purposiveness, in the final analysis have their end not in
life, but in the expression of its nature, in the representation of its
significance. Translation thus ultimately serves the purpose of ex-

pressing the central reciprocal relationship between languages. It cannot possibly reveal or establish this hidden relationship itself; but it can represent it by realizing it in embryonic or intensive form. This representation of hidden significance through an embryonic attempt at making it visible is of so singular a nature that it is rarely met with in the sphere of nonlinguistic life. This, in its analogies and symbols, can draw on other ways of suggesting meaning than intensive—that is, anticipative, intimating—realization. As for the posited central kinship of languages, it is marked by a distinctive convergence. Languages are not strangers to one another, but are, a priori and apart from all historical relationships, interrelated in what they want to express.

With this attempt at an explication our study appears to rejoin, after futile detours, the traditional theory of translation. If the kinship of languages is to be demonstrated by translations, how else can this be done but by conveying the form and meaning of the original as accurately as possible? To be sure, that theory would be hard put to define the nature of this accuracy and therefore could shed no light on what is important in a translation. Actually, however, the kinship of languages is brought out by a translation far more profoundly and clearly than in the superficial and indefinable similarity of two works of literature. To grasp the genuine relationship between an original and a translation requires an investigation analogous to the argumentation by which a critique of cognition would have to prove the impossibility of an image theory. There it is a matter of showing that in cognition there could be no objectivity, not even a claim to it, if it dealt with images of reality; here it can be demonstrated that no translation would be possible if in its ultimate essence it strove for likeness to the original. For in its afterlife—which could not be called that if it were not a transformation and a renewal of something living—the original undergoes a change. Even words with fixed meaning can undergo a maturing process. The obvious tendency of a writer's literary style may in time wither away, only to give rise to immanent tendencies in the literary creation. What sounded fresh once may sound hackneyed later; what was once current may someday sound quaint. To seek the essence of such changes, as well as the equally constant changes in meaning, in the subjectivity of posterity rather than in the very life of language and its works, would mean—even allowing for the crudest psychologism—to confuse the root cause of a thing with its essence. More pertinently, it would mean denying, by an impotence of thought, one of the most powerful and fruitful historical processes. And even if one tried to turn an author's last stroke of the pen into the coup de grâce of his work, this still would not save that dead theory of translation. For just as the tenor and the significance of the great works of literature undergo a complete transformation over the centuries, the mother tongue of the translator is transformed as well. While a poet's words endure in his own language, even the greatest translation is destined to become part of the growth of its own language and eventually to be absorbed by its renewal. Translation is so far removed from being the sterile equation of two dead languages that of all literary forms it is the one charged with the special mission of watching over the maturing process of the original language and the birth pangs of its own.

If the kinship of languages manifests itself in translations, this is not accomplished through a vague alikeness between adaptation and original. It stands to reason that kinship does not necessarily involve likeness. The concept of kinship as used here is in accord with its more restricted common usage: in both cases, it cannot be defined adequately by identity of origin, although in defining the more restricted usage the concept of origin remains indispensable. Wherein resides the relatedness of two languages, apart from historical considerations? Certainly not in the similarity between works of literature or words. Rather, all suprahistorical kinship of languages rests in the intention underlying each language as a whole—an intention, however, which no single language can attain by itself but which is realized only by the totality of their intentions supplementing each other: pure language. While all individual elements of foreign languages—words, sentences, structure—are mutually exclusive, these languages supplement one another in their intentions. Without distinguishing the intended object from the mode of intention, no firm grasp of this basic law of a philosophy of language can be achieved. The words *Brot* and *pain* "intend" the same object, but the modes of this intention are not the same. It is owing to these modes that the word *Brot* means something different to a German than the word *pain* to a Frenchman, that these words are not interchangeable for them, that, in fact, they strive to exclude each other. As to the intended object, however, the two words mean the very same thing. While the modes of intention in these two words are in conflict, intention and object of intention complement each of the two languages from which they are derived; there the object is complementary to the intention. In the individual, unsupplemented languages, meaning is never found in relative independence, as in individual words or sentences; rather, it is in a constant state of flux—until it is able to emerge as pure language from the harmony of all the various modes of intention. Until then, it remains hidden in the languages. If, however, these languages continue to grow in this manner until the end of their time, it is translation which catches fire on the eternal life of the works and the perpetual renewal of language. Translation keeps putting the hallowed growth of languages to the test: How far removed is their hidden meaning from revelation, how close can it be brought by the knowledge of this remoteness?

This, to be sure, is to admit that all translation is only a somewhat provisional way of coming to terms with the foreignness of languages. An instant and final rather than a temporary and provisional solution of this foreignness remains out of the reach of mankind; at any rate, it eludes any direct attempt. Indirectly, however, the growth of religions ripens the hidden seed into a higher development of language. Although translation, unlike art, cannot claim permanence for its products, its goal is undeniably a final, conclusive, decisive stage of all linguistic creation. In translation the original rises into a higher and purer linguistic air, as it were. It cannot live there permanently, to be sure, and it certainly does not reach it in its entirety. Yet, in a singularly impressive manner, at least it points the way to this region: the predestined, hitherto inaccessible realm of reconciliation and fulfillment of languages. The transfer can never be total, but what reaches this region is that element in a translation which goes beyond transmittal of subject matter. This nucleus is best defined as the element that does not lend itself to translation. Even when all the surface content has been extracted and transmitted, the primary concern of the genuine translator remains elusive. Unlike the words of the original, it is not translatable, because the relationship between content and language is quite different in the original and the translation. While content and language form a certain unity in the original, like a fruit and its skin, the language of the translation envelops its content like a royal robe with ample folds. For it signifies a more exalted language than its own and thus remains unsuited to its content, overpowering and alien. This disjunction prevents translation and at the same time makes it superfluous. For any translation of a work originating in a specific stage of linguistic history represents, in regard to a specific aspect of its content, translation into all other languages. Thus translation, ironically, transplants the original into a more definitive linguistic realm since it can no longer be displaced by a secondary rendering. The original can only be raised there anew and at other points of time. It is no mere coincidence that the word "ironic" here brings the Romanticists to mind. They, more than any others, were gifted with an insight into the life of literary works which has its highest testimony in translation. To be sure, they hardly recognized translation in this sense, but devoted their entire attention to criticism, another, if lesser, factor in the continued life of literary works. But even though the Romanticists virtually ignored translation in their theoretical writings, their own great translations testify to their sense of the essential nature and the dignity of this literary mode. There is abundant evidence that this sense is not necessarily most pronounced in a poet; in fact, he may be least open to it. Not even literary history suggests the traditional notion that great poets have been eminent translators and lesser poets have been indifferent translators. A number of the most eminent ones, such as Luther, Voss, and Schlegel, are incomparably more important as translators than as creative writers; some of the great among them, such as Hölderlin and Stefan George, cannot be simply subsumed as poets, and quite particularly not if we consider them as translators. As translation is a mode of its own, the task of the translator, too, may be regarded as distinct and clearly differentiated from the task of the poet.

The task of the translator consists in finding that intended effect [*Intention*] upon the language into which he is translating which produces in it the echo of the original. This is a feature of translation which basically differentiates it from the poet's work, because the effort of the latter is never directed at the language as such, at its totality, but solely and immediately at specific linguistic contextual aspects. Unlike a work of literature, translation does not find itself in the center of the language forest but on the outside facing the wooded ridge; it calls into it without entering, aiming at that single spot where the echo is able to give, in its own language, the reverberation of the work in the alien one. Not only does the aim of translation differ from that of a literary work—it intends language as a whole, taking an individual work in an alien language as a point of departure—but it is a different effort altogether. The intention of the poet is spontaneous, primary, graphic; that of the translator is derivative, ultimate, ideational. For the great motif of integrating many tongues into one true language is at work. This language is one in which the independent sentences, works of literature, critical judgments, will never communicate—for they remain dependent on translation; but in it the languages themselves, supplemented and reconciled in their mode of signification, harmonize. If there is such a thing as a language of truth, the tensionless and even silent depository of the ultimate truth which all thought strives for, then this language of truth is—the true language. And this very language, whose divination and description is the only perfection a philosopher can hope for, is concealed in concentrated fashion in translations. There is no muse of philosophy, nor is there one of translation. But despite the claims of sentimental artists, these two are not banausic. For there is a philosophical genius that is characterized by a yearning for that language which manifests itself in translations.

> Les langues imparfaites en cela que plusieurs, manque la suprême: penser étant écrire sans accessoires, ni chuchotement mais tacite encore l'immortelle parole, la diversité, sur terre, des idiomes empêche personne de proférer les mots qui, sinon se trouveraient, par une frappe unique, elle-même matériellement la vérité.[1]

If what Mallarmé evokes here is fully fathomable to a philosopher, translation, with its rudiments of such a language, is midway between poetry and doctrine. Its products are less sharply defined, but it leaves no less of a mark on history.

If the task of the translator is viewed in this light, the roads toward a solution seem to be all the more obscure and impenetrable. Indeed, the problem of ripening the seed of pure language in a translation seems to be insoluble, determinable in no solution. For is not the ground cut from under such a solution if the reproduction of the sense ceases to be decisive? Viewed negatively, this is actually the meaning of all the foregoing. The traditional concepts in any discussion of translations are fidelity and license—the freedom of faithful reproduction and, in its service, fidelity to the word. These ideas seem to be no longer serviceable to a theory that looks for other things in a translation than reproduction of mean-

---

1. "The imperfection of languages consists in their plurality, the supreme one is lacking: thinking is writing without accessories or even whispering, the immortal word still remains silent; the diversity of idioms on earth prevents everybody from uttering the words which otherwise, at one single stroke, would materialize as truth."

ing. To be sure, traditional usage makes these terms appear as if in constant conflict with each other. What can fidelity really do for the rendering of meaning? Fidelity in the translation of individual words can almost never fully reproduce the meaning they have in the original. For sense in its poetic significance is not limited to meaning, but derives from the connotations conveyed by the word chosen to express it. We say of words that they have emotional connotations. A literal rendering of the syntax completely demolishes the theory of reproduction of meaning and is a direct threat to comprehensibility. The nineteenth century considered Hölderlin's translations of Sophocles as monstrous examples of such literalness. Finally, it is self-evident how greatly fidelity in reproducing the form impedes the rendering of the sense. Thus no case for literalness can be based on a desire to retain the meaning. Meaning is served far better—and literature and language far worse—by the unrestrained license of bad translators. Of necessity, therefore, the demand for literalness, whose justification is obvious, whose legitimate ground is quite obscure, must be understood in a more meaningful context. Fragments of a vessel which are to be glued together must match one another in the smallest details, although they need not be like one another. In the same way a translation, instead of resembling the meaning of the original, must lovingly and in detail incorporate the original's mode of signification, thus making both the original and the translation recognizable as fragments of a greater language, just as fragments are part of a vessel. For this very reason translation must in large measure refrain from wanting to communicate something, from rendering the sense, and in this the original is important to it only insofar as it has already relieved the translator and his translation of the effort of assembling and expressing what is to be conveyed. In the realm of translation, too, the words ἐν ἀρχῇ ἦν ὁ λόγος [in the beginning was the word] apply. On the other hand, as regards the meaning, the language of a translation can—in fact, must—let itself go, so that it gives voice to the *intentio* of the original not as reproduction but as harmony, as a supplement to the language in which it expresses itself, as its own kind of *intentio*. Therefore it is not the highest praise of a translation, particularly in the age of its origin, to say that it reads as if it had originally been written in that language. Rather, the significance of fidelity as ensured by literalness is that the work reflects the great longing for linguistic complementation. A real translation is transparent; it does not cover the original, does not

block its light, but allows the pure language, as though reinforced
by its own medium, to shine upon the original all the more fully.
This may be achieved, above all, by a literal rendering of the syntax
which proves words rather than sentences to be the primary element of the translator. For if the sentence is the wall before the
language of the original, literalness is the arcade.

Fidelity and freedom in translation have traditionally been regarded as conflicting tendencies. This deeper interpretation of the
one apparently does not serve to reconcile the two; in fact, it seems
to deny the other all justification. For what is meant by freedom
but that the rendering of the sense is no longer to be regarded as
all-important? Only if the sense of a linguistic creation may be
equated with the information it conveys does some ultimate, decisive element remain beyond all communication—quite close and
yet infinitely remote, concealed or distinguishable, fragmented or
powerful. In all language and linguistic creations there remains in
addition to what can be conveyed something that cannot be communicated; depending on the context in which it appears, it is
something that symbolizes or something symbolized. It is the former only in the finite products of language, the latter in the evolving of the languages themselves. And that which seeks to represent,
to produce itself in the evolving of languages, is that very nucleus
of pure language. Though concealed and fragmentary, it is an active force in life as the symbolized thing itself, whereas it inhabits
linguistic creations only in symbolized form. While that ultimate
essence, pure language, in the various tongues is tied only to linguistic elements and their changes, in linguistic creations it is
weighted with a heavy, alien meaning. To relieve it of this, to turn
the symbolizing into the symbolized, to regain pure language fully
formed in the linguistic flux, is the tremendous and only capacity
of translation. In this pure language—which no longer means or
expresses anything but is, as expressionless and creative Word, that
which is meant in all languages—all information, all sense, and all
intention finally encounter a stratum in which they are destined to
be extinguished. This very stratum furnishes a new and higher justification for free translation; this justification does not derive from
the sense of what is to be conveyed, for the emancipation from this
sense is the task of fidelity. Rather, for the sake of pure language, a
free translation bases the test on its own language. It is the task of
the translator to release in his own language that pure language
which is under the spell of another, to liberate the language im-

prisoned in a work in his re-creation of that work. For the sake of
pure language he breaks through decayed barriers of his own language. Luther, Voss, Hölderlin, and George have extended the
boundaries of the German language.—And what of the sense in its
importance for the relationship between translation and original?
A simile may help here. Just as a tangent touches a circle lightly
and at but one point, with this touch rather than with the point
setting the law according to which it is to continue on its straight
path to infinity, a translation touches the original lightly and only
at the infinitely small point of the sense, thereupon pursuing its
own course according to the laws of fidelity in the freedom of linguistic flux. Without explicitly naming or substantiating it, Rudolf
Pannwitz has characterized the true significance of this freedom.
His observations are contained in *Die Krisis der europäischen Kultur*
and rank with Goethe's Notes to the *Westöstlicher Divan* as the best
comment on the theory of translation that has been published in
Germany. Pannwitz writes:

> Our translations, even the best ones, proceed from a wrong premise.
> They want to turn Hindi, Greek, English into German instead of
> turning German into Hindi, Greek, English. Our translators have a
> far greater reverence for the usage of their own language than for the
> spirit of the foreign works. . . . The basic error of the translator is that
> he preserves the state in which his own language happens to be in-
> stead of allowing his language to be powerfully affected by the foreign
> tongue. Particularly when translating from a language very remote
> from his own he must go back to the primal elements of language
> itself and penetrate to the point where work, image, and tone con-
> verge. He must expand and deepen his language by means of the
> foreign language. It is not generally realized to what extent this is
> possible, to what extent any language can be transformed, how lan-
> guage differs from language almost the way dialect differs from dia-
> lect; however, this last is true only if one takes language seriously
> enough, not if one takes it lightly.

The extent to which a translation manages to be in keeping
with the nature of this mode is determined objectively by the translatability of the original. The lower the quality and distinction of
its language, the larger the extent to which it is information, the
less fertile a field is it for translation, until the utter preponderance
of content, far from being the lever for a translation of distinctive
mode, renders it impossible. The higher the level of a work, the

more does it remain translatable even if its meaning is touched upon only fleetingly. This, of course, applies to originals only. Translations, on the other hand, prove to be untranslatable not because of any inherent difficulty, but because of the looseness with which meaning attaches to them. Confirmation of this as well as of every other important aspect is supplied by Hölderlin's translations, particularly those of the two tragedies by Sophocles. In them the harmony of the languages is so profound that sense is touched by language only the way an aeolian harp is touched by the wind. Hölderlin's translations are prototypes of their kind; they are to even the most perfect renderings of their texts as a prototype is to a model. This can be demonstrated by comparing Hölderlin's and Rudolf Borchardt's translations of Pindar's Third Pythian Ode. For this very reason Hölderlin's translations in particular are subject to the enormous danger inherent in all translations: the gates of a language thus expanded and modified may slam shut and enclose the translator with silence. Hölderlin's translations from Sophocles were his last work; in them meaning plunges from abyss to abyss until it threatens to become lost in the bottomless depths of language. There is, however, a stop. It is vouchsafed to Holy Writ alone, in which meaning has ceased to be the watershed for the flow of language and the flow of revelation. Where a text is identical with truth or dogma, where it is supposed to be "the true language" in all its literalness and without the mediation of meaning, this text is unconditionally translatable. In such case translations are called for only because of the plurality of languages. Just as, in the original, language and revelation are one without any tension, so the translation must be one with the original in the form of the interlinear version, in which literalness and freedom are united. For to some degree all great texts contain their potential translation between the lines; this is true to the highest degree of sacred writings. The interlinear version of the Scriptures is the prototype or ideal of all translation.

T E N
EZRA POUND
Guido's Relations

The critic, normally a bore and a nuisance, can justify his existence in one or more minor and subordinate ways: he may dig out and focus attention upon matter of interest that would otherwise have passed without notice; he may, in the rare cases when he has any really general knowledge or "perception of relations" (swift or other) locate his finds with regard to other literary inventions; he may, thirdly, or as you might say, conversely and as part and supplement of his activity, construct cloacae to carry off the waste matter, which stagnates about the real work, and which is continuously being heaped up and caused to stagnate by academic bodies, obese publishing houses, and combinations of both, such as the Oxford Press. (We note their particular infamy in a recent reissue of Palgrave.)

Since Dante's unfinished brochure on the common tongue, Italy may have had no general literary criticism, the brochure is somewhat "special" and of interest mainly to practitioners of the art of writing. Lorenzo Valla somewhat altered the course of history by his close inspection of Latin usage. His prefaces have here and there a burst of magnificence, and the spirit of the Elegantiae should benefit any writer's lungs. As he wrote about an ancient idiom, Italian and English writers alike have, when they have heard his name at all, supposed that he had no "message" and, in the case of the Britons, they returned, we may suppose, to Pater's remarks

From the essay "Cavalcanti," in Ezra Pound, *The Literary Essays of Ezra Pound.* Copyright 1935 by Ezra Pound. Reprinted by Permission of New Directions Publishing Company.

Guido Cavalcanti (ca. 1255–1300) was the author of many sonnets and the most important Florentine poet before Dante, his friend and admirer.—Eds.

on Pico. (Based on what the weary peruser of some few other parts
of Pico's output might pettishly denounce as Pico's one remarkable
paragraph.)

The study called "comparative literature" was invented in Germany but has seldom if ever aspired to the study of "comparative
values in letters."

The literature of the Mediterranean races continued in a steady
descending curve of renaissance-ism. There are minor upward fluc-
tuations. The best period of Italian poetry ends in the year 1321.
So far as I know one excellent Italian tennis player and no known
Italian writer has thought of considering the local literature in relation to rest of the world.

Leopardo read, and imitated Shakespeare. The Prince of
Monte Nevoso has been able to build his unique contemporary
position because of barbarian contacts, whether consciously, and
via visual stimulus from any printed pages, or simply because he
was aware of, let us say, the existence of Wagner and Browning. If
Nostro Gabriele started something new in Italian. Hating barba-
rism, teutonism, never mentioning the existence of the ultimate
Britons, unsurrounded by any sort of society or milieu, he ends as
a solitary, superficially eccentric, but with a surprisingly sound standard of values, values, that is, as to the relative worth of a few
perfect lines of writing, as contrasted to a great deal of flub-dub
and "action."

The only living author who has ever taken a city or held up the
diplomatic crapule at the point of machine guns, he is in a position
to speak with more authority than a batch of neurasthenic incom-
petents or of writers who never having swerved from their jobs,
might be, or are, supposed by the scientists and the populace to be
incapable of action. Like other serious characters who have taken
seventy years to live and to learn to live, he has passed through
periods wherein he lived (or wrote) we should not quite say "less
ably," but with less immediately demonstrable result.

This period "nel mezzo," this passage of the "selva oscura"
takes men in different ways, so different indeed that comparison is
more likely to bring ridicule on the comparer than to focus attention on the analogy—often admittedly farfetched.·

In many cases the complete man makes a "very promising
start," and then flounders or appears to flounder for ten years, or
for twenty or thirty (cf. Henry James's middle period) to end, if he
survive, with some sort of demonstration, discovery, or other jus-

tification of his having gone by the route he has (apparently) stumbled on.

When I "translated" Guido eighteen years ago I did *not* see Guido at all. I saw that Rossetti had made a remarkable translation of the *Vita Nuova*, in some places improving (or at least enriching) the original; that he was indubitably the man "sent," or "chosen" for that particular job, and that there was something in Guido that escaped him or that was, at any rate, absent from his translations. A *robustezza*, a masculinity. I had a great enthusiasm (perfectly justified), but I did not clearly see exterior demarcations—Euclid inside his cube, with no premonition of Cartesian axes.

My perception was not obfuscated by Guido's Italian, difficult as it then was for me to read. I was obfuscated by the Victorian language.

If I hadn't been, I very possibly couldn't have done the job at all. I should have seen the too great multiplicity of problems contained in the one problem before me.

I don't mean that I didn't see dull spots in the sonnets. I saw that Rossetti had taken most of the best sonnets, that one couldn't make a complete edition of Guido simply by taking Rossetti's translations and filling in the gaps, it would have been too dreary a job. Even though I saw that Rossetti had made better English poems than I was likely to make by (in intention) sticking closer to the direction of the original. I began by meaning merely to give prose translation so that the reader ignorant of Italian could see what the melodic original meant. It is, however, an illusion to suppose that more than one person in every 300,000 has the patience or the intelligence to read a foreign tongue for its sound, or even to read what are known to be the masterworks of foreign melody, in order to learn the qualities of that melody, or to see where one's own falls short.

What obfuscated me was not the Italian but the crust of dead English, the sediment present in my own available vocabulary—which I, let us hope, got rid of a few years later. You can't go round this sort of thing. It takes six or eight years to get educated in one's art, and another ten to get rid of that education.

Neither can anyone learn English, one can only learn a series of Englishes. Rossetti made his own language. I hadn't in 1910 made a language, I don't mean a language to use, but even a language to think in.

It is stupid to overlook the lingual inventions of precurrent authors, even when they are fools or flapdoodles or Tennysons. It is sometimes advisable to sort out these languages and inventions, and to know what and why they are.

Keats, out of Elizabethans, Swinburne out of a larger set of Elizabethans and a mixed bag (Greeks, *und so weiter*), Rossetti out of Sheets, Kelly, and Co. plus early Italians (written and painted); and so forth, including *King Wenceslas,* ballads and carols.

Let me not discourage a possible reader, or spoil anyone's naive enjoyment, by saying that my early versions of Guido are bogged in Dante Gabriel and in Algernon. It is true, but let us pass by it in silence. Where both Rossetti and I went off the rails was in taking an English sonnet as the equivalent for a sonnet in Italian. I don't mean in overlooking the mild difference in the rhyme scheme. The mistake is "quite natural," very few mistakes are "unnatural." Rime looks very important. Take the rimes off a good sonnet, and there is a vacuum. And besides the movement of *some* Italian sonnets *is* very like that in some sonnets in English. The feminine rhyme goes by the board . . . again for obvious reasons. It had gone by the board, quite often, in Provençal. The French made an ecclesiastical law about using it 50/50.

As a bad analogy, imagine a Giotto or Simone Martini fresco, "translated" into oils by "Sir Joshua," or Sir Frederick Leighton. Something is lost, something is somewhat denatured.

Suppose, however, we have a Cimabue done in oil, not by Holbein, but by some contemporary of Holbein who can't paint as well as Cimabue.

There are about seven reasons why the analogy is incorrect, and six more to suppose it inverted, but it may serve to free the reader's mind from preconceived notions about the English of "Elizabeth" and her British garden of songbirds.—And to consider language as a medium of expression.

(Breton forgives Flaubert on hearing that Father Gustave was trying only to give "l'impression de la couleur jaune" (*Nadja,* p. 12).)

Dr. Schelling has lectured about the Italianate Englishman of Shakespeare's day. I find two Shakespeare plots within ten pages of each other in a forgotten history of Bologna, printed in 1596. We have heard of the effects of the traveling Italian theater companies, *commedia dell' arte,* etc. What happens when you idly attempt to translate early Italian into English, unclogged by the Victorian era, freed from sonnet obsession, but trying merely to sing and to leave out the dull bits in the Italian, or the bits you don't understand?

I offer you a poem that "don't matter," it is attributed to Guido in Codex Barberiniano Lat. 3953. Alacci prints it as Guido's; Simone Occhi in 1740 says that Alacci is a fool or words to that effect and a careless man without principles, and proceeds to print the poem with those of Cino Pistoia. Whoever wrote it, it is, indubitably, not a *capo lavoro*.

Madonna la vostra belta enfolio	
Si li mei ochi che menan lo core	MS. *oghi*
A la bataglia ove l'ancise amore	
Che del vostro placer armato uscio;	*usio*

Si che nel primo asalto che asalio
Passo dentro la mente e fa signore,
E prese l'alma che fuzia di fore
Planzendo di dolor che vi sentio.

Però vedete che vostra beltate
Mosse la folia und e il cor morto
Et a me ne convien clamar pietate,

Non per campar, ma per aver conforto
Ne la morte crudel che far min fate
Et o rason sel non vinzesse il torto.

Is it worth an editor's while to include it among dubious attributions? It is not very attractive: until one starts playing with the simplest English equivalent.

Lady thy beauty doth so mad mine eyes,
Driving my heart to strife wherein he dies.

Sing it of course, don't try to speak it. It thoroughly falsifies the movement of the Italian, it is an opening quite good enough for Herrick or Campion. It will help you to understand just why Herrick, and Campion, and possibly Donne are still with us.

The next line is rather a cliché; the line after more or less lacking in interest. We pull up on:

Whereby thou seest how fair thy beauty is
To compass doom.

That would be very nice, but it is hardly translation.

Take these scraps, and the almost impossible conclusion, a tag of Provençal rhythm, and make them into a plenum. It will help you to understand some of M. de Schloezer's remarks about Stravinsky's trend toward melody. And you will also see what the best Elizabethan lyricists did, as well as what they didn't.

My two lines take the opening and two and a half of the Italian, English more concise; and the octave gets too light for the sestet. Lighten the sestet.

> So unto Pity must I cry
> Not for safety, but to die.
> Cruel Death is now mine ease
> If that he thine envoy is.

We are preserving one value of early Italian work, the cantabile; and we are losing another, that is the specific weight. And if we notice it we fall on a root difference between early Italian, "The philosophic school coming out of Bologna," and the Elizabethan lyric. For in these two couplets, and in attacking this sonnet, I have let go the fervor and the intensity, which were all I, rather blindly, had to carry through my attempt of twenty years gone.

And I think that if anyone now lay, or if we assume that they mostly *then* (in the expansive days) laid, aside care for specific statement of emotion, a dogmatic statement, made with the seriousness of someone to whom it mattered whether he had three souls, one in the head, one in the heart, one possibly in his abdomen, or lungs, or wherever Plato, or Galen, had located it; if the anima is still breath, if the stopped heart is a dead heart, and if it is all serious, much more serious than it would have been to Herrick, the imaginary investigator will see more or less how the Elizabethan modes came into being.

Let him try it for himself, on any Tuscan author of that time, taking the words, not thinking greatly of their significance, not balking at clichés, but being greatly intent on the melody, on the single uninterrupted flow of syllables—as open as possible, that can be sung prettily, that are not very interesting if spoken, that don't even work into a period or an even meter if spoken.

And the mastery, a minor mastery, will lie in keeping this line unbroken, as unbroken in sound as a line in one of Miro's latest drawings is on paper; and giving it perfect balance, with no breaks, no bits sticking ineptly out, and no losses to the force of individual phrases.

Whereby thou seest how fair thy beauty is
To compass doom.

Very possibly too regularly "iambic" to fit in the finished poem.
There is opposition, not only between what M. de Schloezer
distinguishes as musical and poetic lyricism, but in the writing itself there is a distinction between poetic lyricism, the emotional
force of the verbal movement, and melopœic lyricism, the letting
the words flow on a melodic current, realized or not, realizable or
not, if the line is supposed to be sung on a sequence of notes of
different pitch.

But by taking these Italian sonnets, which are not metrically
the equivalent of the English sonnet, by sacrificing, or losing, or
simply not feeling and understanding their cogency, their sobriety,
and by seeking simply that far from quickly or so-easily-as-it-looks
attainable thing, the perfect melody, careless of exactitude of idea,
or careless as to which profound and fundamental idea you, at that
moment, utter, perhaps in precise enough phrases, by cutting away
the apparently nonfunctioning phrases (whose appearance de-
ceives) you find yourself in the English *seicento* songbooks.

Death has become melodious; sorrow is as serious as the night-
ingale's, tombstones are shelves for the reception of rose leaves.
And there is, quite often, a Mozartian perfection of melody, a wisdom, almost perhaps an ultimate wisdom, deplorably lacking in
guts. My phrase is, shall we say, vulgar. Exactly, because it fails in
precision. Guts in surgery refers to a very limited range of internal
furnishings. A thirteenth-century exactitude in search for the exact
organ best illustrating the lack, would have saved me that plunge.
We must turn again to the Latins. When the late T. Roosevelt was
interviewed in France on his return from the jungle, he used a
phrase which was translated (the publication of the interview rather
annoyed him). The French at the point I mention ran: "Ils ont
voulu me briser les *reins* mais je les ai solides."

And now the reader may, if he like, return to the problem of
the "eyes that lead the heart to battle where him love kills." This
was not felt as an inversion. It was 1280, Italian was still in the
state that German is today. How can you have "PROSE" in a country where the chambermaid comes into your room and exclaims:
"Schön ist das Hemd!"

Continue: who is armed with thy delight, is come forth so that
at the first assault he assails, he passes inward to the mind, and lords

it there, and catches the breath (soul) that was fleeing, lamenting the grief I feel.

"Whereby thou seest how thy beauty moves the madness, whence is the heart dead (stopped) and I must cry on Pity, not to be saved but to have ease of the cruel death thou puttest on me. And I am right (?) save the wrong him conquereth."

Whether the reader will accept this little problem in melopœia as substitute for the crossword puzzle I am unable to predict. I leave it on the supposition that the philosopher should try almost everything once.

As second exercise, we may try the sonnet by Guido Orlando which is supposed to have invited Cavalcanti's *Donna mi Prega*.

Say what is Love, whence doth he start   ?
Through what be his courses bent   ?
Memory, substance, accident   ?
A chance of eye or will of heart   ?

Whence he state or madness leadeth   ?
Burns he with consuming pain   ?
Tell me, friend, on what he feedeth   ?
How, where, and o'er whom doth he reign   ?

Say what is Love, hath he a face   ?
True form or vain similitude   ?
Is the Love life, or is he death   ?

Thou shouldst know for rumour saith:
Servant should know his master's mood—
Oft art thou ta'en in his dwelling-place.

I give the Italian to show that there is no deception, I have invented nothing, I have given a *verbal* weight about equal to that of the original, and arrived at this equality by dropping a couple of syllables per line. The great past master of pastiche has, it would seem, passed this way before me. A line or two of this, a few more from Lorenzo Medici, and he has concocted one of the finest gems in our language.

Onde si move e donde nasce Amore
qual è suo proprio luogo, ov' ei dimora
Sustanza, o accidente, o ei memora?
E cagion d'occhi, o è voler di cuore?

Da che procede suo stato o furore?
Come fuoco si sente che divora?
Di che si nutre domand' io ancora,
Come, e quando, e di cui si fa signore?

Che cosa è, dico, amor? ae figura?
A per se forma o pur somiglia altrui?
E vita questo amore ovvero e morte?

Ch 'l serve dee saver di sua natura:
Io ne domando voi, Guido, di lui:
Odo che molto usate in la sua corte.

We are not in a realm of proofs, I suggest, simply, the way in which early Italian poetry has been utilized in England. The Italian of Petrarch and his successors is of no interest to the practicing writer or to the student of comparative dynamics in language, the collectors of bric-a-brac are outside our domain.

There is no question of giving Guido in an English contemporary to himself, the ultimate Britons were at that date unbreeched, painted in woad, and grunting in an idiom far more difficult for us to master than the Langue d'Oc of the Plantagenets or the Lingua di Si.

If, however, we reach back to pre-Elizabethan English, of a period when the writers were still intent on clarity and explicitness, still preferring them to magniloquence and the thundering phrase, our trial, or mine at least, results in:

Who is she that comes, makying turn every man's eye
And makying the air to tremble with a bright clearenesse
That leadeth with her Love, in such nearness
No man may proffer of speech more than a sigh?

Ah God, what she is like when her owne eye turneth, is
Fit for Amor to speake, for I cannot at all;
Such is her modesty, I would call
Every woman else but an useless uneasiness.

No one could ever tell all of her pleasauntness
In that every high noble vertu leaneth to herward,
So Beauty sheweth her forth as her Godhede;

Never before so high was our mind led,
Nor have we so much of heal as will afford
That our mind may take her immediate in its embrace.

The objections to such a method are: the doubt as to whether one has the right to take a serious poem and turn it into a mere exercise in quaintness; the "misrepresentation" not of the poem's antiquity, but of the proportionate feel of that antiquity, by which I mean that Guido's thirteenth-century language is to twentieth-century Italian sense much less archaic than any fourteenth-, fifteenth-, or early sixteenth-century English is for us. It is even doubtful whether my bungling version of twenty years back isn't more "faithful," in the sense at least that it tried to preserve the fervor of the original. And as this fervor simply does not occur in English poetry in those centuries there is no ready-made verbal pigment for its objectification.

In the long run the translator is in all probability impotent to do *all* of the work for the linguistically lazy reader. He can show where the treasure lies, he can guide the reader in choice of what tongue is to be studied, and he can very materially assist the hurried student who has a smattering of a language and the energy to read the original text alongside the metrical gloze.

This refers to "interpretative translation." The "other sort." I mean in cases where the "translator" is definitely making a new poem, falls simply in the domain of original writing, or if it does not it must be censured according to equal standards, and praised with some sort of just deduction, assessable only in the particular case.

E L E V E N
José Ortega y Gasset
The Misery and the Splendor of Translation
Translated by Elizabeth Gamble Miller

1. The Misery

During a colloquium attended by professors and students from the Collège de France and other academic circles, someone spoke of the impossibility of translating certain German philosophers. Carrying the proposition further, he proposed a study that would determine the philosophers who could and those who could not be translated.

"This would be to suppose, with excessive conviction," I suggested, "that that-there are philosophers and, more generally speaking, writers who can, in fact, be translated. Isn't that an illusion? Isn't the act of translating necessarily a utopian task? The truth is, I've become more and more convinced that everything Man does is utopian. Although he is principally involved in trying to know, he never fully succeeds in knowing anything. When deciding what is fair, he inevitably falls into cunning. He thinks he loves and then discovers he only promised to. Don't misunderstand my words to be a satire on morals, as if I would criticize my colleagues because they don't do what they propose. My intention is, precisely, the opposite; rather than blame them for their failure, I would suggest that none of these things can be done, for they are impossible in their very essence, and they will always remain mere intention, vain aspiration, an invalid posture. Nature has simply endowed each creature with a specific program of actions he can execute satisfactorily. That's why it's so unusual for an animal to be sad. Only

From "La Miseria y el esplendor de la traducción," *La Nación* (Buenos Aires), May–June 1937. Reprinted in José Ortega y Gasset, *Obras Completas: Tomo V (1933–1941)* (Madrid: Revista de Occidente, 1947), pp. 429–48.

occasionally may something akin to sadness be observed in a few higher species—the dog or the horse—and that's when they seem closest to us, seem most human. Perhaps Nature, in the mysterious depths of the jungle, offers its most surprising spectacle—surprising because of its equivocal aspect—the melancholic orangutan. Animals are normally happy. We have been endowed with an opposite nature. Always melancholic, frantic, manic, men are ill-nurtured by all those illnesses Hippocrates called divine. And the reason for this is that human tasks are unrealizable. The destiny of Man—his privilege and honor—is never to achieve what he proposes, and to remain merely an intention, a living utopia. He is always marching toward failure, and even before entering the fray he already carries a wound in his temple.

"This is what occurs whenever we engage in that modest occupation called translating. Among intellectual undertakings, there is no humbler one. Nevertheless, it is an excessively demanding task.

"To write well is to make continual incursions into grammar, into established usage, and into accepted linguistic norms. It is an act of permanent rebellion against the social environs, a subversion. To write well is to employ a certain radical courage. Fine, but the translator is usually a shy character. Because of his humility, he has chosen such an insignificant occupation. He finds himself facing an enormous controlling apparatus, composed of grammar and common usage. What will he do with the rebellious text? Isn't it too much to ask that he also be rebellious, particularly since the text is someone else's? He will be ruled by cowardice, so instead of resisting grammatical restraints he will do just the opposite: he will place the translated author in the prison of normal expression; that is, he will betray him. *Traduttore, traditore.*"

"And, nevertheless, books on the exact and natural sciences can be translated," my colleague responded.

"I don't deny that the difficulty is less, but I do deny that it doesn't exist. The branch of mathematics most in vogue in the last quarter century was Set Theory. Fine, but its creator, Cantor, baptized it with a term that has no possibility of being translated into our language. What we have had to call 'set' he called 'quantity' (*Menge*), a word whose meaning is not encompassed in 'set.' So, let's not exaggerate the translatability of the mathematical and physical sciences. But, with that proviso, I am disposed to recognize that a version of them may be more precise than one from another discipline."

"Do you, then, recognize that there are two classes of writings: those that can be translated and those that cannot?"

"Speaking *grosso modo*, we must accept that distinction, but when we do so we close the door on the real problem every translation presents. For if we ask ourselves the reason certain scientific books are easier to translate, we will soon realize that in these the author himself has begun by translating from the authentic tongue in which he 'lives, moves and has his being' into a pseudolanguage formed by technical terms, linguistically artificial words which he himself must define in his book. In short, he translates himself from a language into a terminology."

"But a terminology is a language like any other! Furthermore, according to our Condillac, the best language, the language that is 'well constructed,' is science."

"Pardon me for differing radically from you and from the good father. A language is a system of verbal signs through which individuals may understand each other without a previous accord, while a terminology is only intelligible if the one who is writing or speaking and the one who is reading or listening have previously and *individually* come to an agreement as to the meaning of the signs. For this reason, I call it pseudolanguage, and I say that the scientist has to begin by translating his own thoughts into it. It is a *Volapuk*, an Esperanto established by a deliberate convention between those who cultivate that discipline. That is why these books are easier to translate from one language to another. Actually, in every country these are written almost entirely in the same language. That being the case, men who speak the authentic language in which they are apparently written often find these books to be hermetic, unintelligible, or at least very difficult to understand."

"In all fairness, I must admit you are right and also tell you I am beginning to perceive certain mysteries in the verbal relationships between individuals that I had not previously noticed."

"And I, in turn, perceive you to be the sole survivor of a vanished species, like the last of the Abencerrajes, since when faced with another's belief you are capable of thinking him, rather than you, to be right. It is a fact that the discussion of translation, to whatever extent we may pursue it, will carry us into the most recondite secrets of that marvelous phenomenon that we call speech.

Just examining questions that our topic obviously presents will be sufficient for now. In my comments up to this point, I have based the utopianism of translation on the fact that an author of a book— not of mathematics, physics, or even biology—is a writer in a positive sense of the word. This is to imply that he has used his native tongue with prodigious skill, achieving two things that seem impossible to reconcile: simply, to be intelligible and, at the same time, to modify the ordinary usage of language. This dual operation is more difficult to achieve than walking a tightrope. How can we demand it of the average translator? Moreover, beyond this first dilemma that personal style presents to the translator, we perceive new layers of difficulties. An author's personal style, for example, is produced by his slight deviation from the habitual meaning of the word. The author forces it to an extraordinary usage so that the circle of objects it designates will not coincide exactly with the circle of objects which that same word customarily means in its habitual use. The general trend of these deviations in a writer is what we call his style. But, in fact, each language compared to any other also has its own linguistic style, what von Humboldt called its 'internal form.' Therefore, it is utopian to believe that two words belonging to different languages, and which the dictionary gives us as translations of each other, refer to exactly the same objects. Since languages are formed in different landscapes, through different experiences, their incongruity is natural. It is false, for example, to suppose that the thing the Spaniard calls a *bosque* [forest] the German calls a *Wald,* yet the dictionary tells us that *Wald* means *bosque.* If the mood were appropriate this would be an excellent time to interpolate an *aria di bravura* describing the forest in Germany in contrast to the Spanish forest. I am jesting about the singing, but I proclaim the result to be intuitively clear, that is, that an enormous difference exists between the two realities. It is so great that not only are they exceedingly incongruous, but almost all their resonances, both emotive and intellectual, are equally so.

"The shapes of the meanings of the two fail to coincide as do those of a person in a double-exposed photograph. This being the case, our perception shifts and wavers without actually identifying with either shape or forming a third; imagine the distressing vagueness we experience when reading thousands of words affected in this manner. These are the same causes, then, that produce the phenomenon of *flou* [blur, haziness] in a visual image and in linguistic expression. Translation is the permanent literary *flou,* and since what we usually call nonsense is, on the other hand, but the *flou* of thoughts, we shouldn't be surprised that a translated author always seems somewhat foolish to us."

2. The Two Utopianisms

"When conversation is not merely an exchange of verbal mechanisms, wherein men act like gramophones, but rather consists of a true interchange, a curious phenomenon is produced. As the conversation evolves, the personality of each speaker becomes progressively divided: one part listens agreeably to what is being said, while the other, fascinated by the subject itself, like a bird with a snake, will increasingly withdraw and begin thinking about the matter. When we converse, we live within a society; when we think, we remain alone. But in this case, in this kind of conversation, we do both at once, and as the discussion continues we do them with growing intensity: we pay attention to what is being said with almost melodramatic emotion and at the same time we become more and more immersed in the solitary well of our meditation. This increasing disassociation cannot be sustained in a permanent balance. For this reason, such conversations characteristically reach a point when they suffer a paralysis and lapse into a heavy silence. Each speaker is self-absorbed. Simply as a result of thinking, he isn't able to talk. Dialogue has given birth to silence, and the initial social contact has fallen into states of solitude.

"This happened at our conference—after my last statement. Why then? The answer is clear: this sudden tide of silence wells up over dialogue at that point when the topic has been developed to its extreme in one direction and the conversation must turn around and set the prow toward another quadrant."

"This silence that has risen among us," someone said, "has a funereal character. You have murdered translation, and we are sullenly following along for the burial."

"Oh, no!" I replied. "Not at all! It was most important that I emphasize the miseries of translating; it was especially important that I define its difficulty, its improbability, but not so as to remain there. On the contrary, it was important so that this might act as a ballistic spring to impel us toward the possible splendor of the art of translation. This is the opportunity to cry out: 'Translation is dead! Long live translation!' Now we must advocate the opposite position and, as Socrates said on similar occasions, recant."

"I fear that will be rather difficult for you," said Mr. X. "For we haven't forgotten your initial statement to us setting forth the task of translating as a utopian operation and an impossible proposition."

"In fact, I said that and a little more: all specific tasks that Man undertakes are of similar character. Don't fear that I now intend to tell you why I think so. I know that in a French conversation one must always avoid the principal point and it's preferable to remain in the temperate zone of intermediate questions. You've been more than amiable in tolerating me, and even in forcing this disguised monologue upon me, despite the fact that the monologue is, perhaps, the most grievous crime one can commit in Paris. For that reason I am somewhat inhibited and conscience-stricken by the impression I have now of committing something like a rape. The only thing that comforts me is the conviction that my French stumbles along and would never allow the contredanse of dialogue. But let's return to our subject, the essentially utopian condition of everything human. Instead of confirming this belief by truly solid reasoning, I will simply invite you, for the pure pleasure of an intellectual experiment, to accept it as a basic principle and in that light to contemplate the endeavors of Man."

"Nevertheless," said my dear friend Jean Baruzi, "your quarrel with utopianism frequently appears in your work."

"Frequently and substantially! There is a false utopianism that is the exact inverse of the one I am now describing, a utopianism consistent in its belief that what man desires, projects and proposes is, obviously, possible. Nothing is more repugnant to me, for I see this false utopianism as the major cause of all the misfortunes taking place now on this planet. In this humble matter in which we are now engaged, we can appreciate the opposing meanings of the two utopianisms. Both the bad and the good utopians consider it desirable to correct the natural reality that places men within the confines of diverse languages and impedes communication between them. The bad utopian thinks that because it is *desirable,* it is possible. Believing it to be easy is just moving one step further. With such an attitude, he won't give much thought to the question of how one must translate, and without further ado he will begin the task. This is the reason why almost all translations done until now are bad ones. The good utopian, on the other hand, thinks that *because* it would be desirable to free men from the divisions imposed by languages, there is little probability that it can be attained; therefore, it can only be achieved to an approximate measure. But this approximation can be greater or lesser, to an infinite degree, and the efforts at execution are not limited, for there always exists the possibility of bettering, refining, perfecting: 'progress,' in short. All human existence consists of activities of this type. Imagine the opposite: that you should be condemned to doing only those activities deemed possible of achievement, possible in themselves. What profound anguish! You would feel as if your life were emptied of all substance. Precisely because your activity had attained what it was supposed to, you would feel as if you had done nothing. Man's existence has a sporting character, with pleasure residing in the effort itself, and not in the results. World history compels us to recognize Man's continuous, inexhaustible capacity to invent unrealizable projects. In the effort to realize them, he achieves many things, he creates innumerable realities that so-called Nature is incapable of producing for itself. The only thing that Man does not achieve is, precisely, what he proposes to—let it be said to his credit. This wedding of reality with the demon of what is impossible supplies the universe with the only growth it is capable of. For that reason, it is very important to emphasize that everything—that is, everything worthwhile, everything truly human—is difficult, very difficult; so much so, that it is impossible.

"As you see, to declare its impossibility is not an argument against the possible splendor of the translator's task. On the contrary, this characterization admits it to the highest rank and lets us infer that it is meaningful."

An art historian interrupted, "Accordingly, you would tend to think, as I do, that Man's true mission, what gives meaning to his undertakings, is to oppose Nature."

"In fact, I am very close to such an opinion, as long as we don't forget the previous distinction between the two utopianisms—the good and the bad—which, for me, is fundamental. I say this because the essential character of the good utopian in radically opposing Nature is to be aware of its presence and not to be deluded. The good utopian promises himself to be, primarily, an inexorable realist. Only when he is certain of not having acceded to the least illusion, thus having gained the total view of a reality stripped stark naked, may he, fully arrayed, turn against that reality and strive to reform it, yet acknowledging the impossibility of the task, which is the only sensible approach.

"The inverse attitude, which is the traditional one, consists of believing that what is desirable is already there, as a spontaneous fruit of reality. This has blinded us *a limine* in our understanding of human affairs. Everyone, for example, wants Man to be good, but your Rousseau, who has caused the rest of us to suffer, thought the desire had long since been realized, that Man was good in himself by nature. This idea ruined a century and a half of European history which might have been magnificent. We have required infinite anguish, enormous catastrophes—even those yet to come—in order to rediscover the simple truth, known throughout almost all previous centuries, that Man, in himself, is nothing but an evil beast.

"Or, to return definitively to our subject: to emphasize its impossibility is very far from depriving the occupation of translating of meaning, for no one would even think of considering it absurd for us to speak to each other in our mother tongue yet, nevertheless, that is also a utopian exercise."

This statement produced, in turn, a sharpening of opposition and protests. "That is an exaggeration or, rather, what grammarians call 'an abuse,' " said a philologist, previously silent. "There is too much supposition and paradox in that," exclaimed a sociologist.

"I see that my little ship of audacious doctrine runs the risk of running aground in this sudden storm. I understand that for French ears, even your so benevolent ones, it is hard to hear the statement that talking is a utopian exercise. But what am I to do if such is undeniably the truth?"

3. About Talking and Keeping Silent

Once the storm my last remarks had elicited subsided, I continued: "I well understand your indignation. The statement that talking is an illusory activity and a utopian action has all the air of a paradox, and a paradox is always irritating. It is especially so for the French. Perhaps the course of this conversation takes us to a point where we need to clarify why the French spirit is such an enemy of paradox. But you probably recognize that it is not always within our power to avoid it. When we try to rectify a fundamental opinion that seems quite erroneous to us, there is little probability that our words will be free of a certain paradoxical insolence. Who is to say whether the intellectual, who has been inexorably prescribed to be one even against his desire or will, has not been commissioned in this world to declare paradox! If someone had bothered to clarify for us in depth and once and for all why the intellectual exists, why he has been here since the time that he has, and if someone would put before us some simple data of how the oldest ones perceived their mission—for example, the ancient thinkers of Greece, the first prophets of Israel, etc.—perhaps my suspicions would turn out to be obvious and trivial. After all, *doxa* means public opinion, and it doesn't seem justifiable for there to be a class of men whose particular office consists of giving an opinion if their opinion is to coincide with that of the public. Is this not redundancy or, as is said in our Spanish language, which is more the product of muleteers than lord chamberlains, a packsaddle over a packsaddle? Doesn't it seem more likely that the intellectual exists in order to oppose public opinion, the *doxa,* by revealing and maintaining a front against the commonplace with true opinion, the *paradoxa?* More than likely the intellectual's mission is essentially an unpopular one.

"Consider these suggestions simply as my defense before your irritation, but let it be said in passing that with them I believe I am touching matters of primary importance, although they are still scandalously untouched. Let it be evident, furthermore, that this new digression is your responsibility for having incited me.

"And the fact is that my statement, despite its paradoxical physiognomy, is rather obvious and simple. We usually understand by the term *speech* the exercise of an activity through which we succeed in making our thinking known to our fellowman. Speech is, of course, many other things besides this, but all of them suppose or imply this to be a primary function of speech. For example, through speech we try to persuade another, to influence him, at times to deceive him. A lie is speech which hides our authentic thought. But it is evident that a lie would be impossible if normal speech were not primarily sincere. Counterfeit money circulates sustained by sound money. In the end, deceit turns out to be a humble parasite of innocence.

"Let us say, then, that Man, when he begins to speak, does so *because* he thinks that he is going to be able to say what he thinks. Well, this is illusory. Language doesn't offer that much. It says, a little more or less, a portion of what we think, while it sets an insurmountable obstacle in place, blocking a transmission of the rest. It is rather useful for mathematical statements and proofs, but the language of physics is already beginning to be equivocal or insufficient. As soon as conversation begins to revolve around themes that are more important, more human, more 'real' than the latter, its imprecision, its awkwardness and its convolutedness increase. Infected by the entrenched prejudice that through speech we understand each other, we make our remarks and listen in such good faith that we inevitably misunderstand each other much more than if we had remained silent and had guessed. Furthermore, since our thought is in great measure attributable to the tongue—although I cannot help but doubt that the attribution is absolute, as it is usually purported to be—it turns out that thinking is talking to oneself and, consequently, misunderstanding oneself and running a great risk of becoming completely muddled."

"Aren't you exaggerating a bit?" scoffed Mr. Z.

"Perhaps, perhaps . . . but in any case it would be a question of a medicinal, compensatory exaggeration. In 1922 there was a session at the Philosophical Society of Paris dedicated to discussing the question of progress in language. In addition to the philosophers of the Seine, those participating were the great teachers of the French Linguistics School, which, at least as a school, is certainly the most illustrious in the world. Well, while reading the summary of the discussion, I ran across some phrases from Meillet that left me dumbfounded—from Meillet, consummate master of contemporary linguistics—'Every language,' he said, 'expresses whatever is necessary for the society of which it is an organ. . . . With any phonetics, any grammar, one can express anything.' Don't you think, with all due respect to the memory of Meillet, that there is also evidence of exaggeration in those words? How has Meillet become informed about the truth of such an absolute assertion? It can't be as a linguist. As a linguist he only knows the languages of peoples, not their thoughts, and his dogma supposes the measurement of the latter to coincide with the former. Even so it would not be sufficient to say that every language can formulate every thought, but to say that all can do it with the same facility and immediacy. The Basque language may be however perfect Meillet wishes, but the fact is that it forgot to include in its vocabulary a term to designate God and it was necessary to pick a phrase that meant 'lord over the heights'—*Jaungoikua*. Since centuries ago lordly authority disappeared, *Jaungoikua* today means God directly, but we must place ourselves in the time when one was obliged to think of God as a political, worldly authority, to think of God as a civil governor or the like. To be exact, this case reveals to us that lacking a name for God made it very difficult for the Basques to think about God. For that reason they were very slow in being converted to Christianity; the word *Jaungoikua* also indicates that police intervention was necessary in order to put the mere idea of the divinity in their heads. So language not only makes the expression of certain thoughts difficult, but it also impedes their reception by others; it paralyzes our intelligence in certain directions.

"We are not going to discuss now the truly basic questions— and the most provocative ones!—that this extraordinary phenomenon, language, elicits. In my judgment, we haven't even had an inkling of those questions, precisely because we were blinded to them by the persistent ambiguity hidden in the idea that the function of speech is to manifest our thoughts."

"What ambiguity are you referring to? I don't really understand," questioned the art historian.

"That phrase can mean two radically different things: that when we speak we try to express our ideas or inner states but *only partially* succeed in doing so, or, on the other hand, that speech attains this intention *fully*. As you see, the two utopianisms we stumbled upon before, in our involvement with translation, reappear here. And in the same way they will appear in every human act, according to the general thesis that I invited you to apply: 'everything that Man does is utopian.' This principle alone will open our eyes to the basic questions of language. Because if, in fact, we are cured of believing that speech succeeds in expressing *all* that we think, we will recognize what, in fact, is obviously constantly happening to us: that when speaking or writing we refrain constantly from saying many things because language doesn't allow them to be said. The effectiveness of speech does not simply lie in speaking, in making statements, but, at the same time and of necessity, in a relinquishing of speech, a keeping quiet, a being silent! The phenomenon could not be more frequent or unquestionable. Remember what happens to you when you have to speak in a foreign language. Very distressing! It is what I am feeling now when I speak in French: the distress of having to quiet four-fifths of what occurs to me, because those four-fifths of my Spanish thoughts can't be said well in French, in spite of the fact that the two languages are so closely related. Well, don't believe that it is not the same, of course to a lesser extent, when we think in our own language; only our contrary preconception prevents our noticing it. With this declaration I find myself in the terrible situation of provoking a second storm much more serious than the first. In fact, everything said is necessarily summed up in a formula that frankly displays the insolent biceps of paradox. The fact is that the stupendous reality, which is language, will not be understood at its root if one doesn't begin by noticing that speech is composed above all of silences. A person incapable of quieting many things would not be capable of talking. And each language is a different equation of statements and silences. All peoples silence some things in order to be able to say others. Otherwise, everything would be unsayable. From this we deduce the enormous difficulty of translation: in it one tries to say in a language precisely what that language tends to silence. But, at the same time, one glimpses a possible marvelous aspect of the enterprise of translating: the revelation of the mutual secrets that peoples and epochs keep to themselves and which contribute so much to their separation and hostility; in short—an audacious integration of Humanity. Because, as Goethe said: 'Only between all men can that which is human be lived fully.' "

4. We Don't Speak Seriously

My prediction didn't transpire. The tempest that I had expected did not materialize. The paradoxical statement penetrated my listeners' minds without provoking quakes or tremors, like a hypodermic injection that, fortunately, fails to hit a nerve. So it was an excellent occasion to execute a retreat.

"While I had been expecting the fiercest rebellion on your part, I find myself engulfed in tranquility. You will probably not be surprised if I take this opportunity to cede to another the floor I've been unwillingly monopolizing. Almost all of you are better acquainted with these matters than I. There is one especially great scholar of linguistics who belongs to the new generation, and it would be very interesting for us all to hear his thoughts on the subjects we've been discussing."

"A great scholar I am not," the linguist began; "I am only enthusiastic about my profession, which I think is reaching its first period of maturation, a time of maximum harvest. And it pleases me to assert that, in general, what you have said, and even further what I intuit and sense behind what is being expressed, rather coincides with my thinking and with what, in my judgment, is going to dominate the immediate future of the science of language. Of course, I would have avoided the example of the Basque word for designating God because it's a very controversial question. But, in general, I agree with you. Let us look carefully at what the primary operation of any language is.

"Modern man is too proud of the sciences he has created. Certainly through them the world takes on a new shape. But, relatively speaking, this innovation is not very profound. Its substance is a delicate film stretched over other shapes developed in other ages of humanity, which we project as our innovation. We draw from this gigantic wealth at every opportunity, but we don't realize it, because we haven't produced it; rather we have inherited it. Like most good heirs, we are usually rather stupid. The telephone, internal combustion engine and drilling rig are prodigious discoveries, but they would have been impossible if twenty thousand years ago human genius had not invented the way to make fire, the ax, the hammer, and the wheel. In a similar manner, the scientific interpretation of the world has been supported and nurtured by other precedents, especially by the oldest, the original one, which is language. Present-day science would be impossible without language, not because of the cliché that to produce science is to speak, but, on the contrary, because language is the original science. Precisely because this is a fact, modern science lives in a perpetual dispute with language.

"Would this make any sense if language were not a science in itself, a knowledge we try to improve because it seems insufficient to us? We don't clearly see this that is evident because for a long, long time humanity, at least Western humanity, has not spoken seriously. I don't understand why linguists have not duly paused before this surprising phenomenon. Today, when we speak, we don't say what the language in which we speak says, but instead, by conventionally using, as if joking, what our words say for themselves, we say, in the manner of our language, what we want to say. My paragraph has become a stupendous tongue twister, hasn't it? I will explain: if I say that *el sol* [the sun, masculine] *sale* [comes out or rises] *por Oriente* [in the East], what my words, and as such the language in which I express myself, are actually saying is that an entity of the masculine sex, capable of spontaneous actions—the so-called sun—executes the action of 'coming out,' that is, being born, and that he does so in a place from among other places that is the one where births occur—the East. Well now, I don't seriously want to say any of that; I don't believe that the sun is a young man nor a subject capable of spontaneous activities, nor that the action, its 'coming out,' is something it does by itself, nor that births happen especially in that part of space. When I use such an expression in my mother tongue, I am behaving ironically; I discredit what I am saying, and I take it as a joke. Language is today a mere joke. But it is clear that there was a time in which Indo-European man thought, in fact, that the sun was a male, that natural phenomena were spontaneous actions of willful entities, and that the beneficent star was born and reborn every morning in a region of space. Because he believed it, he searched for symbols to say it, and he created language. To speak was then, in such an epoch, a very different thing from what it is today: it was to speak seriously. The words, the morphology, the syntax, enjoyed full meaning. The expressions were saying what seemed to be the truth about the world, were announcing new knowledge, learning. They were the exact opposite of jokes. In fact, both in the ancient language from which Sanskrit evolved and also in Greek the words for 'word' and 'say'—*brahman, logos*—have sacred value.

"The structure of the Indo-European phrase transcribes an interpretation of reality in which events in the world are always the actions of an agent having a specific sex. Thus the structure necessarily consists of a masculine or feminine subject and an active verb. But there are other languages in which the structure of the phrase differs and which supposes interpretations of what is real that are very different from the Indo-European.

"The fact is that the world surrounding Man has never been definable in unequivocal articulations. Or said more clearly, the world, such as we find it, is not composed of 'things' definitively separated and frankly different. We find in it infinite differences, but these differences are not absolute. Strictly speaking, everything is different from everything else, but also everything looks somewhat like everything else. Reality is a limitless continuum of diversity. In order not to get lost in it, we have to slice it, portion it out, and separate the parts; in short, we have to allocate an absolute character to differentiations that actually are only relative. For that reason Goethe said that things are differences that we establish. The first action that Man has taken in his intellectual confrontation with the world is to classify the phenomena, to divide what he finds before him into classes. To each one of these classes is attributed a signifier for his voice, and this is language. But the world offers us innumerable classifications, and does not impose any on us. That being the case, each people must carve up the volatile part of the world in a different way, must make a different incision, and for that reason there are such diverse languages with different grammars and vocabularies and semantics. That original classification is the first supposition to have been made about what the truth of the world is; it was, therefore, the first knowledge. Here is the reason why, as a principle, speaking was knowing.

"The Indo-European believed that the most important difference between 'things' was sex, and he gave every object, a bit indecently, a sexual classification. The other great division that he imposed on the world was based on the supposition that everything that existed was either an action—therefore, the verb—or an agent—therefore, the noun.

"Compared to our paltry classification of nouns—into masculine, feminine and neuter—African peoples who speak the Bantu languages offer much greater enrichment. In some of these languages there are twenty-four classifying signifiers—that is, compared to our three genders, no less than two dozen. The things that move, for example, are differentiated from the inert ones, the vegetable from the animal, etc. While one language scarcely establishes distinctions, another pours out exuberant differentiation. In Eise there are thirty-three words for expressing that many different forms of human movement, of 'going.' In Arabic there are 5,714 names for the camel. Evidently, it's not easy for a nomad of the Arabian desert and a manufacturer from Glasgow to come to an agreement about the humpbacked animal. Languages separate us and discommunicate, not simply because they are different languages, but because they proceed from different mental pictures, from disparate intellectual systems—in the last instance, from divergent philosophies. Not only do we speak, but we also think in a specific language, and intellectually slide along preestablished rails prescribed by our verbal destiny."

The linguist stopped talking and stood with his sharply pointed nose tilted up to a vague quadrant in the heavens. In the corners of his mouth was the hint of a possible smile. I immediately understood that this perspicacious mind was one that took the dialectic path, striking a blow on one side and then the other. As I am of the same breed, I took pleasure in revealing the enigma that his discourse presented to us.

"Surreptitiously and with astute tactics," I said, "you have carried us to the precipice of a contradiction, doubtless in order to make us acutely sensitive to it. You, in fact, have sustained two opposing theses: one, that each language imposes a circumscribed table of categories, of mental routes; another, that the original tables devised by each language no longer have validity, that we use them conventionally and jokingly, that no longer is our speech appropriately saying what we think but is only a manner of speaking. As both theses are convincing, their confrontation leads us to set forth a problem that until now has not been studied by the linguist: what is alive in our language and what is dead; which grammatical categories continue informing our thought and which ones have lost their validity. Because, out of all you have told us, what is most evident is this scandalous proposition that would make Meillet's and Vendryes's hair stand on end: our languages are anachronisms."

"Exactly," exclaimed the linguist. "That is the proposition I wished to suggest, and that is my thinking. Our languages are anachronistic instruments. When we speak, we are humble hostages to the past."

5. The Splendor

"Time is moving along," I said to the great linguist, "and this meeting must be concluded. But I would not like to leave without knowing what you think about the task of translating."

"I think as you do," he replied; "I think it's very difficult, it's unlikely, but, for the same reasons, it's very meaningful. Furthermore, I think that for the first time we will be able to try it in depth and on a broad scale. One should note, in any case, that what is essential concerning the matter has been said more than a century ago by the dear theologian Schleiermacher in his essay 'On the Different Methods of Translating.' According to him, a translation can move in either of two directions: either the author is brought to the language of the reader, or the reader is carried to the language of the author. In the first case, we do not translate, in the proper sense of the word; we, in fact, do an imitation, or a paraphrase of the original text. It is only when we force the reader from his linguistic habits and oblige him to move within those of the author that there is actually translation. Until now there has been almost nothing but pseudotranslations.

"Proceeding from there, I would dare formulate certain principles that would define the new enterprise of translating. Later, if

there is time, I will state the reasons why we must dedicate ourselves more than ever to this task.

"We must begin by correcting at the outset the idea of what a
translation can and ought to be. Should we understand it as a
magic manipulation through which the work written in one language suddenly emerges in another language? If so, we are lost,
because this transubstantiation is impossible. Translation is not a
duplicate of the original text; it is not—it shouldn't try to be—the
work itself with a different vocabulary. I would say translation
doesn't even belong to the same literary genre as the text that was
translated. It would be appropriate to reiterate this and affirm that
translation is a literary genre apart, different from the rest, with its
own norms and own ends. The simple fact is that the translation is
not the work, but a path toward the work. If this is a poetic work,
the translation is no more than an apparatus, a technical device that
brings us closer to the work without ever trying to repeat or replace it.

"In an attempt to avoid confusion, let's consider what in my
judgment is most urgent, the kind of translation that would be
most important to us: that of the Greeks and Romans. For us these
have lost the character of models. Perhaps one of the strangest and
most serious symptoms of our time is that we live without models,
that our faculty to perceive something as a model has atrophied. In
the case of the Greeks and Romans, perhaps our present irrever-
ence will become fruitful, because when they die as norms and
guides they are reborn for us as the only case of civilizations radically different from ours into which—thanks to the number of
works that have been preserved—we can delve. The only definitive
voyage into time that we can make is to Greece and Rome. And
today this type of excursion is the most important that can be
undertaken for the education of Western man. The effects of two
centuries of pedagogy in mathematics, physics and biology have
demonstrated that these disciplines are not sufficient to humanize
man. We must integrate our education in mathematics and physics
through an authentic education in history, which does not consist
of knowing lists of kings and descriptions of battles or statistics of
prices and daily wages in this or the other century, but requires a
voyage to the foreign, to the absolutely foreign, which another
very remote time and another very different civilization comprise.

"In order to confront the natural sciences today, the humanities must be reborn, although under a different sign than the one before. We need to approach the Greek and the Roman again, but not as models—on the contrary, as exemplary errors. Because Man is a historical entity and like every historical reality—not definitively, but for the time being—he is an error. To acquire a historical consciousness of oneself and to learn to see oneself as an error are the same thing. And since—for the time being and relatively speaking—always being an error is the truth of Man, only a historical consciousness can place him into his truth and rescue him. But it is useless to hope that present Man by simply looking at himself will discover himself as an error. One can only educate his optics for human truth, for authentic humanism, by making him look closely and well at the error that others were and, especially, at the error that the best ones were. That is why I have been obsessed, for many years, with the idea that it is necessary to make all Greco-Roman antiquity available for reading—and for that purpose a gigantic task of new translation is absolutely necessary. Because now it would not be a question of emptying into today's languages only literary pieces that were valued as models of their genres, but rather all works, without distinction. We are interested in them, they are important to us, I repeat, as errors, not as examples. We don't need to learn from Greeks and Romans because of what they said, thought, sang, but simply because they were, because they existed, because, like us, they were poor men who swam desperately as we do against the tides in the perennial disaster of living.

"With that in mind, it's important to provide orientation for the translation of the classics along those lines. Since I said before that a repetition of a work is impossible and that the translation is only an apparatus that carries us to it, it stands to reason that diverse translations are fitting for the same text. It is, at least it almost always is, impossible to approximate all the dimensions of the original text at the same time. If we want to give an idea of its aesthetic qualities, we will have to relinquish almost all the substance of the text in order to carry over its formal graces. For that reason, it will be necessary to divide the work and make divergent translations of the same work according to the facets of it that we may wish to translate with precision. But, in general, the interest in those texts is so predominantly concerned with their significance in regard to ancient life that we can dispense with their other qualities without serious loss.

"Whenever a translation of Plato, even the most recent translation, is compared with the text, it will be surprising and irritating, not because the voluptuousness of the Platonic style has vanished on being translated but because of the loss of three-fourths of those very things in the philosopher's phrases that are compelling, that he has stumbled upon in his vigorous thinking, that he has in the back of his mind and insinuates along the way. For that reason— not, as is customarily believed, because of the amputation of its beauty—does it interest today's reader so little. How can it be interesting when the text has been emptied beforehand and all that remains is a thin profile without density or excitement? And let it be stated that what I am saying is not mere supposition. It is a notoriously well-known fact that only one translation of Plato has been really fruitful. This translation is, to be sure, Schleiermacher's, and it is so precisely because, with deliberate design, he refused to do a beautiful translation and tried, as a primary approach, to do what I have been saying. This famous version has been of great service even for philologists. It is false to believe that this kind of work serves only those who are ignorant of Greek and Latin.

"I imagine, then, a form of translation that is ugly, as science has always been; that does not intend to wear literary garb; that is not easy to read but is very clear indeed (although this clarity may demand copious footnotes). The reader must know beforehand that when reading a translation he will not be reading a literarily beautiful book but will be using an annoying apparatus. However, it will truly help him transmigrate within poor Plato, who twenty-four centuries ago, in his way, made an effort to stay afloat on the surface of life.

"Men of other times had need of the ancients in a pragmatic sense. They needed to learn many things from the ancients in order to apply those things to daily life. So it was understandable for translation to try to modernize the ancient text, to accommodate it to the present. But it is advisable for us to do otherwise. We need the ancients precisely to the degree they are dissimilar to us, and translation should emphasize their exotic, distant character, making it intelligible as such.

"I don't understand how any philologist can fail to consider himself obliged to leave some ancient work translated in this form. In general, no writer should denigrate the occupation of translating, and he should complement his own work with some version of an ancient, medieval, or contemporary text. It is necessary to restore the prestige of this labor and value it as an intellectual work of the first order. Doing this would convert translating into a discipline sui generis which, cultivated with continuity, would devise its own techniques that would augment our network of intellectual approaches considerably. And if I have paid special attention to the translations of Greek and Latin, it has only been because the general question is most obvious in their case. But in one way or another, the conclusions to be drawn are the same regarding any other epoch or people. What is imperative is that, in translating, we try to leave our language and go to the other—and not the reverse, which is what is usually done. Sometimes, especially in treating contemporary authors, it will be possible for the version to have, besides its virtues as translation, a certain aesthetic value. That will be icing on the cake or, as you Spaniards say, honey on top of *hojuelas*—probably without having an idea of what *hojuelas* are."

"I've been listening with considerable pleasure," I said, to bring the discussion to a conclusion. "It is clear that a country's reading public do not appreciate a translation made in the style of their own language. For this they have more than enough native authors. What is appreciated is the inverse: carrying the possibilities of their language to the extreme of the intelligible so that the ways of speaking appropriate to the translated author seem to cross into theirs. The German versions of my books are a good example of this. In just a few years, there have been more than fifteen editions. This would be inconceivable if one did not attribute four-fifths of the credit to the success of the translation. And it is successful because my translator has forced the grammatical tolerance of the German language to its limits in order to carry over precisely what is not German in my way of speaking. In this way, the reader effortlessly makes mental turns that are Spanish. He relaxes a bit and for a while is amused at being another.

"But this is very difficult to do in the French language. I regret that my last words at this meeting are involuntarily abrasive, but the subject of our talk forces them to be said. They are these: of all the European languages, the one that least facilitates the task of translating is French."

TWELVE
PAUL VALÉRY
Variations on the *Eclogues*
Translated by Denise Folliot

One of my friends asked me, on behalf of certain persons who wish to produce a fine book, to translate the *Eclogues* in my own fashion. And desiring a symmetry that would make visible to the eye their plan to compose noble, firm, and well-balanced pages, they decided that it would be well if the Latin and French were to correspond line for line. They therefore set me this problem of the equality of appearance and numbers.

*

Latin is, in general, a more compact language than our own. It has no articles; it is chary of auxiliaries (at least during the classical period); it is sparing of prepositions. It can say the same things in fewer words and, moreover, is able to arrange these with an enviable freedom almost completely denied to us. This latitude is most favorable to poetry, which is an art of continuously constraining language to interest the ear directly (and through the ear, everything sounds may provoke of themselves) at least as much as it does the mind. A *line* is both a succession of syllables and a combination of words; and just as the latter ought to form a probable meaning, so the succession of syllables ought to form for the ear a kind of audible shape, which, with a special and as it were peculiar compulsion, should impress itself simultaneously on both voice and memory. The poet must therefore constantly fulfill two sepa-

This translation of the essay "Variations sur Les Bucoliques" (*Traduction en vers des Bucoliques de Virgile* [Paris, 1953]) appeared in Paul Valéry, *Collected Works in English,* vol. 7, The Art of Poetry, pp. 295–312. Copyright © 1985 Princeton University Press. Reprinted with permission of Princeton University Press.

rate demands, just as the painter must present to the simple vision
a harmony, but to the understanding a likeness of things or people.
It is clear that freedom in arranging the words of a sentence, to
which French is curiously hostile, is essential to the game of verse
making. The French poet does what he can within the very narrow
bounds of our syntax; the Latin poet, within the much wider
bounds of his own, does almost what he will.

*

As I therefore had to translate Virgil's famous text into French,
line for line, and as I was inclined to allow, from myself as from
others, only the most faithful translation that the differences in language would admit, my first impulse was to refuse the proposed
task. Nothing marked me out for it. My small amount of schoolboy's Latin had faded, after fifty-five years, to the memory of a
memory; and as so many men, among them the most scholarly and
erudite (not to mention others), had toiled in the course of three
or four centuries at the translation of these poems, I could only
hope to do much worse what they had accomplished so well. In
addition, I must confess that bucolic themes do not excite my interest uncontrollably. Pastoral life is quite foreign to me and strikes
me as tedious. Agricultural industry requires precisely the virtues I
lack. I am depressed by the sight of furrows—including those
made by my pen. The recurrence of the seasons and of their effects
illustrates the stupidity of nature and of life, which can persist only
by repeating itself. I think, too, of the monotonous efforts required
to trace lines in the heavy soil, and I am not surprised that the
obligation inflicted on man of "earning his bread by the sweat of
his brow" should be considered a harsh and degrading punish-
ment. This rule has always seemed to me ignominious. If I am
reproved for this sentiment, which I confess and which I do not
pretend to excuse, I shall say that I was born in a port. No fields
round about, only sand and salt water. Fresh water had to be
brought from a distance. No cattle were seen except as cargo, when
the poor beasts, more dead than alive, hung between heaven and
earth, dangling their hooves in the air, as they were hoisted rapidly
up and deposited, all bewildered, on the dusty quayside. They were
then driven in a herd to the dark trains, trotting and stumbling over
the rails, urged on by the sticks of fluteless herdsmen.

But in the end the sort of challenge posed by the difficulties I have mentioned, together with the very comparisons to be feared, acted as incentives, and so I yielded. My habit is to give way to those agents of fate known as "Others." I have no will, except on two or three absolute and deep-rooted matters. For the rest, I am pliable to the point of weakness and stupidity, as a result of a curious indifference that is founded, possibly, on my conviction that no one knows what he is doing or what he will become, and that to will one thing is at once to will an infinity of other things that will inevitably, when their time comes, appear on the horizon. All the events of my life, though apparently my own acts, were the work of some other, and each is signed with a name. I have observed that there is scarcely more advantage than disadvantage in doing what one wants, and this leads me to ask and to refuse as little as possible. The most reasonable decision, in view of the complexity and confusion of things, is no different from the toss of a coin; if you do not realize it the same day, you will a month later.

*

So I again opened my school Virgil, where, as is usual, there was no lack of notes revealing the erudition of some professor but revealing it to him alone, for on the whole they are wonderfully calculated to entangle the innocent pupil in philology and doubts—if, that is, he should consult them, which he is careful not to do.

O classroom Virgil, who would have thought that I should have occasion to flounder about in you once more?

*

Having sworn on this childhood Virgil to be as faithful as possible to the text of these occasional pieces which nineteen centuries of fame have rendered venerable and almost sacred, and in view of the condition I mentioned of the correspondence line for line between Virgil according to Virgil and Virgil according to me, I decided to write a verse for a verse, an alexandrine opposite each hexameter. However, I did not even consider making the alexandrines rhyme, for this would undoubtedly have led me to make too free with the text, whereas I allowed myself scarcely more than a few omissions of detail. Again, here and there the practice of writing verse made easier, and as it were more natural, the pursuit of a certain harmony, without which, where poetry is concerned, fidelity to meaning alone is a kind of betrayal. How many poetic works, reduced to prose, that is, to their simple meaning, become literally nonexistent! They are anatomical specimens, dead birds! Sometimes, indeed, untrammeled absurdity swarms over these deplorable corpses, their number multiplied by the teaching profession, which claims them as food for what is known as the "Curriculum." Verse is put into prose as though into its coffin.

This is because the finest verses in the world are trivial or senseless once their harmonic flow has been broken and their sonorous substance altered as it develops within the time peculiar to their measured movement, and once they have been replaced by an expression of no intrinsic musical necessity and no resonance. I would even go so far as to say that the more an apparently poetic work survives being put into prose and retains a certain value after this assault, the less is it the work of a poet. A poem, in the modern sense (that is, appearing after a long evolution and differentiation of the functions of speech), should create the illusion of an indissoluble compound of *sound* and *sense,* although there exists no rational relationship between these two constituents of language, which are linked word by word in our memory; that is, by chance, to be called on at need—another effect of chance.

*

I shall now relate quite simply my impressions as a translator, but, according to my peculiar habit of mind, I shall not be able to help first laying down a few principles and turning over a few ideas—for the pleasure of it. . . . Πρὸς Χάριν.

*

Writing anything at all, as soon as the act of writing requires a certain amount of thought and is not a mechanical and unbroken inscribing of spontaneous inner speech, is a work of translation exactly comparable to that of transmuting a text from one language into another. This is because, within the range of any one language, used by everybody to meet the conditions of the moment and of circumstance, our interlocutor, our simple or complex intent, our leisure or haste, and so on, modify our speech. We have one language for ourselves, from which all other ways of speaking differ more or less. One language for our friends, one for general intercourse, one for the rostrum. There is one for love, one for anger, one for command, and one for prayer. There is one for poetry and one of prose, if not several in each category, and all this with the same vocabulary (more or less restricted or extended as the case may be) and subject to the same syntax.

*

If the discourse is a considered one, it is as though composed of halts; it proceeds from point to point. Instead of embracing and permitting the utterance of what comes to it as an immediate result of a stimulus, the mind thinks and rethinks (as though in an aside) the thing it wishes to express, which is not yet in language, and this takes place in the constant presence of the conditions it has set itself.

A man writing verse, poised between his ideal of beauty and his nothingness, is in a state of active and questioning expectation that renders him uniquely and supremely sensitive to the forms and words which the shape of his desire, endlessly resumed and retraced, demands from the unknown, that is from the latent resources of his constitution as a speaker. Meanwhile, an indefinable singing force exacts from him what the bare thought can obtain only through a host of successively tested combinations. The poet chooses among these, not the one which would express his "thought" most exactly (that is the business of prose) and which would therefore repeat what he knows already, but the one which a thought by itself cannot produce, and which appears to him both strange and a stranger, a precious and unique solution to a problem that is formulated only when it is solved. This happy formulation communicates to the poet the same state of emotion which suddenly engendered the formulation: it is not a constructed expression, but a kind of propagation, a matter of resonance. Here language is no longer an intermediary annulled by understanding, once its office is accomplished; it acts through its form, and the effect of form is to be immediately reborn and recognized as itself.

The poet is a peculiar type of translator, who translates ordinary speech, modified by emotion, into "language of the gods," and his inner labor consists less of seeking words for his ideas than of seeking ideas for his words and paramount rhythms.

*

Although I am the least self-assured of Latinists, the slender and mediocre knowledge of the language of Rome that I still retain is very precious to me. One can quite easily write in ignorance of that language, but I do not believe that, if one is ignorant of it, one can feel that one is constructing what one writes as well as if one had a certain awareness of the underlying Latin. One may quite well draw the human body without having the least knowledge of anatomy, but he who has this knowledge is bound to profit somewhat by it, if only by abusing it in order more boldly and successfully to distort the figures in his composition. Latin is not merely the father of French; it is also its tutor in matters of the grand style. All the foolishness and extraordinary reasoning that have been put forward in defense of what are vaguely and untruthfully called the Humanities do but obscure the evidence of the true value for us of a language to which we owe what is most solid and dignified in the monuments of our own tongue. Latin is related to French in two ways, a fact in itself both remarkable and unusual. First of all, Latin gave birth to French through a succession of imperceptible self-modifications, during which evolution a good many other factors and borrowings were irregularly annexed and incorporated down the ages. Later, when our French language was well established and quite distinct from its parent stock, learned men and the most notable authors of their time chose out of the long history of literary Latin one period, rather short but rich in works of the first order, which they hailed as the epoch of perfection in the arts of speaking and writing. One cannot prove that they were right, since this is not a field in which proofs can be made, but it would be easy to show that the close study and assimilation of the writings of Cicero, Livy, or Tacitus were essential to the formation of our abstract prose in the first half of the seventeenth century, which contains the finest and most substantial works produced by France

in the realm of Letters. Poor Latinist though I am, this is what
I feel.

But I should be dealing with poetry and with Virgil.

*

After a while, as I went on with my translation—making, un-
making, remaking, sacrificing here and there, restoring as best I
could what I had first rejected—this labor of approximation with
its little successes, its regrets, its conquests, and its resignations,
produced in me an interesting feeling, of which I was not immediately aware and which it would be better not to confess, if I cared
about other readers than those reflective enough to understand it.

Faced with my Virgil, I had the sensation (well known to me)
of a poet at work. From time to time I argued absently with myself
about this famous book, set in its millennial fame, with as much
freedom as if it had been a poem of my own on the table before
me. At moments, as I fiddled with my translation, I caught myself
wanting to change something in the venerable text. It was a naïve
and unconscious identification with the imagined state of mind of
a writer in the Augustan age. This lasted for one or two seconds of
actual time and amused me. "Why not?" I said to myself, returning
from this short absence. Why not? At bottom there are always the
same problems—that is, the same attitudes: the "inner" ear alert
for the possible, for what will murmur "of itself" and, once mur-
mured, will return to the condition of desire; the same suspense
and the same verbal crystallizations; the same oriented sensitivity
of the subjective vocabulary, as though all the words in the memory were watching their chance to try their luck in reaching the
voice. I was not afraid to reject this epithet, to dislike that word.
Why not?

*

Two coincident remarks may serve to justify this involuntary
amusement. As a diversion the critic may explain himself to himself.

First of all, there is the fact that the *Eclogues* are a work of
youth. Then, there is the state of Latin poetry at the time of their
composition. The man was young, but the art of verse in Rome
had reached the point where it was so conscious of its means that

the temptation to employ them for the pleasure of it and to develop them to the limit outran the true, primitive, and simple need of self-expression. The taste for producing the effect became the cause: put a weapon into the hands of a boy, and flee from him. This is because awareness of strength urges us to use it, and abuse of power is inevitably suggested by the knowledge that one has it. So, in the arts, there appear the virtuosos with their superb indifference to the subject they have to treat or interpret.

But to produce this mental state it is not necessary that technical ability, the possession of supple means, and the free play of an articulate mind be really as assured as the budding artist imagines after making a few attempts whose daring and novelty astonish and enrapture him. It is almost enough to have some inkling of them, and to feel in himself the necessary audacity, for him to experience the sensation of wresting from his probable genius one or two secrets of producing Beauty. . . .

*

I have gone into this subject because anything useful I have to say about Virgil I have gathered from some experience of his craft. Indeed, erudition (which I do not possess) can only point out amid so much uncertainty a few landmarks of biography, reading, or the interpretation of terms. This has its importance, but it is mainly external. It would doubtless be interesting to know whether the poet practiced the kind of love he attributes to some of his shepherds, or whether a certain plant named in his verse has its equivalent in French. Philology can ponder laboriously, and even brilliantly, over these problems. But for myself, I can only wander along quite different paths. I proceed, as is my method, from the finished poem, crystallized as it were in its fame, back to its nascent state. I agree that this is a matter of pure imagination, but imagination tempered by reliable memories.

*

I cannot, then, think of Virgil as a young poet without remembering the time when I, too, was a beginner. The work of translation, done with regard for a certain approximation of form, causes us in some way to try walking in the tracks left by the author; and not to fashion one text upon another, but from the latter to work back to the virtual moment of its formation, to the phase when the mind is in the same state as an orchestra whose instruments begin to waken, calling to each other and seeking harmony before beginning their concert. From that vividly imagined state one must make one's way down toward its resolution in a work in a different tongue.

The *Eclogues,* drawing me for a moment out of my old age, took me back to the time of my first verses. They seemed to give me the same impressions. I believed I could see in the text a mixture of perfections and imperfections, of felicitous combinations and graces of form together with palpably clumsy expressions and sometimes rather surprising commonplaces, of which I shall give an example. I recognized in this unevenness of execution a talent in its youth, and one, moreover, that had budded at a critical age of poetry. When I was twenty, our own poetry, after four centuries of magnificent production, was prey to a restless search for entirely new developments. The widest variety of forms and modes of expression was permitted, and our art was given over to every possible experiment that could be suggested, by both the wish to break with the poetic systems followed till then and the positive idea of enriching it with inventions that were sometimes bizarre, born of the subtlest analyses of the stimulating powers of language.

I was attracted by research of this kind. Soon I had more liking for it than was perhaps necessary merely for the making of verse. My passionate interest in the creative process itself detached me from the initial motive of works, now become a pretext, and in the end gave me a sensation of freedom toward "ideas," and of the supremacy of form over them, which satisfied my belief in the sovereignty of the mind over its functions. I made up my mind that thought is only an accessory to poetry and that the chief thing in a work in verse, a thing proclaimed by the very use of verse, is the whole, the power resulting from effects compounded of all the attributes of language.

*

These explanations, far too personal perhaps, are intended to show that I found myself assuming an attitude of familiarity, rather shocking but inevitable, towards a work of my own trade.

I might also observe that Latin verse differs much more from prose than does French verse, which grazes it and even blends too

easily with it, in spite of being subject, in general, to the law of
rhyme, which is unknown in "classical" Latin. French verse will
stand being made from a verbal substance that does not necessarily
display the musical quality of the "language of the gods." Our syllables follow one another without any rules requiring them to do
so as harmoniously as possible. This was where Malherbe and Boileau erred, forgetting the essential part of their code while proscrib-
ing the unfortunate hiatus, and thus sometimes making life very
difficult for us and depriving us of charming effects such as the
most necessary *tutoiements*. Only a few poets have spent their energy in the search for continuous euphony in their verses, which in
most cases is infrequent and almost incidental. I admit that I have
attached prime importance to euphony and made great sacrifices to
obtain it. I have often said: for me, since the language of the gods
should be as distinct as possible from the language of men, all
means of differentiating it should be retained as long as they also
conduce to harmony. I am a partisan of inversions.

*

Being imbued with these sentiments, I could not help looking
at the text of the *Eclogues,* as I translated them, with the same critical eye as at French verse, my own or another's. I may disapprove,
may regret, or may admire; I may envy or delete; I may reject,
erase, then rediscover, confirm my discovery, and looking on it
with more favor the second time, adopt it.

When an illustrious work is in question, this way of treating it
by analogy may, and indeed probably does, appear naive and presumptuous. I can only contend that it was quite natural for me to
do so, for the reasons I have mentioned. Moreover, I thought that
by thus imagining the still fluid state of a work now far beyond
being merely completed, I could most feelingly share in the very
life of that work, for a work dies by being completed. When a
poem compels one to read it with passion, the reader feels he is
momentarily its author, and that is how he knows the poem is
beautiful. Finally, my illusory identification all at once dispelled the
schoolroom atmosphere of boredom, the recollection of wasted
hours and rigid programs that brood over those unhappy shepherds, their flocks, and their loves (of various kinds), and which the
sight of my "classic" brings back to me. I know of nothing more
barbarous, pointless, and consequently more stupid than a system

of education that confuses the so-called acquisition of a language with the so-called comprehension and enjoyment of a literature. Marvels of poetry or prose are droned out by children who stumble over each word, lost in a vocabulary and syntax that teach them nothing but their ignorance, whereas they know only too well that this forced labor leads to nothing and that they will abandon with relief all these great men who have been turned into instruments of torture for them and all these beauties whose too early and peremptory acquaintance engenders, for the most part, nothing but distaste.

*

Let us now face the *Eclogues* as readers tempted to play the poet. One needs some courage to be this particular poet. In age he is between a youth and a young man. He knows the pleasure of writing verse. He is already able to sing of whatever he likes; he finds a thousand "motifs" in his Italic countryside—both nurse and mother. He is its son and lives by it, body and soul. Besides being well versed in letters, he is more familiar than anyone with the people, the customs, the works and days of this very varied land, where wheat and vines are cultivated, where there are fields and marshes, wooded mountains and bare, stony patches. The elm and cypress grow there, each in its own particular majesty. There are also oaks, sometimes struck by lightning—which signifies something. Moreover, the whole region is haunted or inhabited by deities or divinities who each have some part to play in the strange economy of nature found in Latium, which was a singular combination of the mystical and practical sides of existence. The common task of this mythical population was to animate men's relations with the products, metamorphoses, caprices and laws, benefits and hardships, regularities and irregularities they observed in the world around them. In those days nothing was inanimate, nothing was senseless and deaf unless deliberately, for those Latin peasants, who gave their real names to the springs, the woods, and the grottoes and knew how to speak to things, to invoke and adjure them and call them to witness. So between things and men there grew up an intercourse of mystery and service that we cannot call to mind without thinking: "Poetry"—thus eliminating the whole value and seriousness of this system of exchanges. But what we call Poetry is in fact only what remains to us of an epoch that knew only how to create. All poetry derives from a period of innocent creative awareness and has gradually emerged from a primary and spontaneous state in which thought was fiction in all its force. I fancy that this power has become progressively weaker in towns, where nature is ill received and badly treated, where fountains obey the magistrates, nymphs have dealings with the vice squad, satyrs are looked at askance, and seasons are thwarted. Later on, the countryside also became depopulated, not only of its charming and redoubtable ghosts but also of its credulous and dreaming men. The peasant became an "agriculturist."

But, to return to our poet of the year 40 B.C., it must be admitted that one sings of fauns, dryads, Silenus, and Priapus more gracefully when one believes much less in their existence than in the magic of accomplished verse and in the charm of exquisitely formed figures of speech.

     *

Virgil, the small landowner—though very different from many modern ones, who are moved only by the conversion of their toil and sweat into hard cash, and who cut down a fine tree on the edge of a field as though the preservation of that magnificence were a crime against their virtuous economy—Virgil, who felt himself divided between the different ways of looking at the country around him, Virgil, whose view was double, sometimes invested the countryside with the contentment, fears, and hopes of a man who possesses and is often obsessed by the cares of the property that provides him with a living. At other times a different consideration assailed him. His ambitions ceased to be rural; he was no longer a simple man; there emerged in him a polished spirit, learned in Greek refinements and attracted by subtler compositions than these songs of the artless herdsmen. He could have written an eleventh eclogue between him and himself. But then he was, or had just become, a victim of the disorders that civil war and its brutal consequences had brought into the orbit of his life.

So: a poet, whose desire and artifices are developing, a man of the fields, yet a man threatened with expropriation and practically ruined by the exactions of the victorious soldiery, reduced to appealing to the powers of the day and arranging for protectors— such is the threefold state of the author of the *Eclogues*. Virgil's whole poetic career was to be the most graceful development of the

Latin language and its musical and plastic means in a field of political forces, with his native soil at once a foster mother, a bearer of history or legend, and a treasure house of images, furnishing him with the different pretexts, settings, episodes, and personages of his successive works.

*

This would be a good place for a short consideration of the poet's relations with the authorities. It is a vast subject, a perennial question. If I had not so often teased History, I should suggest a thesis or treatise: "On the Relations of Poetry with Various Regimes or Governments." One could also conceive of a Fable in the manner of La Fontaine: "The Poet and the State," on the lines of "The Cobbler and the Financier." Or make a commentary on the famous saying of the Gospel: "Render unto Caesar," etc.

This problem admits of as many solutions as the mood and state of each man, or the circumstances, suggest. There are economic solutions—for one must live. Others are of a moral order. And some are purely affective. A regime attracts either by its material perfections or by its glory and triumphs; one leader by his genius; another by his liberality, sometimes a mere smile. In other cases opposition is provoked by the state of public affairs. The man of intellect rebels more or less openly or shuts himself up in a work that secretes a kind of intellectual insulation about his sensibility. In fact, every type can be observed. Racine adores his King. Chénier curses his tyrants. Hugo goes into exile. Corneille begs proudly. Goethe prefers injustice to disorder. Majesty dazzles. Authority impresses. Freedom intoxicates. Anarchy terrifies. Personal interest speaks with its powerful voice. One must not forget, either, that every individual distinguished by his talents places himself in his heart among a certain aristocracy. Whether he wishes it or not, he cannot confuse himself with the masses, and this unavoidable feeling has the most various consequences. He notices that democracy, egalitarian in its essence, is incapable of pensioning a poet. Or else, judging the men in power and the men dominated by these, he despises both but feels the temptation to appear in politics himself and to take part in the conduct of affairs. This temptation is not infrequent among lyric poets. It is remarkable that the purest of human occupations, that of taming and elevating beings by song, as Orpheus did, should so often lead to coveting the impurest of occupations. What is one to think? There are examples of everything, since we are speaking of History. . . .

*

Virgil cannot stand disorder and exactions. He sees himself plundered, torn from his home, deprived of his means of existence by measures of political expediency. He sees a threat to his leisure to be himself and to become what he dreams of—that most precious possession, that treasure of free time, rich in latent beauties that he is sure of bringing forth. He sees no further. How should one expect him not to welcome the favors of a tyrant, not to sing of the man who assures him peaceful days and thus restores his reason for living?

Ludere quae vellem calamo permisit agresti

Virgil did not hesitate between the independence of the citizen and that of the creator of poems. Perhaps he did not even think that he was sacrificing anything in professing to praise Caesar, even to deifying him:

Erit ille semper deus . . .

Just imagine all the sentences that could be written for or against that attitude, according as one judged as a modern or took account of the relativity of feelings and circumstances. In those days there was yet no question of the Rights of Man.

The problem of conscience that might be introduced here, insoluble though it is, becomes particularly interesting if it is transformed into a problem of values. If the submission to a despot, the acceptance of his favors, which degenerates into, or reveals itself in, expressions of gratitude and praise, is a condition of the production of works of the first order, what is one to decide, to do, to think? This problem is hardly introduced before it develops into endless arguments. I shall take care not to enter upon them.

THIRTEEN
VLADIMIR NABOKOV
Problems of Translation: *Onegin* in English

I constantly find in reviews of verse translations the following kind of thing that sends me into spasms of helpless fury: "Mr. (or Miss) So-and-so's translation reads smoothly." In other words, the reviewer of the "translation," who neither has, nor would be able to have, without special study, any knowledge whatsoever of the original, praises as "readable" an imitation only because the drudge or the rhymster has substituted easy platitudes for the breathtaking intricacies of the text. "Readable," indeed! A schoolboy's boner is less of a mockery in regard to the ancient masterpiece than its commercial interpretation or poetization. "Rhyme" rhymes with "crime," when Homer or *Hamlet* are rhymed. The term "free translation" smacks of knavery and tyranny. It is when the translator sets out to render the "spirit"—not the textual sense—that he begins to traduce his author. The clumsiest literal translation is a thousand times more useful than the prettiest paraphrase.

For the last five years or so I have been engaged, on and off, in translating and annotating Pushkin's *Onegin*. In the course of this work I have learned some facts and come to certain conclusions. First, the facts.

The novel is concerned with the afflictions, affections, and fortunes of three young men—Onegin, the bitter lean fop, Lenski, the temperamental minor poet, and Pushkin, their friend—and of three young ladies—Tatiana, Olga, and Pushkin's Muse. Its events take place between the end of 1819 and the spring of 1825. The scene shifts from the capital to the countryside (midway between

From *Partisan Review* 22, no. 4 (Fall 1955) pp. 498–512. Reprinted by arrangement with the Estate of Vladimir Nabokov.

Opochka and Moscow), and thence to Moscow and back to Petersburg. There is a description of a young rake's day in town; rural
landscapes and rural libraries; a dream and a duel; various festivities
in country and city; and a variety of romantic, satirical and biblio-
graphic digressions that lend wonderful depth and color to the
thing.

Onegin himself is, of course, a literary phenomenon, not a local or historical one. Childe Harold, the hero of Byron's "romaunt"
(1812), whose "early youth [had been] misspent in maddest
whim," who has "moping fits," who is bid to loath his present state
by a "weariness which springs from all [he] meets," is really only a
relative, not the direct prototype, of Onegin. The latter is less "a
Muscovite in Harold's cloak" than a descendant of many fantastic
Frenchmen such as Chateaubriand's *René,* who was aware of existing only through a "profond sentiment d'ennui." Pushkin speaks of
Onegin's spleen or "chondria" (the English "hypo" and the Russian
"chondria" or "handra" represent a neat division of linguistic labor
on the part of two nations) as of "a malady the cause of which it
seems high time to find." To this search Russian critics applied
themselves with commendable zeal, accumulating during the last
one hundred and thirty years one of the most somniferous masses
of comments known to civilized man. Even a special term for Onegin's "sickness" has been invented *(Oneginstvo);* and thousands of
pages have been devoted to him as a "type" of something or other.
Modern Soviet critics standing on a tower of soapboxes provided
a hundred years ago by Belinski, Herzen, and many others, diag-
nosed Onegin's sickness as the result of "Tzarist despotism." Thus
a character borrowed from books but brilliantly recomposed by a
great poet to whom life and library were one, placed by that poet
within a brilliantly reconstructed environment, and played with by
him in a succession of compositional patterns—lyrical impersona-
tions, tomfooleries of genius, literary parodies, stylized epistles,
and so on—is treated by Russian commentators as a sociological
and historical phenomenon typical of Alexander the First's regime:
alas, this tendency to generalize and vulgarize the unique fancy of
an individual genius has also its advocates in this country.

Actually there has never been anything especially local or time-
significant in hypochondria, misanthropy, ennui, the blues, *Welt-
schmerz,* etc. By 1820, ennui was a seasoned literary cliché of characterization which Pushkin could toy with at his leisure. French
fiction of the eighteenth century is full of young characters suffer-

ing from the spleen. It was a convenient device to keep one's hero on the move. Byron gave it a new thrill; René, Adolphe, and their co-sufferers received a transfusion of demon blood.

*

Evgeniy Onegin is a Russian novel in verse. Pushkin worked at it from May 1823 to October 1831. The first complete edition appeared in the spring of 1833 in St. Petersburg; there is a well-preserved specimen of this edition at the Houghton Library, Harvard University. *Onegin* has eight chapters and consists of 5,551 lines, all of which, except a song of eighteen unrhymed lines (in trochaic trimeter), are in iambic tetrameter, rhymed. The main body of the work contains, apart from two freely rhymed epistles, 366 stanzas, each of fourteen lines, with a fixed rhyme pattern: ababeecciddiff (the vowels indicate the feminine rhymes, the consonants the masculine ones). Its resemblance to the sonnet is obvious. Its octet consists of an elegiac quatrain and of two couplets, its sestet of a closed quatrain and a couplet. This hyperborean freak is far removed from the Petrarchan pattern, but is distinctly related to Malherbe's and Surrey's variations.

The tetrametric, or "anacreontic," sonnet was introduced in France by Scévole de Sainte-Marthe in 1579; and it was once tried by Shakespeare (Sonnet CXLV: "Those lips that Love's own hand did make," with a rhyme scheme "make-hate-sake: state-come-sweet-doom-greet: end-day-fiend-away. Threw-you"). The *Onegin* stanza would be technically an English anacreontic sonnet had not the second quatrain consisted of two couplets instead of being closed or alternate. The novelty of Pushkin's freak sonnet is that its first twelve lines include the greatest variation in rhyme sequence possible within a three-quatrain frame: alternate, paired, and closed. However, it is really from the French, not from the English, that Pushkin derived the idea for this new kind of stanza. He knew his Malherbe well—and Malherbe had composed several sonnets (see for example, "A Rabel, peintre, sur un livre de fleurs," 1630) in tetrameter, with four rhymes in the octet and assymetrical quatrains (the first alternately rhymed, the second closed), but of course Malherbe's sestet was the classical one, never clinched with a couplet in the English fashion. We have to look elsewhere for Pushkin's third quatrain and for his epigrammatic couplet—namely in French light verse of the seventeenth and eighteenth cen-

tury. In one of Gresset's *Epîtres* ("Au Père Bougeant, jésuite") the
Onegin sestet is exactly represented by the lines

> Mais pourquoi donner au mystère,
> Pourquoi reprocher au hazard
> De ce prompt et triste départ
> La cause trop involontaire?
> Oui, vous seriez encore à nous
> Si vous étiez vous-même à vous.

Theoretically speaking, it is not impossible that a complete
Onegin stanza may be found embedded somewhere in the endless
"Epistles" of those periwigged bores, just as its sequence of rhymes
is found in La Fontaine's *Contes* (e.g., "Nicaise," 48–61) and in
Pushkin's own freely-rhymed *Ruslan i Lyudmila,* composed in his
youth (see the last section of Canto Three, from *Za otdalyonnïmi
godami* to *skazal mne vazhno Chernomor*). In this Pushkinian pseu-
dosonnet the opening quatrain, with its brilliant alternate rhymes,
and the closing couplet, with its epigrammatic click, are in greater
evidence than the intermediate parts, as if we were being shown
first the pattern on one side of an immobile sphere which would
then start to revolve, blurring the colors, and presently would come
to a stop, revealing clearly again a smaller pattern on its opposite
side.

As already said, there are in *Onegin* more than 300 stanzas of
this kind. We have moreover fragments of two additional chapters
and numerous stanzas canceled by Pushkin, some of them spar-
kling with more originality and beauty than any in the Cantos from
which he excluded them before publication. All this matter, as well
as Pushkin's own commentaries, the variants, epigraphs, dedica-
tions, and so forth, must be of course translated too, in appendices
and notes.

II

Russian poetry is affected by the following six characteristics
of language and prosody:
1. The number of rhymes, both masculine and feminine (i.e.,
single and double), is incomparably greater than in English and
leads to the cult of the rare and the rich. As in French, the *consonne
d'appui* is obligatory in masculine rhymes and aesthetically valued

in feminine ones. This is far removed from the English rhyme, Echo's poor relation, a genteel pauper whose attempts to shine result merely in doggerel garishness. For if in Russian and French the feminine rhyme is a glamorous lady friend, her English counterpart is either an old maid or a drunken hussy from Limerick.

2. No matter the length of a word in Russian it has but one stress; there is never a secondary accent or two accents as occurs in English—especially American English.

3. Polysyllabic words are considerably more frequent than in English.

4. All syllables are fully pronounced; there are no elisions and slurs as there are in English verse.

5. Inversion, or more exactly pyrrhichization of trochaic words—so commonly met with in English iambics (especially in the case of two-syllable words ending in -er or -ing)—is rare in Russian verse: only a few two-syllable prepositions and the trochaic components of compound words lend themselves to shifts of stress.

6. Russian poems composed in iambic tetrameter contain a larger number of modulated lines than of regular ones, while the reverse is true in regard to English poems.

By "regular line" I mean an iambic line in which the metrical beat coincides in each foot with the natural stress of the word: *Of cloudless climes and starry skies* (Byron). By "modulated line" I mean an iambic line in which at least one metrical accent falls on the unstressed syllable of a polysyllabic word (such as the third syllable in "reasonable") or on a monosyllabic word unstressed in speech (such as "of," "the," "and" etc.). In Russian prosody such modulations are termed "half-accents," and both in Russian and English poetry a tetrametric iambic line may have one such half-accent on the first, second, or third foot, or two half-accents in the first and third, or in adjacent feet. Here are some examples (the Roman figure designates the foot where the half-accent occurs).

I	Make the delighted spirit glow (Shelley);
	My apprehensions come in crowds (Wordsworth);
II	Of forests and enchantments drear (Milton);
	Beyond participation lie (Wordsworth);
III	Do paint the meadows with delight (Shakespeare);
	I know a reasonable woman (Pope);
I + II	And on that unforgotten shore (Bottomly);
II + III	When icicles hang by the wall (Shakespeare);

I + III   Or in the chambers of the sea (Blake);
            An incommunicable sleep (Wordsworth).

It is important to mark that, probably in conjunction with
characteristic 3, the half-accent in the third foot occurs three or
four times more frequently in Russian iambic tetrameters than in
English ones, and that the regular line is more than twice rarer. If,
for instance we examine Byron's *Mazeppa,* Scott's *The Lady of the
Lake,* Keats's *The Eve of Saint Mark* and Tennyson's *In Memoriam,*
we find that the percentage of regular lines there is around 65, as
against only some 25 in *Onegin.* There is, however, one English
poet whose modulations, if not as rich in quantity and variety as
Pushkin's, are at least an approach to that richness. I refer to An-
drew Marvell. It is instructive to compare Byron's snip-snap mon-
otonies such as

> One shade the more one ray the less
> Had half impaired the nameless grace
> Which waves in every raven tress
> Or softly lightens o'er her face

with any of the lines addressed by Marvell "To His Coy Mistress":

> And you should if you please refuse,
> Till the conversion of the Jews
> My vegetable love should grow
> Vaster than empires and more slow,

—four lines in which there are six half-accents against Byron's
single one.

It is among such melodies that one should seek one's model
when translating Pushkin in verse.

III

I shall now make a statement for which I am ready to incur the
wrath of Russian patriots: Alexandr Sergeyevich Pushkin (1799–
1837), the national poet of Russia, was as much a product of
French literature as of Russian culture; and what happened to be
added to this mixture, was individual genius which is neither Russian nor French, but universal and divine. In regard to Russian

influence, Zhukovski and Batyushkov were the immediate predecessors of Pushkin: harmony and precision—this was what he
learned from both, though even his boyish verses were more vivid
and vigorous than those of his young teachers. Pushkin's French
was as fluent as that of any highly cultured gentleman of his day.
Gallicisms in various stages of assimilation populate his poetry with
the gay hardiness of lucern and dandelion invading a trail in the
Rocky Mountains. *Coeur flétri, essaim de désirs, transports, alarmes,
attraits, attendrissement, fol amour, amer regret* are only a few—my
list comprises about ninety expressions that Pushkin as well as his
predecessors and contemporaries transposed from French into melodious Russian. Of special importance is *bizarre, bizarrerie* which
Pushkin rendered as *stranniy, strannost'* when alluding to the oddity
of Onegin's nature. The *douces chimères* of French elegies are as
close to the *sladkie mechti* and *sladostnie mechtaniya* of Pushkin as
they are to the "delicious reverie" and "sweet delusions" of
eighteenth-century English poets. The *sombres bocages* are Pushkin's
sumrachnïe dubrovï and Pope's "darksome groves." The English
translator should also make up his mind how to render such significant nouns and their derivatives as *toska (angoisse), tomnost' (langueur)* and *nega (mollesse)* which constantly recur in Pushkin's
idiom. I translate *toska* as "heart-ache" or "anguish" in the sense of
Keats's "wakeful anguish." *Tomnost'* with its adjective *tomnïy* is
among Pushkin's favorite words. The good translator will recall
that "languish" is used as a noun by Elizabethan poets (e.g., Sam-
uel Daniel's "relieve my languish"), and in this sense is to "anguish"
what "pale" is to "dark." Blake's "her languished head" takes care
of the adjective, and the "languid moon" of Keats is nicely dupli-
cated by Pushkin's *tomnaya luna*. At some point *tomnost'* (languor)
grades into *nega (molle langueur)*, soft luxury of the senses, slum-
berous tenderness. Pushkin was acquainted with English poets only
through their French models or French versions; the English translator of *Onegin,* while seeking an idiom in the Gallic diction of
Pope and Byron, or in the romantic vocabulary of Keats, must constantly refer to the French poets.

In his early youth, Pushkin's literary taste was formed by the
same writers and the same *Cours de Littérature* that formed Lamartine and Stendhal. This manual was the *Lycée ou Cours de Littérature, ancienne et moderne* by Jean François Laharpe, in sixteen volumes, 1799–1805. To the end of his days, Pushkin's favorite
authors were Boileau, Bossuet, Corneille, Fénelon, Lafontaine,

Molière, Pascal, Racine, and Voltaire. In relation to his contemporaries, he found Lamartine melodious but monotonous, Hugo gifted but on the whole second-rate; he welcomed the lascivious verse of young Musset, and rightly despised Béranger. In *Onegin* one finds echoes not only of Voltaire's *Le Mondain* (various passages in chapter one) or Millevoye's *Elégies* (especially in passages related to Lenski), but also of Parny's *Poésies Erotiques,* Gresset's *Vert-vert,* Chénier's melancholy melodies and of a host of *petits poètes français,* such as Baïf, Gentil Bernard, Bernis, Bertin, Chaulieu, Colardeau, Delavigne, Delille, Desbordes-Valmore, Desportes, Dorat, Ducis, Gilbert, Lattaignant, Lebrun, Le Brun, Legouvé, Lemierre, Léonard, Malfilâtre, Piron, Jean-Baptiste Rousseau, and others.

As to German and English, he hardly had any. In 1821, translating Byron into gentleman's French for his own private use, he renders "the wave that rolls below the Athenian's grave" (beginning of the *Giaour*) as "ce flot qui roule sur la grêve d'Athène." He read Shakespeare in Guizot's and Amedée Pichot's revision of Letourneur's edition (Paris, 1821) and Byron in Pichot's and Eusèbe de Salle's versions (Paris, 1819–21). Byron's command of the cliché was singularly dear to Russian poets as echoing the minor and major French poetry on which they had been brought up.

It would have been a flat and dry business indeed, if the verbal texture of *Onegin* were reduced to these patterns in faded silks. But a miracle occurred. When, more than a hundred and fifty years ago, the Russian literary language underwent the prodigious impact of French, the Russian poets made certain inspired selections and matched the old and the new in certain enchantingly individual ways. French stock epithets, in their Russian metamorphosis, breathe and bloom anew, so delicately does Pushkin manipulate them as he disposes them at strategic points of his meaningful harmonies. Incidentally, this does not lighten our task.

IV

The person who desires to turn a literary masterpiece into another language, has only one duty to perform, and this is to reproduce with absolute exactitude the whole text, and nothing but the text. The term "literal translation" is tautological since anything but that is not truly a translation but an imitation, an adaptation or a parody.

The problem, then, is a choice between rhyme and reason: can a translation while rendering with absolute fidelity the whole text, and nothing but the text, keep the form of the original, its rhythm and its rhyme? To the artist whom practice within the limits of one language, his own, has convinced that matter and manner are one, it comes as a shock to discover that a work of art can present itself to the would-be translator as split into form and content, and that the question of rendering one but not the other may arise at all. Actually what happens is still a monist's delight: shorn of its primary verbal existence, the original text will not be able to soar and to sing; but it can be very nicely dissected and mounted, and scientifically studied in all its organic details. So here is the sonnet, and there is the sonneteer's ardent admirer still hoping that by some miracle of ingenuity he will be able to render every shade and sheen of the original and somehow keep intact its special pattern in another tongue.

Let me state at once that in regard to mere meter there is not much trouble. The iambic measure is perfectly willing to be combined with literal accuracy for the curious reason that English prose lapses quite naturally into an iambic rhythm.

Stevenson has a delightful essay warning the student against the danger of transferring one's prose into blank verse by dint of polishing and pruning; and the beauty of the thing is that Stevenson's discussion of the rhythmic traps and pitfalls is couched in pure iambic verse with such precision and economy of diction that readers, or at least the simpler readers, are not aware of the didactic trick.

Newspapers use blank verse as commonly as Monsieur Jourdain used prose. I have just stretched my hand toward a prostrate paper, and reading at random I find

> Debate on European Army interrupted: the Assembly's
> Foreign Affairs Committee by a vote
> Of twenty-four to twenty has decided
> To recommend when the Assembly
> Convenes this afternoon
> That it adopt the resolution
> To put off the debate indefinitely.
> This, in effect, would kill the treaty.

> The New York Yankees aren't conceding
> The American League flag to Cleveland

But the first seed of doubt
Is growing in the minds of the defending champions.

Nebraska city proud of jail:
Stromsburg, Nebraska (Associated Press).
They're mighty proud here of the city jail,
A building that provides both for incarceration
And entertainment. The brick structure houses
The police station and the jail. The second story
Has open sides and is used as a band stand.

V

Onegin has been mistranslated into many languages. I have
checked only the French and English versions, and some of the
rhymed German ones. The three complete German concoctions I
have seen are the worst of the lot. Of these Lippert's (1840) which
changes Tatiana into Johanna, and Seubert's (1873) with its Max-
und-Moritz tang, are beneath contempt; but Bodenstedt's fluffy
product (1854) has been so much praised by German critics that it
is necessary to warn the reader that it, too, despite a more laudable
attempt at understanding if not expression, bristles with incredible
blunders and ridiculous interpolations. Incidentally, at this point,
it should be noted that Russians themselves are responsible for the
two greatest insults that have been hurled at Pushkin's masterpiece—the vile Chaykovski (Tschaykowsky) opera and the equally
vile illustrations by Repin which decorate most editions of the
novel.

Onegin fared better in French—namely in Turgenev and Viardot's fairly exact prose version (in *La Revue Nationale*, Paris 1863).
It would have been a really good translation had Viardot realized
how much Pushkin relied on the Russian equivalent of the stock
epithets of French poetry, and had he acted accordingly. As it is,
Dupont's prose version (1847), while crawling with errors of a
textual nature, is more idiomatic.

There are four English complete versions unfortunately available to college students: *Eugene Onéguine,* translated by Lieut.-Col.
Spalding (Macmillan, London, 1881); *Eugene Onegin,* translated
by Babette Deutsch in *The Works of Alexander Pushkin,* selected and
edited by Abraham Yarmolinski (Random House, New York,
1936); *Evgeny Onegin,* translated by Oliver Elton (*The Slavonic Revue,* London, January 1936 to January 1938, and The Pushkin

Press, London, 1937); *Eugene Onegin,* translated by Dorothea
Prall Radin and George Z. Patrick (University of California Press,
Berkeley, 1937).

All four are in meter and rhyme; all are the result of earnest
effort and of an incredible amount of mental labor; all contain here
and there little gems of ingenuity; and all are grotesque travesties
of their model, rendered in dreadful verse, teeming with mistrans-
lations. The least offender is the bluff, matter-of-fact Colonel; the
worst is Professor Elton, who combines a kind of irresponsible
verbal felicity with the most exuberant vulgarity and the funniest
howlers.

One of the main troubles with would-be translators is their
ignorance. Only by sheer unacquaintance with Russian life in the
'twenties of the last century can one explain, for instance, their per-
sistently translating *derevnya* by "village" instead of "countryseat,"
and *skakat'* by "to gallop" instead of "to drive." Anyone who wishes
to attempt a translation of Onegin should acquire exact information in regard to a number of relevant subjects, such as the Fables
of Krïlov, Byron's works, French poets of the eighteenth century,
Rousseau's *La Nouvelle Héloïse,* Pushkin's biography, banking
games, Russian songs related to divination, Russian military ranks
of the time as compared to western European and American ones,
the difference between cranberry and lingenberry, the rules of the
English pistol duel as used in Russia, and the Russian language.

VI

To illustrate some of the special subtleties that Pushkin's translators should be aware of, I propose to analyze the opening quatrain of stanza 39 in Chapter 4, which describes Onegin's life in
the summer of 1820 on his country estate situated some three hundred miles west of Moscow:

> Progúlki, chtén'e, son glubókoy,
> Lesnáya ten', zhurchán'e struy,
> Poróy belyánki cherno-ókoy
> Mladóy i svézhiy potzelúy . . .

In the first line,

progulki, chten'e, son glubokoy

(which Turgenev-Viardot translated correctly as "la promenade, la lecture, un somneil profond et salutaire"), *progulki* cannot be rendered by the obvious "walks" since the Russian term includes the additional idea of riding for exercise or pleasure. I did not care for "promenades" and settled for "rambles" since one can ramble about on horseback as well as on foot. The next word means "reading," and then comes a teaser: *glubokoy son* means not only "deep sleep" but also "sound sleep" (hence the double epithet in the French translation) and of course implies "sleep by night." One is tempted to use "slumber," which would nicely echo in another key the alliterations of the text (*progulki-glubokoy*, rambles-slumber), but of these elegancies the translator should beware. The most direct rendering of the line seems to be:

> rambles, and reading, and sound sleep . . . [1]

In the next line

> lesnaya ten', zhurchan'e struy . . .

lesnaya ten' is "the forest's shade," or, in better concord "the sylvan shade" (and I confess to have toyed with (Byron's) "the umbrage of the wood"); and now comes another difficulty: the catch in *zhurchan'e struy,* which I finally rendered as "the bubbling of the streams," is that *strui* (nominative plural) has two meanings: its ordinary one is the old sense of the English "streams" designating not bodies of water but rather limbs of water, the shafts of a running river (for example as used by Kyd in "Cornelia": "O beautious Tyber with thine easie streams that glide . . . ," or by Anne Bradstreet in "Contemplations": "a [River] where gliding streams" etc.), while the other meaning is an attempt on Pushkin's part to express the French *ondes,* waters; for it should be clear to Pushkin's translator that the line

> the sylvan shade, the bubbling of the streams . . .

(or as an old English rhymster might have put it "the green-wood shade, the purling rillets") deliberately reflects an idyllic ideal dear

---

1. Compare Pope's "sound sleep by night, study and ease," in "Solitude," or James Thomson's "retirement, rural quiet, friendship, books," in "The Seasons: Spring."

to the Arcadian poets. The wood and the water, "les ruisseaux et les bois," can be found together in countless "éloges de la campagne" praising the "green retreats" that were theoretically favored by eighteenth-century French and English poets. Antoine Bertin's "le silence des bois, le murmure de l'onde" *(Elégie 22)* or Evariste Parny's "dans l'épaisseur du bois, au doux bruit des ruisseaux" *(Fragment d'Alcée)* are typical commonplaces of this kind. With the assistance of these minor French poets, we have now translated the first two lines of the stanza. Its entire first quatrain runs:

> Rambles, and reading, and sound sleep,
> the sylvan shade, the bubbling of the streams;
> sometimes a white-skinned dark-eyed girl's
> young and fresh kiss.

> Poroy belyanki cherno-okoy
> Mladoy i svezhiy potzeluy

The translator is confronted here by something quite special. Pushkin masks an autobiographical allusion under the disguise of a literal translation from André Chénier, whom however he does not mention in any appended note. I am against stressing the human-interest angle in the discussion of literary works; and such emphasis would be especially incongruous in the case of Pushkin's novel where a stylized, and thus fantastic, Pushkin is one of the main characters.

However there is little doubt that our author camouflaged in the present stanza, by means of a device which in 1825 was unique in the annals of literary art, his own experience: namely a brief intrigue he was having that summer on his estate in the Province of Pskov with Olga Kalashnikov, a meek, delicate-looking slave girl, whom he made pregnant and eventually bundled away to a second demesne of his, in another province. If we now turn to André Chénier, we find, in a fragment dated 1789 and published by Latouche as "Epitre VII, à de Pange ainé" (lines 5–8):

> ... Il a dans sa paisible et sainte solitude,
> Du loisir, due sommeil, et les bois, et l'étude,
> Le banquet des amis, et quelquefois, les soirs,
> Le baiser jeune et frais d'une blanche aux yeux noirs.

None of the translators of Pushkin, English, German or French, have noticed what several Russian students of Pushkin discovered independently (a discovery first published, I think, by Savchenko—"Elegiya Lenskogo i frantzuskaya elegiya," in *Pushkin v mirovoy literature*, note, p. 362, Leningrad, 1926), that the two first lines of our stanza 39 are a paraphrase, and the next two a metaphrase of Chénier's lines. Chénier's curious preoccupation with the whiteness of a woman's skin (see for example *Elégie 22*) and Pushkin's vision of his own frail young mistress, fuse to form a marvelous mask, the disguise of a personal emotion; for it will be noted that our author, who was generally rather careful about the identification of his sources, nowhere reveals his direct borrowing here, as if by referring to the literary origin of these lines he might impinge upon the mystery of his own romance.

English translators, who were completely unaware of all the implications and niceties I have discussed in connection with this stanza, have had a good deal of trouble with it. Spalding stresses the hygienic side of the event

> the uncontaminated kiss
> of a young dark-eyed country maid;

Miss Radin produces the dreadful:

> a kiss at times from some fair maiden
> dark-eyed, with bright and youthful looks;

Miss Deutsch, apparently not realizing that Pushkin is alluding to Onegin's carnal relations with his serf girls, comes up with the incredibly coy:

> and if a black-eyed girl permitted
> sometimes a kiss as fresh as she;

and Professor Elton, who in such cases can always be depended upon for grotesque triteness and bad grammar, reverses the act and peroxides the concubine:

> at times a fresh young kiss bestowing
> upon some blond and dark-eyed maid.

Pushkin's line is, by-the-by, an excellent illustration of what I mean by "literalism, literality, literal interpretation." I take literalism to mean "absolute accuracy." If such accuracy sometimes results in the strange allegoric scene suggested by the phrase "the letter has killed the spirit," only one reason can be imagined: there must have been something wrong either with the original letter or with the original spirit, and this is not really a translator's concern. Pushkin has literally (i.e., with absolute accuracy) rendered Chénier's *une blanche* by *belyanka* and the English translator should reincarnate here both Pushkin and Chénier. It would be false literalism to render *belyanka (une blanche)* as "a white one"—or, still worse, "a white female"; and it would be ambiguous to say "fair-faced." The accurate meaning is "a white-skinned female," certainly "young," hence a "white-skinned girl," with dark eyes and, presumably, dark hair enhancing by contrast the luminous fairness of unpigmented skin.

Another good example of a particularly "untranslatable" stanza is 33 in Chapter 1:

I recollect the sea before a storm:
O how I envied
the waves-that ran in turbulent succession
to lie down at her feet with love!

Ya pómnyu móre pred grozóyu:
kak ya zavídoval volnám
begúshchim búrnoy cheredóyu
s lyukóv'yu lech k eyó nogám!

Russian readers discern in the original here two sets of beautifully onomatopoeic alliterations: *begushchim burnoy* . . . which renders the turbulent rush of the surf, and *s lyubov'yu lech*—the liquid lisp of the waves dying in adoration at the lady's feet. Whomsoever the recollected feet belonged to (thirteen-year-old Marie Raevski paddling near Taganrog, or her father's godchild, a young *dame de compagnie* of Tatar origin, or what is more likely—despite Marie's own memoirs—Countess Elise Vorontzov, Pushkin's mistress in Odessa, or, most likely, a retrospective combination of reflected ladies), the only relevant fact here is that these waves come from Lafontaine through Bogdanovich. I refer to "L'onde pour toucher . . . [Vénus] à longs flots s'entrepousse et d'une égale ardeur chaque flot à son tour s'en vient baiser les pieds de la mère d'Amour" (Jean

de la Fontaine, "Les Amours de Psiche et de Cupidon," 1669) and
to a close paraphrase of this by Ippolit Bogdanovich, in his "Sweet
Psyche" (*Dushen'ka*, 1783–1799) which in English should read
"the waves that pursue her jostle jealously to fall humbly at her
feet."

Without introducing various changes, there is no possibility
whatsoever to make of Pushkin's four lines an alternately rhymed
tetrametric quatrain in English, even if only masculine rhymes be
used. The key words are: *collect, sea, storm, envied, waves, ran, turbulent, succession, lie, feet, love;* and to these eleven not a single addition can be made without betrayal. For instance, if we try to end
the first line in "before"—*I recollect the sea before* (followed by a
crude enjambement)—and graft the rhyme "shore" to the end of
the third line (the *something* waves that storm the shore), this one
concession would involve us in a number of other changes completely breaking up the original sense and all its literary associations. In other words, the translator should constantly bear in mind
not only the essential pattern of the text but also the borrowings
with which that pattern is interwoven. Nor can anything be added
for the sake of rhyme or meter. One thinks of some of those task
problems in chess tourneys to the composition of which special
restrictive rules are applied, such as the stipulation that only certain
pieces may be used. In the marvelous economy of an *Onegin* stanza,
the usable pieces are likewise strictly limited in number and kind:
they may be shifted around by the translator but no additional men
may be used for padding or filling up the gaps that impair a unique
solution.

VII

To translate an *Onegin* stanza does not mean to rig up fourteen
lines with alternate beats and affix to them seven jingle rhymes
starting with pleasure-love-leisure-dove. Granted that rhymes can
be found, they should be raised to the level of *Onegin*'s harmonies
but if the masculine ones may be made to take care of themselves,
what shall we do about the feminine rhymes? When Pushkin
rhymes *devï* (maidens) with *gde vï* (where are you?), the effect is
evocative and euphonious, but when Byron rhymes "maidens"
with "gay dens," the result is burlesque. Even such split rhymes in
Onegin as the instrumental of Childe Harold and the instrumental
of "ice" (*Garol'-dom—so-l'dom*), retain their aonian gravity and

have nothing in common with such monstrosities in Byron as "new skin" and "Pouskin" (a distortion of the name of Count Musin-Pushkin, a binominal branch of the family).

So here are three conclusions I have arrived at: (1) It is impossible to translate *Onegin* in rhyme. (2) It is possible to describe in a series of footnotes the modulations and rhymes of the text as well as all its associations and other special features. (3) It is possible to translate *Onegin* with reasonable accuracy by substituting for the fourteen rhymed tetrameter lines of each stanza fourteen unrhymed lines of varying length, from iambic dimeter to iambic pentameter.

These conclusions can be generalized. I want translations with copious footnotes, footnotes reaching up like skyscrapers to the top of this or that page so as to leave only the gleam of one textual line between commentary and eternity. I want such footnotes and the absolutely literal sense, with no emasculation and no padding—I want such sense and such notes for all the poetry in other tongues that still languishes in "poetical" versions, begrimed and beslimed by rhyme. And when my *Onegin* is ready, it will either conform exactly to my vision or not appear at all.

FOURTEEN
ROMAN JAKOBSON
On Linguistic Aspects of Translation

According to Bertrand Russell, "no one can understand the word 'cheese' unless he has a nonlinguistic acquaintance with cheese."[1] If, however, we follow Russell's fundamental precept and place our "emphasis upon the linguistic aspects of traditional philosophical problems," then we are obliged to state that no one can understand the word "cheese" unless he has an acquaintance with the meaning assigned to this word in the lexical code of English. Any representative of a cheese-less culinary culture will understand the English word "cheese" if he is aware that in this language it means "food made of pressed curds" and if he has at least a linguistic acquaintance with "curds." We never consumed ambrosia or nectar and have only a linguistic acquaintance with the words "ambrosia," "nectar," and "gods"—the name of their mythical users; nonetheless, we understand these words and know in what contexts each of them may be used.

The meaning of the words "cheese," "apple," "nectar," "acquaintance," "but," "mere," and of any word or phrase whatsoever is definitely a linguistic—or to be more precise and less narrow—a semiotic fact. Against those who assign meaning *(signatum)* not to the sign, but to the thing itself, the simplest and truest argument would be that nobody has ever smelled or tasted the meaning of "cheese" or of "apple." There is no *signatum* without *signum*. The meaning of the word "cheese" cannot be inferred from a nonlin-

Reprinted by permission of the publishers from *On Translation*, Reuben Brower, editor (Cambridge, Mass.: Harvard University Press. Copyright © 1959 by the President and Fellows of Harvard College; © renewed 1987 by Helen P. Brower.

1. Bertrand Russell, "Logical Positivism," *Revue Internationale de Philosophie* 4 (1950): 18; cf. p. 3.

guistic acquaintance with cheddar or with camembert without the assistance of the verbal code. An array of linguistic signs is needed to introduce an unfamiliar word. Mere pointing will not teach us whether "cheese" is the name of the given specimen, or of any box of camembert, or of camembert in general or of any cheese, any milk product, any food, any refreshment, or perhaps any box irrespective of contents. Finally, does a word simply name the thing in question, or does it imply a meaning such as offering, sale, prohibition, or malediction? (Pointing actually may mean malediction; in some cultures, particularly in Africa, it is an ominous gesture.)

For us, both as linguists and as ordinary word-users, the meaning of any linguistic sign is its translation into some further, alternative sign, especially a sign "in which it is more fully developed," as Peirce, the deepest inquirer into the essence of signs, insistently stated.[2] The term "bachelor" may be converted into a more explicit designation, "unmarried man," whenever higher explicitness is required. We distinguish three ways of interpreting a verbal sign: it may be translated into other signs of the same language, into another language, or into another, nonverbal system of symbols. These three kinds of translation are to be differently labeled:

1. Intralingual translation or *rewording* is an interpretation of verbal signs by means of other signs of the same language.

2. Interlingual translation or *translation proper* is an interpretation of verbal signs by means of some other language.

3. Intersemiotic translation or *transmutation* is an interpretation of verbal signs by means of signs of nonverbal sign systems.

The intralingual translation of a word uses either another, more or less synonymous, word or resorts to a circumlocution. Yet synonymy, as a rule, is not complete equivalence: for example, "every celibate is a bachelor, but not every bachelor is a celibate." A word or an idiomatic phrase-word, briefly a code-unit of the highest level, may be fully interpreted only by means of an equivalent combination of code-units, i.e., a message referring to this code-unit: "every bachelor is an unmarried man, and every unmarried man is a bachelor," or "every celibate is bound not to marry, and everyone who is bound not to marry is a celibate."

Likewise, on the level of interlingual translation, there is ordinarily no full equivalence between code-units, while messages may serve as adequate interpretations of alien code-units or messages.

2. Cf. John Dewey, "Peirce's Theory of Linguistic Signs, Thought, and Meaning," *The Journal of Philosophy* 43 (1946): 91.

The English word "cheese" cannot be completely identified with
its standard Russian heteronym "сыр," because cottage cheese is a
cheese but not a сыр. Russians say: принеси сыру и творогу,
"bring cheese and [sic] cottage cheese." In standard Russian, the
food made of pressed curds is called сыр only if ferment is used.

Most frequently, however, translation from one language into
another substitutes messages in one language not for separate code-
units but for entire messages in some other language. Such a translation is a reported speech; the translator recodes and transmits a
message received from another source. Thus translation involves
two equivalent messages in two different codes.

Equivalence in difference is the cardinal problem of language
and the pivotal concern of linguistics. Like any receiver of verbal
messages, the linguist acts as their interpreter. No linguistic specimen may be interpreted by the science of language without a translation of its signs into other signs of the same system or into signs
of another system. Any comparison of two languages implies an
examination of their mutual translatability; widespread practice of
interlingual communication, particularly translating activities,
must be kept under constant scrutiny by linguistic science. It is
difficult to overestimate the urgent need for and the theoretical and
practical significance of differential bilingual dictionaries with careful comparative definition of all the corresponding units in their
intension and extension. Likewise differential bilingual grammars
should define what unifies and what differentiates the two languages in their selection and delimitation of grammatical concepts.

Both the practice and the theory of translation abound with
intricacies, and from time to time attempts are made to sever the
Gordian knot by proclaiming the dogma of untranslatability. "Mr.
Everyman, the natural logician," vividly imagined by B. L. Whorf,
is supposed to have arrived at the following bit of reasoning: "Facts
are unlike to speakers whose language background provides for
unlike formulation of them."[3] In the first years of the Russian revolution there were fanatic visionaries who argued in Soviet peri-
odicals for a radical revision of traditional language and particularly
for the weeding out of such misleading expressions as "sunrise" or
"sunset." Yet we still use this Ptolemaic imagery without implying
a rejection of Copernican doctrine, and we can easily transform our

3. Benjamin Lee Whorf, *Language, Thought, and Reality* (Cambridge, Mass.,
1956), p. 235.

customary talk about the rising and setting sun into a picture of the earth's rotation simply because any sign is translatable into a sign in which it appears to us more fully developed and precise. A faculty of speaking a given language implies a faculty of talking about this language. Such a "metalinguistic" operation permits revision and redefinition of the vocabulary used. The complementarity of both levels—object-language and metalanguage—was brought out by Niels Bohr: all well-defined experimental evidence must be expressed in ordinary language, "in which the practical use of every word stands in complementary relation to attempts of its strict definition."[4]

All cognitive experience and its classification is conveyable in any existing language. Whenever there is deficiency, terminology may be qualified and amplified by loanwords or loan-translations, neologisms or semantic shifts, and finally, by circumlocutions. Thus in the newborn literary language of the Northeast Siberian Chukchees, "screw" is rendered as "rotating nail," "steel" as "hard iron," "tin" as "thin iron," "chalk" as "writing soap," "watch" as "hammering heart." Even seemingly contradictory circumlocutions, like "electrical horsecar" (Электрическая конка), the first Russian name of the horseless street car, or "flying steamship" (*jena paragot*), the Koryak term for the airplane, simply designate the electrical analogue of the horse-car and the flying analogue of the steamer and do not impede communication, just as there is no semantic "noise" and disturbance in the double oxymoron—"cold beef-and-pork hot dog."

No lack of grammatical device in the language translated into makes impossible a literal translation of the entire conceptual information contained in the original. The traditional conjunctions "and," "or" are now supplemented by a new connective—"and/or"—which was discussed a few years ago in the witty book *Federal Prose: How to Write in and/or for Washington*.[5] Of these three conjunctions, only the latter occurs in one of the Samoyed languages.[6] Despite these differences in the inventory of conjunctions, all three varieties of messages observed in "federal prose" may be

---

4. Niels Bohr, "On the Notions of Causality and Complementarity," *Dialectica* 1 (1948): 317f.

5. James R. Masterson and Wendell Brooks Phillips, *Federal Prose* (Chapel Hill, N.C., 1948), p. 40f.

6. Cf. Knut Bergsland, "Finsk-ugrisk og almen språkvitenskap," *Norsk Tidsskrift for Sprogvidenskap* 15 (1949): 374f.

distinctly translated both into traditional English and into this Sa-
moyed language. Federal prose: (1) John and Peter, (2) John or
Peter, (3) John and/or Peter will come. Traditional English: (3)
John and Peter or one of them will come. Samoyed: John and/or
Peter both will come, (2) John and/or Peter, one of them will come.

If some grammatical category is absent in a given language, its
meaning may be translated into this language by lexical means.
Dual forms like Old Russian брата are translated with the help of
the numeral: "two brothers." It is more difficult to remain faithful
to the original when we translate into a language provided with a
certain grammatical category from a language devoid of such a category. When translating the English sentence "She has brothers"
into a language which discriminates dual and plural, we are compelled either to make our own choice between two statements "She
has two brothers"—"She has more than two" or to leave the decision to the listener and say: "She has either two or more than two
brothers." Again in translating from a language without grammatical number into English one is obliged to select one of the two
possibilities—"brother" or "brothers" or to confront the receiver
of this message with a two-choice situation: "She has either one or
more than one brother."

As Boas neatly observed, the grammatical pattern of a language (as opposed to its lexical stock) determines those aspects of
each experience that must be expressed in the given language: "We
have to choose between these aspects, and one or the other must
be chosen."[7] In order to translate accurately the English sentence
"I hired a worker," a Russian needs supplementary information,
whether this action was completed or not and whether the worker
was a man or a woman, because he must make his choice between
a verb of completive or noncompletive aspect—нанял or
нанимал—and between a masculine and feminine noun—
работника or работницу. If I ask the utterer of the English sentence whether the worker was male or female, my question may be
judged irrelevant or indiscreet, whereas in the Russian version of
this sentence an answer to this question is obligatory. On the other
hand, whatever the choice of Russian grammatical forms to translate the quoted English message, the translation will give no answer
to the question of whether I "hired" or "have hired" the worker, or
whether he/she was an indefinite or definite worker ("a" or "the").

7. Franz Boas, "Language," *General Anthropology* (Boston, 1938), p. 132f.

Because the information required by the English and Russian grammatical pattern is unlike, we face quite different sets of two-choice situations; therefore a chain of translations of one and the same isolated sentence from English into Russian and vice versa could entirely deprive such a message of its initial content. The Geneva linguist S. Karcevski used to compare such a gradual loss with a circular series of unfavorable currency transactions. But evidently the richer the context of a message, the smaller the loss of information.

Languages differ essentially in what they *must* convey and not in what they *may* convey. Each verb of a given language imperatively raises a set of specific yes-or-no questions, as for instance: is the narrated event conceived with or without reference to its completion? Is the narrated event presented as prior to the speech event or not? Naturally the attention of native speakers and listeners will be constantly focused on such items as are compulsory in their verbal code.

In its cognitive function, language is minimally dependent on the grammatical pattern because the definition of our experience stands in complementary relation to metalinguistic operations—the cognitive level of language not only admits but directly requires recoding interpretation, i.e., translation. Any assumption of ineffable or untranslatable cognitive data would be a contradiction in terms. But in jest, in dreams, in magic, briefly, in what one would call everyday verbal mythology and in poetry above all, the grammatical categories carry a high semantic import. In these conditions, the question of translation becomes much more entangled and controversial.

Even such a category as grammatical gender, often cited as merely formal, plays a great role in the mythological attitudes of a speech community. In Russian the feminine cannot designate a male person, nor the masculine specify a female. Ways of personifying or metaphorically interpreting inanimate nouns are prompted by their gender. A test in the Moscow Psychological Institute (1915) showed that Russians, prone to personify the weekdays, consistently represented Monday, Tuesday, and Thursday as males and Wednesday, Friday, and Saturday as females, without realizing that this distribution was due to the masculine gender of the first three names (понедельник, вторник, четверг) as against the feminine gender of the others (среда, пятница, суббота). The fact that the word for Friday is masculine in some

Slavic languages and feminine in others is reflected in the folk traditions of the corresponding peoples, which differ in their Friday ritual. The widespread Russian superstition that a fallen knife presages a male guest and a fallen fork a female one is determined by the masculine gender of нож "knife" and the feminine of вилка "fork" in Russian. In Slavic and other languages where "day" is masculine and "night" feminine, day is represented by poets as the lover of night. The Russian painter Repin was baffled as to why Sin had been depicted as a woman by German artists: he did not realize that "sin" is feminine in German *(die Sünde),* but masculine in Russian (грех). Likewise a Russian child, while reading a translation of German tales, was astounded to find that Death, obviously a woman (Russian смерть, fem.), was pictured as an old man (German *der Tod,* masc.). *My Sister Life,* the title of a book of poems by Boris Pasternak, is quite natural in Russian, where "life" is feminine (жизнь), but was enough to reduce to despair the Czech poet Josef Hora in his attempt to translate these poems, since in Czech this noun is masculine *(život).*

What was the initial question which arose in Slavic literature at its very beginning? Curiously enough, the translator's difficulty in preserving the symbolism of genders, and the cognitive irrelevance of this difficulty, appears to be the main topic of the earliest Slavic original work, the preface to the first translation of the *Evangeliarium,* made in the early 860s by the founder of Slavic letters and liturgy, Constantine the Philosopher, and recently restored and interpreted by A. Vaillant.[8] "Greek, when translated into another language, cannot always be reproduced identically, and that happens to each language being translated," the Slavic apostle states. "Masculine nouns as ποταμός 'river' and ἀστήρ 'star' in Greek, are feminine in another language as pъка and звъзда in Slavic." According to Vaillant's commentary, this divergence effaces the symbolic identification of the rivers with demons and of the stars with angels in the Slavic translation of two of Matthew's verses (7:25 and 2:9). But to this poetic obstacle, Saint Constantine resolutely opposes the precept of Dionysius the Areopagite, who called for chief attention to the cognitive values (силъ разуму) and not to the words themselves.

In poetry, verbal equations become a constructive principle of

---

8. André Vaillant, "Le Préface de L'Évangeliaire vieux-slave," *Revue des Études Slaves* 24 (1948): 5f.

the text. Syntactic and morphological categories, roots, and affixes, phonemes and their components (distinctive features)—in short, any constituents of the verbal code—are confronted, juxtaposed, brought into contiguous relation according to the principle of similarity and contrast and carry their own autonomous signification. Phonemic similarity is sensed as semantic relationship. The pun, or to use a more erudite, and perhaps more precise term—paronomasia, reigns over poetic art, and whether its rule is absolute or limited, poetry by definition is untranslatable. Only creative transposition is possible: either intralingual transposition—from one poetic shape into another, or interlingual transposition—from one language into another, or finally intersemiotic transposition—from one system of signs into another, e.g., from verbal art into music, dance, cinema, or painting.

If we were to translate into English the traditional formula *Traduttore, traditore* as "the translator is a betrayer," we would deprive the Italian rhyming epigram of all its paronomastic value. Hence a cognitive attitude would compel us to change this aphorism into a more explicit statement and to answer the questions: translator of what messages? betrayer of what values?

FIFTEEN
OCTAVIO PAZ
Translation: Literature and Letters
Translated by Irene del Corral

When we learn to speak, we are learning to translate; the child who
asks his mother the meaning of a word is really asking her to translate the unfamiliar term into the simple words he already knows.
In this sense, translation within the same language is not essentially
different from translation between two tongues, and the histories
of all peoples parallel the child's experience. Even the most isolated
tribe, sooner or later, comes into contact with other people who
speak a foreign language. The sounds of a tongue we do not know
may cause us to react with astonishment, annoyance, indignation,
or amused perplexity, but these sensations are soon replaced by
uncertainties about our own language. We become aware that language is not universal; rather, there is a plurality of languages, each
one alien and unintelligible to the others. In the past, translation
dispelled the uncertainties. Although language is not universal, languages nevertheless form part of a universal society in which, once
some difficulties have been overcome, all people can communicate
with and understand each other. And they can do so because in any
language men always say the same things. Universality of the spirit
was the response to the confusion of Babel: many languages, one
substance. It was through the plurality of religions that Pascal became convinced of the truth of Christianity; translation responded
to the diversity of languages with the concept of universal intelli-
gibility. Thus, translation was not only a confirmation but also a
guarantee of the existence of spiritual bonds.

The modern age destroyed that assurance. As he rediscovered
the infinite variety of temperaments and passions, as he observed

From Octavio Paz, *Traducción: Literatura y Literalidad* (Barcelona: Tusquets, 1971).

the vast array of customs and societies, man began to find it difficult to recognize himself in other men. Until that time, the heathen had been a deviant to be suppressed through conversion or extermination, baptism or the sword, but the heathen presented in eighteenth-century salons was a new creature who, although he might speak his hosts' language to perfection, nevertheless embodied an inexorable foreignness. He was not subjected to conversion but to controversy and criticism; the originality of his views, the simplicity of his customs, and even the violence of his passions verified the absurdity and futility, to say nothing of the infamy, of baptism and conversion. A new course was taken: the religious quest for spiritual universality was superseded by an intellectual curiosity intent upon unearthing equally universal differences. Foreignness was no longer the exception, but the rule. This shift in perception is both paradoxical and revealing. The savage represented civilized man's nostalgia, his alter ego, his lost half. And translation reflected this shift: no longer was it an effort to illustrate the ultimate sameness of men; it became a vehicle to expose their individualities. Translation had once served to reveal the preponderance of similarities over differences; from this time forward translation would serve to illustrate the irreconcilability of differences, whether these stem from the foreignness of the savage or of our neighbor.

During his travels, Dr. Johnson once made an observation that expressed the new attitude very aptly: "A blade of grass is always a blade of grass, whether in one country or another. . . . Men and women are my subjects of inquiry; let us see how these differ from those we have left behind." Dr. Johnson's words convey two thoughts, and both foretell the dual road the modern age was to follow. The first refers to the separation of man from nature, a separation that would be transformed into confrontation and conflict: man's mission was no longer his own salvation but the mastery of nature. The second refers to the separation of man from man. The world is no longer a world, an indivisible whole; there is a split between nature and civilization, a split compounded by further subdivisions into separate cultures. A plurality of languages and societies: each language is a view of the world, each civilization is a world. The sun praised in an Aztec poem is not the sun of the Egyptian hymn, although both speak of the same star. For more than two centuries, philosophers and historians, and more recently anthropologists and linguists as well, have been accumulating examples of the insurmountable differences between individuals, societies, and eras. The greatest schism, scarcely less profound than that between nature and culture, separates primitives from the civilized; further divisions arise from the variety and diversity of civilizations. Within each civilization, more differences emerge: the language that enables us to communicate with one another also encloses us in an invisible web of sounds and meanings, so that each nation is imprisoned by its language, a language further fragmented by historical eras, by social classes, by generations. As for the intercourse among individuals belonging to the same community, each one is hemmed in by his own self-concern.

With all this, one would have expected translators to accept defeat, but this has not been the case; instead, there has been a contradictory and complementary trend to translate even more. This is paradoxical because, while translation overcomes the differences between one language and another, it also reveals them more fully. Thanks to translation, we become aware that our neighbors do not speak and think as we do. On the one hand, the world is presented to us as a collection of similarities; on the other, as a growing heap of texts, each slightly different from the one that came before it: translations of translations of translations. Each text is unique, yet at the same time it is the translation of another text. No text can be completely original because language itself, in its very essence, is already a translation—first from the nonverbal world, and then, because each sign and each phrase is a translation of another sign, another phrase. However, the inverse of this reasoning is also entirely valid. All texts are originals because each translation has its own distinctive character. Up to a point, each translation is a creation and thus constitutes a unique text.

The discoveries of anthropology and linguistics do not impeach translation itself, but a certain ingenuous notion of translation, the word-for-word translation suggestively called *servil* (servile) in Spanish. I do not mean to imply that literal translation is impossible; what I am saying is that it is not translation. It is a mechanism, a string of words that helps us read the text in its original language. It is a glossary rather than a translation, which is always a literary activity. Without exception, even when the translator's sole intention is to convey meaning, as in the case of scientific texts, translation implies a transformation of the original. That transformation is not—nor can it be—anything but literary, because all translations utilize the two modes of expression to which, according to Roman Jakobson, all literary procedures are reduced: metonym and metaphor. The original text never reappears in the new language (this would be impossible); yet it is ever present because the translation, without saying it, expresses it constantly, or else converts it into a verbal object that, although different, reproduces it: metonym or metaphor. Both, unlike explicative translations and paraphrase, are rigorous forms that are in no way inconsistent with accuracy. The metonym is an indirect description, and the metaphor a verbal equation.

The greatest pessimism about the feasibility of translation has been concentrated on poetry, a remarkable posture since many of the best poems in every Western language are translations, and many of those translations were written by great poets. Some years ago the critic and linguist Georges Mounin wrote a book about translation. He pointed out that it is generally, albeit reluctantly, conceded that it is possible to translate the denotative meanings of a text but that the consensus is almost unanimous that the translation of connotative meanings is impossible. Woven of echoes, reflections, and the interaction of sound with meaning, poetry is a fabric of connotations and, consequently, untranslatable. I must confess that I find this idea offensive, not only because it conflicts with my personal conviction that poetry is universal, but also because it is based on an erroneous conception of what translation is. Not everyone shares my view, and many modern poets insist that poetry is untranslatable. Perhaps their opinion comes from their inordinate attachment to verbal matter, or perhaps they have become ensnared in the trap of subjectivity. A mortal trap, as Quevedo warns: "the waters of the abyss / where I came to love myself." Unamuno, in one of his lyric-patriotic outbursts, provides an example of this kind of verbal infatuation:

Avila, Málaga, Cáceres,
Játiva, Mérida, Córdoba,
Cuidad Rodrigo, Sepúlveda,
Ubeda, Arévalo, Frómista,
Zumárraga, Salamanca,
Turéngano, Zaragoza,
Lérida, Zamarramala,
you are the names that stand tall,
free, untarnished, an honor roll,
the untranslatable marrow
of our Spanish tongue.

"The untranslatable marrow / of our Spanish tongue" is an outrageous metaphor (marrow and tongue?), but a perfectly translatable one since its image is universal. Many poets have utilized Unamuno's stylistic device in other languages: the lists of words differ, but the context, the emotion, and the meaning are comparable. It is remarkable that the untranslatable essence of Spain should consist of a succession of Roman, Arabic, Celtiberian and Basque names. It is equally remarkable that Unamuno should have translated the name of the Catalonian city Lleida into Castilian (Lérida). And what is perhaps most surprising of all is that he quoted the following lines by Victor Hugo as an epigraph to his poem, apparently not realizing that by doing so he was contradicting his own assertion that the names were untranslatable:

> Et tout tremble, Irun, Coïmbre,
> Santander, Almodovar,
> sitôt qu'on entend le timbre
> des cymbals de Bivar.

> And everything trembles, Irún, Coímbra,
> Santander, Almodóvar,
> once we hear the timbre
> of the cymbals of Bivar.

In both Spanish and French, the meanings and the emotions are the same. Since, strictly speaking, the proper nouns cannot be translated, Hugo merely recites them in Spanish, making no attempt to gallicize them. The recitation is effective because the words, stripped of precise meaning and converted into verbal castanets, true mantras, echo through the French text even more exotically than in the Spanish. . . . Translation is very difficult—no less difficult than writing so-called original texts—but it is not impossible. The poems of Hugo and Unamuno illustrate that connotative meanings can be preserved if the poet-translator successfully reproduces the verbal situation, the poetic context, into which they are mounted. Wallace Stevens has given us a sort of model image of that situation in a fine passage:

> . . . the hard hidalgo
> Lives in the mountainous character of his speech;

> And in that mountainous mirror Spain acquires
> The knowledge of Spain and of the hidalgo's hat—

A seeming of the Spaniard, a style of life,
The invention of a nation in a phrase. . . .

Here language has become a landscape, and that landscape, in turn, is a creation, the metaphor of a nation or of an individual—a verbal topography that communicates fully, that translates fully. Phrases form a chain of mountains, and the mountains are the characters, the ideograms of a civilization. But not only is the interaction between echoes and words overwhelming; it holds an inescapable threat. The moment comes when, surrounded by words on all sides, we feel intimidated by the distressing bewilderment of living among names and not among things, the bewilderment of even having a name:

Amid the reeds and the late afternoon,
how strange that I am named Federico!

In this case, too, the experience is universal: García Lorca would have felt the same uneasiness if he had been called Tom, Jean, or Chuang Tzu. To lose our name is like losing our shadow; to be only our name is to be reduced to a shadow. The absence of any correlation between things and their names is doubly intolerable: either the meanings evaporate or the things vanish. A world of pure meanings is as inhospitable as a world of things without meaning—without names. It is language that makes the world habitable. The instant of perplexity at the oddness of being called Federico or Sô Ji is immediately followed by the invention of another name, a name that is, in a way, a translation of the first: the metaphor or metonym that, without saying it, says it.

In recent years, perhaps because of the increasing primacy of linguistics, there has been a tendency to deemphasize the decidedly literary nature of translation. There is no such thing—nor can there be—as a science of translation, although translation can and should be studied scientifically. Just as literature is a specialized function of language, so translation is a specialized function of literature. And what, we might ask, of the machines that translate? If they ever really *translate,* they too will perform a literary operation, and they too will produce what translators now do: literature. Translation is an exercise in which what is decisive, given the necessary linguistic proficiency, is the translator's initiative, whether that translator be

a machine programmed by man or a living human being surrounded by dictionaries. Arthur Waley has put it well:

> A French scholar wrote recently with regard to translators: *"Qu'ils
> s'effacent derrière les textes et ceux-ci, s'ils ont été vraiment compris, parle-
> ront d'eux-mêmes."* [They should make themselves invisible behind the
> texts and, if fully understood, the texts will speak for themselves.]
> Except in the rather rare case of plain concrete statements such as
> "The cat chases the mouse," there are seldom sentences that have exact
> word-to-word equivalents in another language. It becomes a question
> of choosing between various approximations. . . . I have always found
> that it was I, not the texts, that had to do the talking.

It would be difficult to improve upon this statement.

In theory, only poets should translate poetry; in practice, poets
are rarely good translators. They almost invariably use the foreign
poem as a point of departure toward their own. A good translator
moves in the opposite direction: his intended destination is a poem
analogous although not identical to the original poem. He moves
away from the poem only to follow it more closely. The good translator of poetry is a translator who is also a poet—like Arthur
Waley—or a poet who is also a good translator—like Nerval when
he translated the first Faust. Nerval also wrote some fine, truly original imitations of Goethe, Jean Paul, and other German poets. The
"imitation" is the twin sister of translation: they are similar, but we
should not mistake one for the other. They are like Justine and
Juliette, the two sisters in Sade's novels. . . . The reason many poets
are unable to translate poetry is not purely psychological, although
egoism has a part in it, but functional: poetic translation, as I intend to demonstrate, is a procedure analogous to poetic creation,
but it unfolds in the opposite direction.

Every word holds a certain number of implicit meanings;
when a word is combined with others to make up a phrase, one of
those meanings is activated and becomes predominant. In prose
there tends to be a single meaning, while, as has often been noted,
one of the characteristics of poetry, and perhaps its distinguishing
trait, is the preservation of a plurality of meanings. What we are
seeing here is actually a general property of language; poetry accen-
tuates it, but, to a lesser degree, it is also present in common speech
and even in prose. (This circumstance confirms that prose, in the
strictest sense of the term, has no real existence: it is a concept
required by the intellect.) Critics have devoted a good deal of at-

tention to this disturbing peculiarity of poetry, but they have dis-
regarded the equally fascinating peculiarity that corresponds to this
kind of mobility and ambiguity of meanings: the immobility of
signs. Poetry radically transforms language, and it does so in a direction opposite to that of prose. In one case, the mobility of characters tends to fix a single meaning; in the other, the plurality of
meanings tends to fix the characters. Language, of course, is a system of mobile signs that may be interchangeable to some degree;
one word can be replaced by another, and each phrase can be expressed (translated) by another. To paraphrase Peirce, we might say
that the meaning of a word is always another word. Whenever we
ask, "What does this phrase mean?" the reply is another phrase. Yet
once we move into the terrain of poetry, we find that words have
lost their mobility and their interchangeability. The meanings of a
poem are multiple and changeable; the words of that poem are
unique and irreplaceable. To change them would be to destroy the
poem. Poetry is expressed in language, but it goes beyond language.

The poet, immersed in the movement of language, in constant
verbal preoccupation, chooses a few words—or is chosen by them.
As he combines them, he constructs his poem: a verbal object made
of irreplaceable and immovable characters. The translator's starting
point is not the language in movement that provides the poet's raw
material but the fixed language of the poem. A language congealed,
yet living. His procedure is the inverse of the poet's: he is not constructing an unalterable text from mobile characters; instead, he is
dismantling the elements of the text, freeing the signs into circula-
tion, then returning them to language. In its first phase, the translator's activity is no different from that of a reader or critic: each
reading is a translation, and each criticism is, or begins as, an interpretation. But reading is translation within the same language, and
criticism is a free version of the poem or, to be more precise, a
transposition. For the critic, the poem is the starting point toward
another text, his own, while the translator, in another language and
with different characters, must compose a poem analogous to the
original. The second phase of the translator's activity is parallel to
the poet's, with this essential difference: as he writes, the poet does
not know where his poem will lead him; as he translates, the translator knows that his completed effort must reproduce the poem he
has before him. The two phases of translation, therefore, are an
inverted parallel of poetic creation. The result is a reproduction of

the original poem in another poem that is, as I have previously mentioned, less a copy than a transmutation. The ideal of poetic translation, as Valéry once superbly defined it, consists of producing analogous effects with different implements.

Translation and creation are twin processes. On one hand, as the works of Baudelaire and Pound have proven, translation is often indistinguishable from creation; on the other, there is constant interaction between the two, a continuous, mutual enrichment. The greatest creative periods of Western poetry, from its origins in Provence to our own day, have been preceded or accompanied by intercrossings between different poetic traditions. At times these intercrossings have taken the form of imitation, and at others they have taken the form of translation. In this respect, the history of European poetry might be viewed as a chronicle of the convergences of the various traditions that compose what is known as Western literature, not to mention the presence of the Arabic tradition in Provençal poetry, or the presence of haiku, and the Chinese tradition in modern poetry. Critics study "influences," but the term is not exact. It would be more sensible to consider Western literature as an integral whole in which the central protagonists are not national traditions—English, French, Portuguese, German poetry—but styles and trends. No trend, no style has ever been national, not even the so-called artistic nationalism. Styles have invariably been translinguistic: Donne is closer to Quevedo than to Wordsworth; there is an evident affinity between Góngora and Marino while nothing, save their common language, unites Góngora with Juan Ruiz, the archpriest of Hita, who, in turn, is sometimes reminiscent of Chaucer. Styles are coalescent and pass from one language to another; the works, each rooted in its own verbal soil, are unique . . . unique, but not isolated: each is born and lives in relation to other works composed in different languages. Thus, the plurality of languages and the singularity of the works produce neither complete diversity nor disorder, but quite the opposite: a world of interrelationships made up of contradictions and harmonies, unions and digressions.

Throughout the ages, European poets—and now those of both halves of the American continent as well—have been writing the same poem in different languages. And each version is an original and distinct poem. True, the synchronization is not perfect, but if we take a step backward, we can understand that we are hearing a concert, and that the musicians, playing different instruments, following neither conductor nor score, are in the process of collectively composing a symphony in which improvisation is inseparable from translation and creation is indistinguishable from imitation. At times, one of the musicians will break out into an inspired solo; soon the others pick it up, each introducing his own variations that make the original motif unrecognizable. At the end of the last century, French poetry amazed and scandalized Europe with the solo begun by Baudelaire and brought to a close by Mallarmé. Hispano-American "modernist" poets were among the first to develop an ear for this new music; in imitating it, they made it their own, they changed it, and they sent it on to Spain where it was once again re-created. A little later the English-language poets performed something similar but on different instruments in a different key and tempo: a more sober and critical version in which Laforgue, not Verlaine, occupied the central position. Laforgue's special status helps explain the character of Anglo-American modernism, a movement that was simultaneously symbolist and antisymbolist. Pound and Eliot, following Laforgue's lead, introduced criticism of symbolism into symbolism itself, in ridicule of what Pound termed the "funny symbolist trappings." This critical perception set the framework for their writing, and a little later they produced poetry that was not modernist but modern, and thus they initiated, together with Wallace Stevens, William Carlos Williams, and others, a new solo—the solo of contemporary Anglo-American poetry.

Laforgue's legacy to English and Spanish poetry is a prime example of the interdependence between creation and imitation, translation and original work. The French poet's influence on Eliot and Pound is a matter of common knowledge, but what is less often appreciated is his influence on Hispano-American poets. In 1905, the Argentinian Leopoldo Lugones, a great poet whose work has not attracted the critical attention it deserves, published a volume of poems, *Los crepúsculos del jardín*, in which some Laforguean features appeared for the first time in Spanish: irony, the clash of colloquial with literary language, violent images that juxtaposed urban absurdity with nature depicted as a grotesque matron. Some of his poems seem to have been written on one of those *dimanches bannis de l'Infini*, the fin-de-siècle Sundays of the Hispano-American bourgeoisie. In 1909 Lugones published *Lunario sentimental*. Although it imitated Laforgue, this volume was one of the most original of its time, and even today can be read with admiration and delight. *Lunario sentimental* exerted a tremendous influence on Hispano-American poets, but it was particularly beneficial and inspiring to the Mexican poet López Velarde. In 1919 López Velarde published *Zozobra*, the principal volume of Hispano-American "postmodernism," that is, our own antisymbolist symbolism. Two years earlier, Eliot had published *Prufrock and Other Observations*. In Boston, a Protestant Laforgue had emerged from Harvard; in Zacatecas, a Catholic Laforgue had slipped out of a seminary. Sensuality, blasphemy, humor, what López Velarde called an "intimate reactionary sadness." The Mexican poet died not long afterward in 1921, at the age of thirty-three. His work ended where Eliot's began . . . Boston and Zacatecas: the coupling of these two names brings a smile as if it were one of those incongruent associations Laforgue so greatly enjoyed. Two poets writing in different languages, neither even suspecting the existence of the other, almost simultaneously produced different but equally original versions of the poetry written some years earlier by a third poet in yet another language.

SIXTEEN
PETER SZONDI
The Poetry of Constancy: Paul Celan's Translation of Shakespeare's Sonnet 105
Translated by Harvey Mendelsohn

Shakespeare's sonnet 105, a poem about the virtues of the author's young friend and, simultaneously, a poem about the poetic writing that extols them, ends with the couplet:

Fair, kind, and true, have often lived alone.
Which three till now, never kept seat in one.

Celan's translation of this sonnet concludes with the verses:

"Schön, gut und treu" so oft getrennt, geschieden.
In Einem will ich drei zusammenschmieden.[1]

Beauty, goodness, and fidelity are the three virtues that the poet ascribes to his friend in the preceding quatrains, and it is to their expression that he wishes to confine his writing, indeed, even its vocabulary. Whereas in these strophes Shakespeare speaks not only of his friend but also of his own love and of his own songs, the final couplet is devoted entirely to the three virtues, which are granted an independent life through the device of personification. Yet this independent life is accorded to beauty, goodness, and fi-

Originally published as "Poetry of Constancy—Poetik der Beständigkeit: Celans Übertragung von Shakespeares Sonett 105," *Sprache im technischen Zeitalter* 37 (1971): 9–25. Reprinted by permission of the publisher from Theory and History of Literature, vol. 15: Peter Szondi, *On Textual Understanding and Other Essays* (Minneapolis: University of Minnesota Press, 1986), pp. 161–78. © 1986 by the University of Minnesota. All rights reserved.

1. William Shakespeare, *Einundzwanzig Sonette*, trans. Paul Celan (Frankfurt am Main, 1967), p. 35. (This is book no. 898 in the series Insel-Bücherei.)

delity only so that the poet may affirm that their separation, which previously was the rule, is henceforth overcome. The "till now" of the dispersion of "fair, kind, and true" is the history of humanity until the appearance of that W. H. who is celebrated in the majority of Shakespeare's sonnets. The last two verses of Celan's translation say something different. They do not contrast the long separation of the three "virtues" with the place in which they finally have all come together. The union of "fair, kind, and true" *("Schön, gut und treu")* is due not to the appearance of the friend, but to a literary work, to the future work of the poet, who intends to "forge" the three "together" *(zusammenschmieden will)*. If Shakespeare's concluding verses are silent about the friend, this is only in order to invoke him all the more strikingly through the negation "never" and above all, through the sonnet's inconspicuous last word, "one," which is a circumlocution for him in whom "fair, kind, and true" have taken up common residence. In contrast, Celan's *in Einem* ("in one"), in which the poet "intends to forge together fair, kind, and true" *("Schön, gut und treu" zusammenschmieden will)*, is not "the one *person*" (der *Eine*) extolled by the poem but "the one *thing*" (das *Eine*), most probably the *one* image that the poet sketches of him, if indeed it is not the unity of the poem, which has entirely absorbed its subject matter. To be sure, in the three quatrains of the Shakespearian sonnet the poet speaks so explicitly about his work ("my songs and praises," "my verse," "my invention"—in the third verse of each quatrain) that, despite the emphatic silence of the concluding couplet, we may interpret the "now," before which moment "fair," "kind," and "true" were separated, as being simultaneously the "now" of Shakespeare's composition of the poem. That the place where beauty, goodness, and fidelity unite could be the friend as well as the poem about him is an ingenious piece of ambiguity based on the relationship between friend and poem established by other poems in the sonnet cycle. In contrast, we may note the explicitness and pathos evident in Celan's translation, in which the poet, through the image of the "forging together," claims that what Shakespeare expresses in the form of a description—and what is linked with the act of its being described only inasmuch as it is a *described* reality—is the product solely of his own will, the result of his poetic activity alone.

This same approach, which characterizes Celan's version of the final two verses, is a decisive element of his entire translation of Shakespeare's sonnet 105:

Let not my love be called idolatry,
Nor my beloved as an idol show,
Since all alike my songs and praises be
To one, of one, still such, and ever so.

Kind is my love to-day, to-morrow kind,
Still constant in a wondrous excellence,
Therefore my verse to constancy confined,
One thing expressing, leaves out difference.

Fair, kind, and true, is all my argument,
Fair, kind, and true, varying to other words,
And in this change is my invention spent,
Three themes in one, which wondrous scope affords.

Fair, kind, and true, have often lived alone,
Which three till now, never kept seat in one.[2]

Ihr sollt, den ich da lieb, nicht Abgott heissen,
nicht Götzendienst, was ich da treib und trieb.
All dieses Singen hier, all dieses Preisen:
von ihm, an ihn und immer ihm zulieb.

Gut ist mein Freund, ists heute und ists morgen,
Und keiner ist beständiger als er.
In der Beständigkeit, da bleibt mein Vers geborgen,
spricht von dem Einen, schweift mir nicht umher.

"Schön, gut und treu," das singe ich und singe.
"Schön, gut und treu"—stets anders und stets das.
Ich find, erfind—um sie in eins zu bringen,
sie einzubringen ohne Unterlass.

"Schön, gut und treu" so oft getrennt, geschieden.
In Einem will ich drei zusammenschmieden.

In the first quatrain, Celan's use of the active voice leads to the introduction of the poet's own activity into the subject matter, even though the translation, too, appears to have only the friend in view. The substantival infinitive forms of the verbs (*Singen,* "singing," and *Preisen,* "praising, extolling") replace the corresponding substantives ("my songs and praises"). Where the passive form "be called" appears in the original, in Celan's version the poet speaks of what he himself is doing (the sequence of verses 1 and 2 is re-

2. William Shakespeare, *The Sonnets,* ed. John Dover Wilson (Cambridge, 1966), p. 55.

versed). And this impression is strengthened by repetition, specifically by the preservation of lexical identity (*treib/trieb,* "do/did"), coexisting with morphological difference (present tense, imperfect tense), as well as by the rhyme on *zulieb* ("for the love of").

In the second quatrain, the poet's activity comes to the fore, since the translator, using both syntax and semantics to achieve his effect, assigns a more active function to a verse that is already personified in Shakespeare. In this way he also intensifies the personification of his own work, which increasingly takes the place of the person extolled by Shakespeare. Celan gives *Da bleibt mein Vers geborgen* ("there lies my verse sheltered") for *my verse to constancy confined;* and he gives *schweift mir nicht umher* ("does not wander round about") for *leaves out difference.*

Finally, in the third quatrain, the poet's more active role, the result of the specific accumulation of verbs referring to his own doings (*Ich find, erfind*—"I discover, invent" for "is my invention spent"; *zu bringen, einzubringen*—"to bring, to harvest") is supplemented by greater semantic specification. Thus, in place of "is all my argument," originally a standard rhetorical phrase, the translation gives *das singe ich und singe* ("that [is what] I sing and sing"), preparing the reader for the repetitions to come in verses 11 and 12.

*

It may seem that the main point involved here is a shift in accent from the person who is being praised to the act of praising or composing. What we are actually dealing with, however, is more than merely the "bolder display" (as Hölderlin expressed it in connection with his translations of Sophocles)[3] of a theme already present in the original, in which, however, it is entirely subordinate to the themes of the "fair friend"[4] and of the poet's love for him. The relationship of Celan's translation to the original can be appropriately described neither as a change in thematic interest or style, nor as the kind of change which, according to the tenets of traditional theories of translation, would be pertinent in judging the fidelity and success of the translation. Rather, the movement from original to translation is a change in what Walter Benjamin, in his

3. Letter of 2 April 1804 to Friedrich Wilmans.
4. Sonnet 104, v. 1.

essay on "The Task of the Translator," calls "intention toward language *(Intention auf die Sprache)*.[5] Where a translation not only may but should differ from the original is in its mode of signification *(Art des Meinens)*.[6] The concept of "significatio" pertains to the structure of language, to a relationship whose two members, however, should not be assigned fixed names, since such names always imply a specific relationship between the two, that is, a precise conception of the structure of signification in language. Michel Foucault calls the two elements of this relationship simply *Words and Things*—a formula that serves as the title of the book in which he interprets the historical change in this relationship as a change in the epistemological "conditions of possibility" governing the specific historical forms assumed by the various "human sciences."[7] Any less general notion would hinder the discovery of the relevant mode of signification; and this would be a serious loss, since it is always this mode that constitutes the historicity of a given linguistic constellation and thus also the goal of philological understanding.[8] Accordingly, a translation does not primarily indicate the his-

5. Charles Baudelaire, *Tableaux Parisiens,* Ger. trans. with a preface on "The Task of the Translator" ("Die Aufgabe des Übersetzers") by Walter Benjamin (Heidelberg, 1923), pp. xi ff. Repr. in Charles Baudelaire, *Ausgewählte Gedichte,* Ger. trans. by Walter Benjamin (Frankfurt am Main, 1970), pp. 14ff. [An English translation of this preface is included in this volume.—Eds.]

In Benjamin's essay, "intention" *(Intention)* does not mean "purpose" *(Absicht)*. What Benjamin means can perhaps best be understood from the following passage from Fritz Mauthner: "Throughout the Middle Ages the concept of *intentio* did not [apply] to the will, but rather to knowing, or to the energy or tension involved in knowing. The Schoolmen's Latin was bad, and in *intentio* they could still detect the original meaning, the metaphor of the taut bow and the aiming of the arrow; hence for them *intentio* was directedness of attention or of consciousness to a perceived or perceptible object" (F. Mauthner, *Wörterbuch der Philosophie: Neue Beiträge zu einer Kritik der Sprache* [Munich, 1910], vol. 1, pp. 584–85). In the following discussion the concept of "intention toward language" is not used strictly in Benjamin's sense, insofar as it has been divorced from the theoretical background of Benjamin's views on language and contains ideas deriving from modern linguistics. For our present purposes "intention toward language" may be defined as the directedness of consciousness toward language, that is, as the linguistic conception preceding all speech; in other words, it may be seen as the mode of signification that stamps linguistic usage.

6. Ibid.

7. *Les mots et les choses* (Paris, 1966); Eng. trans. as *The Order of Things* (New York, 1973).

8. [See the essay "On Textual Understanding," in P. Szondi, *On Textual Understanding and Other Essays,* trans. Harvey Mendelsohn. Theory and History of Literature, vol. 15 (Minneapolis, 1986).—Eds.]

torical state of a language (indeed, primarily it does not indicate this at all); it gives evidence, rather, of the use of language. The translation points not so much to a definite linguistic state as to a definite conception of language. Thus Benjamin saw the legitimacy, indeed the necessity, of translating as lying in the different intentions toward language and modes of signification displayed by an original text and its translation. This very difference, moreover, invalidates the premises underlying debates over the issue of fidelity versus freedom in translating.

*

The way in which Celan's mode of signification differs from Shakespeare's can be gathered by comparing the concluding couplet of sonnet 105 as it stands in the original and in the translation:

> Fair, kind, and true, have often lived alone.
> Which three till now, never kept seat in one.

> "Schön, gut und treu" so oft getrennt, geschieden.
> In Einem will ich drei zusammenschmieden.

The theme in both versions is the separation of the three "virtues" and their unification, the two states being contrasted in the antithetical structure of the couplet. The difference in intention toward language at work in Celan's version and in Shakespeare's text can be inferred from the way Celan expresses the dispersion, as well as the contrast between this dispersion and the ensuing union. In translating "have often lived alone" by *so oft getrennt, geschieden* ("so often separated, divided"), he enriches the discursive mode of expression with another whose poetic energy overwhelms discursiveness. What traditional stylistic criticism would consider as a varied repetition used for emphasis—*getrennt, geschieden*—serves here to express the caesurae between "Schön, gut, und treu" in other than simply a lexical manner. Modern linguistics has conceptualized that which the reader of earlier times could have perceived in analyzing the impression made on him by a phrase like *getrennt, geschieden,* if—and that is the real question—such a turn of phrase and such an intention toward language appeared at all *before* the advent of modern literature. If it is true that the understanding of language consists primarily in making distinctions, in registering "distinctive features," then the phrase *getrennt, geschieden,* is not so much an instance of varied repetition as it is, when spoken aloud as *ge-trennt, ge-schieden*, the union of the common prefix *ge* with two different, although synonymous lexemes, *trennt* and *schieden*. Understanding, which depends upon distinctions, sees intended meaning less in the literal sense of separating and dividing than in the caesura, which splits the word *geschieden* into two parts, by virtue on the one hand, of the identity of the prefix, and, on the other, of the phonological quasi-identity (the paronomasia) of *schieden* and its rhyme word *schmieden*. This separation of *ge* and *schieden* may be seen as a metadiscursive representation of the separation of *"Schön, gut und treu."*

The final rhymes of the English and German versions display a similar phenomenon. The opposition appearing in the original—"lived alone / kept seat in one"—is, of course, reproduced in the translation, namely, in the opposition of separating and dividing, on the one hand and forging together, on the other. Nevertheless, it is clear that in the German version the opposition is conveyed not only through lexical means but also through the difference between *schieden* ("divided") and *schmieden* ("forged"). Just as understanding, sensitive to distinctions, perceives *geschieden* coming after *getrennt* as *ge-schieden*, so, too, does it register the difference between *geschieden* and *zusammenschmieden* as the minimal consonantal variation of the rhymed syllables *schieden* and *schmieden*. The normative identity of the rhymed words, which in the German text starts from the last stressed vowel *(-ieden)*, is reinforced by the *sch*-sound; yet this identity is disrupted by the variation arising from the *m*-sound in *schmieden* (inserted between the *sch*-sound and the rhymed syllable [*-ieden*] and anticipated by the separable prefix *zusammen*). Thus the metadiscursive realization of both the separation and union of the three "virtues" consists in this minimal variation, the near-identity of *schieden* and *schmieden*. In other words, the opposition is expressed by its own antithesis, paronomasia. This device, employed in the rhyme of the final couplet, enables the poem's language to go beyond the dimension of meaning and *speak* the opposition, instead of expressing it (which would represent a recourse to the literal sense); and it can do this all the more so since the only difference, except for the context (*zusammen*, "together"), between the paronomasia and total homonymy lies in the consonant.

The mode of signification which is documented here, and which stamps Celan's translation throughout, may be contrasted with the mode found in Shakespeare, which likewise exploits the possibilities offered by rhyme, although in a different fashion. In Shakespeare, the opposition is already emphasized, not, however, by near-identity but by relation, namely, between "alone" (derived from "all one") and "one." Unlike Celan's, this contrastive technique, which is confined to the lexical and etymological realm, is incapable of generating a determinate negation of discursiveness, i.e., of recourse to literal sense. More important, however, is the fact that the etymological relationship between "alone" and "one" remains external to the opposition that the poem is meant to express and in fact does express on the discursive level. Thus the relationship is an abstract point of maneristic origin. The same may be said, with even greater justification, of the following paradox: separateness is evoked by the very word ("alone") that originally reinforced the word expressing union ("one"). These remarks are not meant as criticism,[9] but simply as an indication of a particular mode of signification that may be seen as the basic premise of much of traditional rhetoric. Just as this intention toward language has changed since Mallarmé, so the very *principles* of rhetoric employed in poetry since Mallarmé differ from those of traditional rhetoric. This fact, which has been noticed by only a few authors such as Derrida[10] and Deguy,[11] becomes evident in comparing Shakespeare's sonnet 105 with Celan's translation.

From the point of view of traditional rhetoric, the sonnet's most ingenious verse is no doubt the fifth:

Kind is my love to-day, to-morrow kind.

This verse is constructed in the form of a chiasmus. The mirror symmetry directly opposes "to-day" and "to-morrow" around a central axis, thereby stressing the present-future antithesis.[12] However, inasmuch as the chiastic sentence structure results, on the lex-

9. An analysis of Shakespeare's sonnet that would do justice to it would have to proceed from its own distinctive features, but that would carry us beyond the bounds of the present essay.

10. See Jacques Derrida, "La double séance," *Tel Quel* 41 (Spring 1970) and 42 (Summer 1970); repr. in *La dissémination* (Paris, 1972).

11. See Michel Deguy, "Vers une théorie de la figure généralisée," *Critique* 269 (October 1969).

12. Cf. Henrich Lausberg, *Handbuch der literarischen Rhetorik* (Munich, 1960), p. 361.

ical level, in the verse's beginning and ending with the same word, "kind," it enables the verse to stress the constancy that cannot be affected by the temporal opposition. The chiasmus in this Shakespearean verse is thus scarcely mere ornament; at the same time, however, it runs entirely counter to the specific relationship of language and "content" found in Celan's translation of this verse:

> Gut ist mein Freund, ists heute und ists morgen.

The chiasmus can be rendered in German, as was shown by Stefan George, whose translation of the verse reads:

> Gut ist heut meine liebe·morgen gut.[13]

If Celan gives up the chiasmus, it is only so as to allow the sentence itself to speak directly that which the chiasmus can express only abstractly and mediated by reflection: constancy. Celan's verse flows easily onward, replacing the antithetically constructed verse, which can only express constancy when it reaches its end in the retrospective glance of synthesis.[14] It is as if Celan's poem heedlessly followed the course of time, in which the friend's goodness persists as unchangingly as the one occurrence of the word *ists* follows the other, as obviously as *morgen* ("tomorrow") follows *heute* ("today"). The difference between Celan's translation and the original is not adequately grasped if one merely notes that the chiasmus is replaced by repetition, as can readily be seen from Celan's German version of the succeeding verse:

> und keiner ist beständiger als er.

In Shakespeare this line reads:

> Still constant in a wondrous excellence.

It appears, though, that Celan does wish to repeat the chiasmus when he follows up *Gut ist mein Freund* with *keiner ist beständiger* in the next verse. But Celan's chiasmus, distributed over two lines

---

13. Stefan George, *Werke* (Munich, 1958), vol. 2, p. 203.
14. Cf. Theodor W. Adorno, *Negative Dialektik* (Frankfurt am Main, 1966), pp. 156ff.

and affecting only parts of these two, lacks that antithesis which only becomes a sign of the intended meaning, i.e., of constancy, when it is surpassed *qua* antithesis through the repetition of the word "kind." In Celan's version, instead of concluding the first verse in a gnomic fashion ("kind is my love to-day, to-morrow kind"), the chiasmus confirms the union of the first verse with the second, in which the impression of a constant onward-flowing motion is preserved by the use of the introductory word *und* ("and") and by the repetition of the word *ist* ("is").

What distinguishes Celan's translation from the original, therefore, is not a renunciation of traditional rhetorical figures but rather a change in basic presuppositions. In other words, his version displays a different mode of signification; and this mode underlies his use of language, both generally and, more particularly, with respect to rhetorical figures, although it can only be discovered by a consideration of the "performance," that is to say, the text itself. As a result, even that type of textual analysis which inquires into these presuppositions may no more dispense with stylistic criticism than it may rely exclusively on the latter.

*

From this point of view, repetition appears as the most consistently employed stylistic device of Celan's translation. Naturally, the fact that in his own poetry Celan frequently repeats words and sentences lends weight to the thesis that Celan translated Shakespeare into his own language; in other words, Celan's translations are Celan poems. While both plausible and likely to find a ready welcome, not necessarily false on that account, such an approach tends to obscure the possible difference in the use of language, that is, in intention toward language, which, according to Benjamin's theory of translation, constitutes the difference between an original text and its translation.[15] Hence we should pursue the comparison of the two poems further still in order to establish the specific mode of signification that informs Celan's language in his translation of the English sonnet.

Shakespeare's own text contains a large number of repetitions, which Celan always retains, however freely he may proceed in other respects. Thus, in the two introductory verses he gives translations

15. Benjamin, "Die Aufgabe des Übersetzers."

of the pairs of corresponding terms "love-beloved" and "idolatry-idol," although *zulieb*, which corresponds to *lieb* (v. 1), does not appear until the conclusion of the first quatrain, though it is anticipated by *trieb* as its rhyming word. This deviation from the parallelism of the two introductory verses is made for the sake of a varied repetition in verse 2 (*was ich da treib und trieb*—"what there I do and did"), which in both its form and underlying intention toward language recalls verse 5 (*Gut ist mein Freund, ists heute und ists morgen*—"kind is my friend, [he] is it today and [he] is it tomorrow"). Celan likewise keeps the slightly modified repetition in verses 6 and 7 ("constant-constancy," *beständiger-Beständigkeit*) as well as the strict repetition of "Fair, kind and true" in verses 9, 10, and 13. One last repetition in the original is made still more emphatic in Celan's version, namely, that found in the final verse of the first quatrain:

> To one, of one, still such, and ever so.

The translation refers, however abstractly, to the "fair friend" a third time:

> von ihm, an ihn und immer ihm zulieb
> ("about him, to him, and always for love of him").

As in the succeeding verse, this type of repetition is qualitatively different from the type we find in Shakespeare; it also serves a different function. What Shakespeare, in the second half of the verse, expresses discursively with the words "still" and "ever" is spoken by Celan's verse *as* verse (with the exception of the word *immer*—"ever"). Unlike Shakespeare's verse 4 ("To one, of one / still such, and ever so"), Celan's is not divided into two parts, but rather proceeds in a continuous fashion, due to the lexical (*ihm-ihm-ihm*) as well as the vocalic periodicity (o-ī-a-ī-u-ī-e-i-u-ī). Here, as in verse 5, constancy is not merely the intended meaning; it characterizes the verse itself. To this extent, Celan's language does not speak *about* something but "speaks" itself. It speaks about things and about language through its very manner of speaking.

In Celan's version, therefore, repetition—the syntagmatic realization of the constancy motif—is not restricted to those passages whose explicit theme is *constancy*, but stamps the sonnet as a whole. Behind the many expressions in the original referring only indirectly to this theme, the translator discerns this same constancy and governs his language accordingly. This is evident from the way he translates *my love* in the first verse of the original:

> Let not my love be called idolatry,

where he makes the constancy implied in "my love" speak through the identity of the lexeme *treib* ("do") in verse 2:

> nicht Götzendienst, was ich da treib und trieb
> ("not idolatry what I do and did").

Furthermore, Celan eliminates the discursive "all alike," which links together "songs" and "praises," and instead introduces these two words by the same phrase:

> All dieses Singen hier, all dieses Preisen
> ("All this singing here, all this praising").

Celan's intention toward language is no less clear when, in the third quatrain, after the identical first part of the two introductory verses, he repeats a word each time in the second part and also makes the sentence structure hinge on this word, as in verse 5 *(Gut ist mein Freund, ists heute und ists morgen)*:

> Fair, kind, and true, is all my argument,
> Fair, kind, and true, varying to other words.

> "Schön, gut und treu," das *singe* ich und *singe*.
> "Schön, gut und treu"—*stets* anders und *stets* das.

In place of the word "argument," which itself suggests discursive, rational language, and its no less logical qualifier "all," Celan offers the stubborn repetition of his own action. By setting the words *und singe* after *das singe ich* (three words that completely disregard the content of the English phrase "is all my argument") he creates a repetition that does not simply say what is expressed in the original by the word "all"; moreover, by reducing *das singe ich* to *singe* through the omission of both subject and object, he hypostatizes, as it were, the poet's action. And this is an action that coincides with the poem instead of being its subject matter, as is the case in Shakespeare.

Even more characteristic is the rendering Celan gives of the phrase "varying to other words": *stets anders und stets das* ("always different and always that"). Varying means "diversifying by change,"[16] "restating in different words."[17] The expression, a rhetorical term, assumes that word and meaning are different and hence distinguishable. It is for this reason alone that the same thing can be designated by different words; it is for this reason alone that it is possible to vary the words without departing from the intended meaning. Celan's intention toward language, by contrast, may be viewed as the determinate negation of this theoretical linguistic premise. What was a stylistic device in traditional rhetoric, and may well have been employed by writers unaware of the conditions that make its use possible, is here recognized by Celan to be a paradox and inserted into the verse as such: *stets anders und stets das*. The continuity is conveyed not merely by the word *stets* itself, but even more by its repetition, while the difference is expressed by the fact that *anders* ("other") is followed by *das* ("that," i.e., that same thing). The paradox itself is maintained in two ways. First, the contradiction between *stets,* on the one hand, and *anders* and *das,* on the other, remains unresolved. Second, and no less important, where one expects to find an answer to the possible question of "*anders* als was?" ("different from what?") there appears a forceful *das*, which, although introduced by the same word, *stets,* is incompatible with *anders*.

Celan's translation of the next verse evinces the same rejection of the traditional conception of language, according to which different signifiers can correspond to the same signified. Indeed, we can sense a desire to abolish the distinction between signifier and signified altogether. In this verse, Shakespeare explicitly mentions that *change* (i.e., the replacement of one word by another, while the intended meaning remains the same) whose premise is precisely this traditional conception of language:

And in this change is my invention spent.

Celan refuses to concede that words may be interchangeable in this way, just as he successfully avoids using a word derived from the

16. Alexander Schmidt, *Shakespeare-Lexikon,* 5th ed. (Berlin, 1962), vol. 2, p. 1310.

17. Gerald Willen and Victor B. Reed, eds., *A Casebook on Shakespeare's Sonnets* (New York, 1964), p. 107.

familiar rhetorical term *inventio* to designate the poet's activity and capacity. Designation is replaced by speaking: *Ich find, erfind*. In linguistic terms, this is one of the boldest passages in Celan's version, surpassed perhaps only by the immediately following one. For here the repetition of the verb, that is, of the word for the activity, does more than simply convey the activity's constancy (which was its sole function in the case of the expressions *Gut ist mein Freund, ists heute und ists morgen* and *das singe ich und singe*). Furthermore, to understand the phrase *Ich find, erfind*, it is not sufficient to read the expansion of "find" in the repetition (*erfind*) as a delayed translation of "invention"; nor should it be viewed as a substitute for the dimension of "change" that Celan refuses to mention explicitly or even to accept as a possible means of expressing variation. To be sure, it is also all that. All the same time, however, with the phrase *Ich find, erfind* Celan pierces the façade of linguistic performance, that is, of *parole* (speech), making it possible to glimpse the inner workings of the linguistic system, of *langue* (language). (He already did this, although in an incomparably less bold fashion, in verse 2: *was ich da treib und trieb*.) What is thereby revealed are parts of the conjugation paradigm, once with respect to tense (*was ich da treib und trieb*) and once with respect to person: *ich find, erfind* (= *er find*). Admittedly, this reading is not compelling in the first case (the change of tense, accompanied by lexical constancy, has its own function, as was seen above); it becomes so only when the first case is considered together with the second (*Ich find, erfind*). Our interpretation of the second case presupposes that, in this position, the prefix *er* carries the connotation of the personal pronoun *er* ("he"). That it actually does so will perhaps be doubted. We may therefore draw attention to two points. Firstly, in the sequence *Ich find, erfind* (as in verse 13: *getrennt, geschieden*), understanding, which is concerned above all with "distinctive features" will depart from the usual pronunciation (*erfind*) to stress the prefix *er* and this is what makes it possible to defend the second meaning (i.e., of *er* as a personal pronoun). Secondly, it will be recalled that there are passages in Celan's own poems in which paradigmatic fragments of *langue* obviously mingle with *parole,* as in the introductory poem of the collection entitled *Die Niemandsrose:*

> I dig, you dig, and the worm, it digs too,
> And that singing over there says: They dig.

Ich grabe, du gräbst, und es gräbt auch der Wurm
und das Singende dort sagt: Sie graben.[18]

The meaning of this questioning of *parole* through the introduction of nonactualized or only partially actualized *faits bruts* of
langue—a technique that is a constitutive element of the most recent, so-called concrete poetry—becomes evident as soon as we
recognize the motivation behind Celan's specific intention toward
language, which emerges ever more clearly from the examples ana-
lyzed. With this end in view, let us analyze one last instance of
varied repetition. At the beginning of the third quatrain Shakespeare states that he wishes to express the theme of "Fair, kind, and
true," which is to be the sole theme of his writing, exclusively by
means of varying words; he then continues:

And in this change is my invention spent,
Three themes in one, which wondrous scope affords.

Celan translates these lines as:

Ich find, erfind—um sie in eins zu bringen,
sie einzubringen ohne Unterlass.

The passage *sie in eins zu bringen,* / *sie einzubringen* is probably
the one in which Celan's method of translating lies most open to
criticism, the one in which it takes the most liberties. Here, more
easily than anywhere else in his German version of Shakespeare's
sonnet, we can perceive the specific intention toward language
underlying this translation from beginning to end. Celan, as we
have seen, does not allow the poet to speak of his own inventive
gifts; similarly, he forbids the poet to mention the *scope* of his poetry writing or to call it "wondrous." These words are replaced by
two half-verses: *um sie in eins zu bringen* and *sie einzubringen.* Each
has its specific content, which can be expressed by other words.
The first, the "bringing-into-one" (which translates *Three themes in
one*), should be understood as the union of *"Schön, gut und treu"*—
as the poetic mimesis of that union embodied in the friend. The
"Three themes" are "One thing" (v. 8). Celan, to be sure, mentions

18. Paul Celan, *Die Niemandsrose* (Frankfurt am Main, 1963), p. 9 [Eng. trans.,
Paul Celan: Poems, trans. Michael Hamburger (New York, 1980), p. 131. Trans.
modified.]

only the unity, the uniting, and not the threefold nature of the manifest reality which, in Shakespeare, is taken for granted. And his *sie* ("they") refers to the group *"Schön, gut und treu,"* which (in contrast to the practice of many critical editions) also appears each time in inverted commas in the English text printed along with Celan's version,[19] with the result that this group is presented as a quotation, that is, as a verbal entity, not as something real. Thus the grouping of the virtues, which, in Shakespeare, serves, in however fictive and fictionalized a manner, as the point of departure of the poet's activity, disappears in Celan's text in two respects: it loses both its threefold nature and its existence as something real.

The second half-verse *sie einzubringen* ("to bring them in," i.e., to harvest them) cannot be understood as a translation of a specific passage of the original. Once again, what is meant is the act of poetic composition. As metaphor, it would have to be linked with the imagery of a harvest or vintage. If one assumes that the term corresponding to the implicit "whither" of the "bringing in" or harvesting is the poem itself, then the resolution of the metaphor may be seen in the "putting in practice" [i.e., of something in a work of art = *Ins Werk Setzen*]. But such an analytic reading, dependent on "retranslation," is overwhelmed by the wave arising from the paronomasia of *sie in eins zu bringen / sie einzubringen* ("to bring them into one / to bring them in"). Unlike the case of the rhyming pair in the final couplet *(schieden / schmieden),* here the paronomasia is not confined to a portion of a word but encompasses an entire syntagma. The sequence *sie in eins zu bringen, / sie einzubringen* also differs from the other paronomasia by the fact that it does not stand in the end-rhyme position; the concordance of sounds is therefore not borne by any schema, but strikes the reader unprepared. These differences, however, constitute merely the preconditions for the really decisive difference; and it is the latter that allows us to grasp the specific character of the passage and thereby the particular motivation of Celan's intention toward language, a motivation that is manifest throughout his translation.

By rhyming *zusammenschmieden* with *geschieden,* Celan brings together two signifiers which not only are different but which have opposite signifieds ("separate" / "join"). He expresses the opposi-

19. The English text printed in the Insel-Bücherei volume was not suggested by Celan, nor did he provide the publisher with it; he did, however, examine and approve it. (This information was kindly given me by Mr. Klaus Reichert.)

tion perhaps even more forcefully through the phonological near-identity, the paronomasia, than through the semantic opposition *e contrario*. In this way he subverts the normative conception of the correspondence, in every case, of the signifieds to the signifiers, the latter of which are assumed to mirror the diversity of the former. (Polysemy is equally the scandal of semiotics, as it is the fundamental fact of poetics.) Now, in contrast to the paronomasia of the final rhyme, the paronomasia of the two syntagmata *sie in eins zu bringen* and *sie einzubringen* is determined not simply by the partial difference between the signifiers *eins* ("one") and *ein* (= *hinein*, "in"), but also through the identity of the signifieds, insofar as Saussure's distinction is at all meaningful and appropriate in the context of Celan's use of language, which seems to be the same one that has been distinctive of modern poetry since Mallarmé.[20] *Ineinsbringen* ("bringing into one," i.e., uniting) and *Einbringen* ("bringing in") do not normally mean the same thing, any more than do "joining" and "putting in practice"; yet, for Celan, to put in practice in a work of art is to unite. The paronomasia of the passage under discussion shows this, and the same is suggested by a reading of the German version of the sonnet as a whole. Here we can plainly see Celan's intention toward language and the poetics of his translation. Its program is formulated in that line which renders Shakespeare's verse

Therefore my verse to constancy confined

by

In der Beständigkeit, da bleibt mein Vers geborgen.

Constancy, the theme of Shakespeare's sonnet, becomes for Celan the medium in which his verse dwells and which impedes the flow of his verse,[21] imposing constancy upon it. Constancy becomes the constituent element of his verse, in contrast to Shakespeare's original, in which constancy is sung about and described by means of a variety of expressions. Celan's intention toward language, in his

20. See Derrida, "La double séance," and also his "Sémiologie et grammatologie," *Information sur les sciences sociales* 7, no. 3 (1968) (Recherches Sémiotiques).
21. See note 26.

version of Shakespeare's sonnet 105, is a realization of constancy
in verse.[22]

*

We have already seen numerous examples of recurrence of the
same elements and of creation of similarities that resist the changes
wrought by the lapse of time, but the catalogue is not yet complete.
Constancy is also conveyed on other linguistic levels than those
considered so far. For example, Celan refrains from using enjambment in his translation, whereas he does employ it in his own poetry and also in others of his translations of Shakespeare's sonnets
(as does Shakespeare himself). Where this device appears in the
original text:

> Since all alike my songs and praises be
> To one, of one, still such, and ever so.

Celan inserts a colon in order to mark the limits of the verse:

> All dieses Singen hier, all dieses Preisen:
> von ihm, an ihn und immer ihm zulieb.

In another instance he replaces a comma (or perhaps a dash)[23] by
a period, and thereby turns the anaphorically linked verses 9 and
10 into two that are merely juxtaposed:

> Fair, kind, and true, is all my argument,
> Fair, kind, and true, varying to other words,

> "Schön, gut und treu," das singe ich und singe.
> "Schön, gut und treu"—stets anders und stets das.

Whereas in the original text this pair of verses ends with a comma,
Celan interrupts this strophe with a period, as he already did in the
first and second strophes and will do in the couplet as well. (None
of Shakespeare's three quatrains consists of more than a single sentence.) It is only in those verses which follow the ones just quoted,

22. It would be worthwhile to examine the function of this program (or experiment) of a poetics of constancy in Celan's own poetry and in its development.
23. See note 19.

and which form the most precarious passage of the entire translation, that one could speak of enjambment. This is with the appearance of the paronomastic sequence *um sie in eins zu bringen,* / *sie einzubringen,* which does not stop at the end of the verse, although, admittedly, the effect of the enjambment is essentially canceled due to internal repetition.

The syntactic constancy, that is, the regular recurrence of the verses as individual sentences, goes still further: it represents a deviation from the original, indeed a determinate negation of the latter's way of shaping language. The syntactic subordination, the hypotaxis, of the original poem disappears, and along with it, the argumentative and logical style. At the turning points of the quatrains and the couplet, Shakespeare places either causal conjunctions (or adverbs):

> v. 3 *Since* all alike my songs and praises be
> v. 7 *Therefore* my verse to constancy confined;

or the conjunction "and" used consecutively:

> v. 11 *And* in this change is my invention spent;

or a relative pronoun:

> v. 14 *Which* three till now, never kept seat in one.

Celan eliminates these connective words. His sentences are not constructed either to refer to each other or to be subordinate to one another. Celan's translation is profoundly marked by the principle of parataxis, in the literal sense as well as in a broader sense similar to the one Adorno introduced in connection with Hölderlin's later poetry.[24] Furthermore, Celan reduces the sharpness of the division of the fourteen lines into three quatrains and a couplet, even though he does set off the quatrains typographically from each other (in accord with the Petrarchan sonnet form) as well as

24. See the reference in note 14. In Hölderlin, to be sure, parataxis serves to isolate individual words, whereas in Celan, at least in this translation, it pertains more to the relationship of the verses and sentences. In Celan's own poetry, parataxis involving individual words plays a decisive role.

preserve the rhyme scheme.[25] For, in contrast to Shakespeare's procedure, Celan divides every quatrain into two in the middle, either
by the sentence structure or by the punctuation. Consequently, in
spite of the rhyme scheme, Celan's quatrains approximate a series
of couplets, whereas his couplet is assimilated to the quatrains,
through syntactic division into two equal parts. In the original we
find dissimilar units (three quatrains and a couplet), and these, by
virtue of the way the sentence-units are interrelated (causal connection between the halves of strophes I and II and consecutive connection in strophe III) are hypotactically structured (even if, in the
strict sense, there are no subordinate clauses in II and III); as a
result they in turn imply inequality. In Celan's translation, on the
other hand, the verses are simply set out one after the other; each
is a unit, which, if it is not autonomous, is nevertheless much less
heteronomous than the corresponding verse of the original. Just
as, on the semantic and phonological levels, Celan's language tends
to reduce change, difference, and variety to a minimum, so, too,
does it strive for syntactic constance—in this translation more than
in any other.

                              *

    Celan's intention toward language, as revealed by a study of his
German version of Shakespeare's sonnet 105, ought not be pre-
maturely generalized. Our investigation dealt with but one sonnet.
Nevertheless, the realization of constancy in verse, which is the
major finding of our analysis, is not merely a feature peculiar to
this one translation. Indeed, it accords with Roman Jakobson's definition of the function of poetic language: "The poetic function
projects the principle of equivalence from the axis of selection into
the axis of combination. Equivalence is promoted to the constitutive device of the sequence."[26] Jakobson's definition is not a de-

25. See note 19. The typographical separation of the quatrains was probably
made in order to have the corresponding lines of the original and the translation
face each other in the dual language.
26. Roman Jakobson, "Linguistics and Poetics," in *Style in Language*, ed. Thomas
A. Sebeok (Cambridge, Mass., 1960), p. 358. In the poetic sequence the equiva-
lences correspond to the passage of time. It is perhaps no accident that sonnets are
the subject both of Jakobson's most important interpretations of poems and of the
present essay: "Le sonnet est fait pour le simultané. Quatorze vers *simultanés*, et
fortement désignés comme tels par l'enchaînement et la conservation des rimes: type
et structure d'un poème *stationnaire*" ["The sonnet is made for the simultaneous.

scription of a poem, but a statement of the principle governing the poetic use of language in the strict sense of the term. This principle can never be fully realized on the linguistic level, if the poem is not to be tautological, in other words, if it is to say anything at all. Celan's translation of Shakespeare's sonnet 105 approaches more closely than any previous poem to the limiting value of a thoroughgoing realization of the principle of the equivalence in the syntagmatic sequence (if one leaves "concrete poetry" aside). This is so not because Celan's poem—and his translation *is* a poem—is more "poetic" than other poems by him or by others (to conclude this would be to misunderstand Jakobson), but because constancy is the theme of his poem, his translation. Of course, it is also the theme of Shakespeare's sonnet, to which, however, the preceding remarks in no way apply. This point brings us back one final time to the difference between the original and the translation, in other words, to the difference between Shakespeare's and Celan's respective intentions toward language.

"Constancy" can be called the theme of Shakespeare's sonnet, insofar as it actually deals with that virtue. Shakespeare asserts and praises the constancy of his "fair friend," and he describes his own writing, whose subject matter is to be exclusively his friend's constancy and the poet's celebration of it. Constancy is, at the same time, conceived of as the means by which this virtue is to be celebrated:

> Therefore my verse to constancy confined,
> One thing expressing, leaves out difference.

But it is as a virtue of the poet's composition that "constancy" figures as the subject matter of the poem. Only in the anaphorical (and thus rhetorically consecrated) repetition of "Fair, kind, and true" does constancy enter the poem's very language.

In Celan's version we find something very different. Consistent

---

Fourteen *simultaneous* verses, and vigorously designated as such by the linking and conserving of rhymes: type and structure of a *stationary* poem"—trans. A. Warminski]. (Paul Valéry, *Tel Quel,* in *Oeuvres,* Pléiade ed. [Paris, 1960], vol. 2, p. 676.) In the framework of Jakobson's definition of the "poetic function," the conjugation paradigm, which was discussed in connection with the passages *was ich da treib und trieb* and *Ich find, erfind,* turns out to be a special case of what modern linguistics terms "paradigmatics."

with his overall approach, Celan leaves untranslated those passages in which Shakespeare describes his own poem, his own style, and the goal of his writing: or else he translates them so "freely" that they no longer seem to deal with these topics:

> Since *all alike* my songs and praises be

> All dieses Singen hier, all dieses Preisen:

> Therefore my verse to constancy *confined*,
> One thing expressing, *leaves out difference*.

> In der Beständigkeit, da bleibt mein Vers geborgen,
> Spricht von dem Einen, schweift mir nicht umher.

> Fair, kind, and true, *is all my argument*,
> Fair, kind, and true, *varying to other words*,
> *And in this change is my invention spent*
> *Three themes in one, which wondrous scope affords.*

> "Schön, gut und treu", das singe ich und singe.
> "Schön, gut und treu"—stets anders und stets das.
> Ich find, erfind—um sie in eins zu bringen,
> sie einzubringen ohne Unterlass.

In Celan's version the poet does not speak of his "argument," his "invention," or his "scope," but instead the verse is arranged in accordance with the exigencies of this theme and of this objective aim. Nor does the poet affirm that this verse leaves out difference; rather he speaks in a language in which differences are simply left out. Celan, writing in the wake of the later Mallarmé and an attentive observer of modern linguistics, philosophy of language, and aesthetics drew the logical consequence from the symbolist conception of poetry, in which a poem is its own subject matter and both invokes and describes itself as a symbol. According to Jakobson there exists a certain kind of constancy which is projected from the paradigmatic axis (of which it is constitutive) into the syntagmatic axis and which distinguishes the poetic sequence from the prosaic in this latter axis. If we accept Jakobson's views, then we may say that in translating a poem whose subject matter is that very constancy, Celan, perhaps without knowing of Jakobson's theorem, replaced the traditional symbolist poem—which deals only with itself and which has itself as its subject matter—with a poem which does not *deal* with itself but which *is* itself! He thus produced a poem which no longer speaks about itself but whose language is *sheltered* in that very place that it assigns to its subject matter, which is none other than itself: it is sheltered "in constancy." [27]

27. The present essay is concerned with Celan's intention toward language. It should be completed by an analysis of his way of fashioning language. Such an analysis would have to devote particular attention to the expressive value and tone of turns of phrase like "den ich *da* lieb," "was ich *da* treib," and "all *dieses* Singen." It would show that with these linguistic means Celan expresses not only the contemplative distance of the melancholic to himself and to the object of his love—and the "I" who speaks in Shakespeare's sonnets may rightly be termed a melancholic; he also expresses the distance between himself and the subjective dimension as such, from which Celan turns away in favor of the objectivity of the poem, which is concerned only with itself. This objectivity is established by a language which, like the one examined here, no longer serves the function of representation. Yet, in the final verse *(In Einem will ich drei zusammenschmieden)* intense light falls on the "I" that sets itself this task, in opposition not only to the "I" standing behind the veil of melancholy, an "I" that lives *there (da)*, but also to the programmatic objectivity of the poem.

SEVENTEEN

YVES BONNEFOY
Translating Poetry

Translated by John Alexander and Clive Wilmer

You can translate by simply declaring one poem the translation of another. For example, Wladimir Weidlé once jokingly said to me that Baudelaire's poem, "Je n'ai pas oublié, voisine de la ville . . . ," renders the *sound* of Pushkin: it has his clarity, it is the "best" translation of him. But is it possible to reduce a poem to its clarity?

The answer to the question, "Can one translate a poem?" is of course no. The translator meets too many contradictions that he cannot eliminate; he must make too many sacrifices.

For example (drawing on my own experience), Yeats's "Sailing to Byzantium": straightaway, the title presents a problem. "L'Embarquement pour Byzance"? Inconceivable. Watteau would get in the way. What's more, "sailing" has the energy of a verb. Baudelaire's "A Honfleur! Le plus tôt possible avant de tomber plus bas" comes to mind, but "A Byzance" would be ridiculous: the myth rules out such brevities. . . . Finally, "to sail" makes one think not only of departure but also of the sea to be crossed—difficult, troubled like passion—and the distant port: commerce, labor, works, the conquest of nature, spirit. None of the things *appareiller* might convey, and *faire voile* isn't strong enough over these distances. I resigned myself to "Byzance—l'autre rive." A certain tension is perhaps salvaged but not the energy, the (at least unconscious) wrenching away that the verb expresses. As so often when

Reprinted from Yves Bonnefoy, *The Act and the Place of Poetry: Selected Essays,* © 1989 by The University of Chicago.

"La Traduction de la poésie" was first given as a lecture to the Association des traducteurs littéraires de France, in Paris, in 1976. This English translation by John Alexander and Clive Wilmer is a slightly revised version of that published in *PN Review* 48 (1985), the "Special Cambridge Poetry Festival Issue."

we pass from the language of Shakespeare to French, still subject as it is to the harsh restrictions Malherbe imposed on it, lived experience is transformed into the timeless and the irrational into the intelligible. Another solution might be to gloss the title with Baudelaire's phrase. Then it would be necessary to experiment with open-ended translation *(traductions developpées)*: one would allow into play all the associations of ideas called up by the work, laid out on the page like Mallarmé's "Coup de dés." But Yeats is *speaking* of the moment—unique, urgent—and one must be faithful to that too.

In the same poem, another sacrifice that can't be avoided: "fish, flesh, and fowl." Yeats crams the variousness of life into three words—its energy, its seeming finality—and does so above all by means of alliteration. Already quite a problem!—but worse is to come. The expression is ready-made, which is why we can dream—and taking it up into the poem suggests this—that everyday language preserves a little of the primordial language, fundamental and transparent, whose return or advent so many poets have longed for. "Sailing to Byzantium" is therefore concerned with the folk wisdom of the race and the here and now, at the very moment when it is a matter of tearing away from these things toward pure spirit. This is a paradox, which in Yeats is profound and ever present, but one that is necessarily lost in French where a comparable concision is not possible: the "felicities" of languages do not coincide. I translated it "tout ce qui nage, vole, s'élance," which retains that vitality in the sense but not in the substance of the words. What is more, the verb form in this instance is weaker than the nouns—"fish, flesh, and fowl"—which seem to repeat the first divine bestowal of names. Where a text has its felicities (accidental or not), its cruxes, its density—its unconscious—the translation must stick to the surface, even if its own cruxes crop up elsewhere. You can't translate a poem.

But that's all to the good, since a poem is less than poetry, and to the extent that one is denied something of the former the effect can be stimulating to the latter. A poem, a certain number of words in a certain order on the page, is a *form,* where all relation to what is other and finite—to what is true—has been suspended. And the author may take pleasure in this: it's satisfying; one likes to bring things into being, things that endure, but one readily regrets having set oneself at odds with the place and time of true reciprocity. The poem is a means, a spiritual statement, which is not, however, an end. Publication puts it to the test: it is a time for reflection which one allows oneself, but this is not to settle for it, to make it hard and fast. And, of course, the best reader is similarly the one who cares for the poem: not as one cares for a being but in response to the irreducible content it addresses, to the *meaning* it bears. Let's neither make an idol of the written page, nor, still less, regard it with that iconoclastic distaste that is inverted idolatry. At its most intense, reading is empathy, shared existence. And, in a sense, how disturbing that is! All that textual richness—ambiguities, wordplay, layers of meaning, etc.—denied the privilege of obliging us to solve their crossword puzzles. In their place, darkness and dull care. I will be reproached for impoverishing the text.

What we gain, however, by way of compensation, is the very thing we cannot grasp or hold: that is to say, the poetry of other languages.

We should in fact come to see what motivates the poem; to relive the act which both gave rise to it and remains enmeshed in it; and released from that fixed form, which is merely its trace, the first intention and intuition (let us say a yearning, an obsession, something universal) can be tried out anew in the other language. The exercise will now be the more genuine because the same difficulty manifests itself: that is to say, as in the original, the language *(langue)* of translation paralyzes the actual, tentative utterance *(parole)*. For the difficulty of poetry is that language *(langue)* is a *system*, while the specific utterance *(parole)* is *presence*. But to understand this is to find oneself back with the author one is translating; it is to see more clearly the duress that bears on him, the maneuvers of thought he deploys against it; and the fidelities that bind him. For words will try to entice us into behaving as they do. Once a good translation has been set in motion, they will rapidly begin to justify the bad poem it turns into, and they will impoverish the experience for the sake of constructing a text. The translator needs to be on his guard and to test the ontological necessity of his new images even more than their term-for-term (and therefore external) resemblance to those of the original poem. This is uphill work, but the translator is rewarded by his author, if it's Yeats, if it's Donne, if it's Shakespeare. And instead of being, as before, up against the body of a text, he finds himself at the source, a beginning rich with possibility, and on this second journey he has the right to be himself. A creative act, in short! Playing tricks with the lacunae of his language, tinkering *(bricoler)*, to use the fashionable word, he now finds himself reexperiencing the restrictions first encountered by his author, insofar as he attends to what the author learned from them: which is to say that you must live before you write. You must realize that the poem is nothing and that translation is possible—which is not to say that it's easy; it is merely poetry re-begun.

＊

Isn't this all out of proportion though, laying claim to a power of invention comparable to Yeats's in order to get back in this way to the source of his poem? But to put yourself forward is not to imply that you feel assured of success. The writing of poetry is invariably ambitious, and, even for the real poet, this ambition must proceed in uncertainty. There is no poetry but that which is impossible. And to fail, let us say, over certain specific details at least leaves one room to attend to unity, or transparency—and destiny.

Indeed, practically, if the translation is not a crib, or mere technique, but an enquiry and an experiment, it can only inscribe itself—write itself—in the course of a life; it will draw upon that life in all its aspects, all its actions. This does not mean that the translator need be in other respects a "poet." But it definitely implies that if he is himself a writer he will be unable to keep his translating separate from his own work.

Some examples of this interdependence—personal ones, since they are nothing to pride oneself on (or to be alarmed at: discrete fragments, with no value except as tokens).

Horatio, talking to Hamlet about his companions of the watch after the ghost has appeared. They were "distilled," he says, "almost to jelly with the act of fear. . . ." The meaning is clear. But "the act of fear" introduces an intensity that is tragic, in which context "jelly" (literally gelatine—so English—in French, *bouillie*) seemed to me problematic. Why? The obscenities at the beginning of *Romeo* are translatable. But an obscenity is a pointed linguistic device, clear-cut and self-contained, while here "jelly" is everyday speech used without special care and not charged with meaning. Now I think my tendency here is very French: given such contexts, which are after all tragic and exemplary, I want a heightened consciousness and, accordingly, an economy of meaning, and so too a vocabulary if not restrained at least tried and tested. Of course, vulgarity must have its place, but simply *as* vulgarity—think of Rabelais and

Rimbaud—and here I am at one again with Racine or Nerval and what is called elevated, or literary, language, but which is no more than language at its tautest, most highly serious. The English (look at Mercutio) expect less from language. They want direct observation and uncomplicated psychology (in short, "jelly" where a soldier would say it) rather than heroic reconstruction.

And I admit they're right. But while I am thus undecided, should I meet the challenge without more ado and speak of *la bouillie*, or even of *l'eau de boudin?* It would cost me almost nothing to be literal. But if it's true that, even in accepting this, I remain however slightly the disciple of Racine, it's also true that what looks like accuracy will lead to quaintness. This is the vice of Romantic translation—badly hewn from an earlier rhetoric—which always seems to me to evade the problem without resolving it. Even Duçis[1] would be better than that! Better still, listen to Shakespeare until I can anticipate him in all my own writing and not merely mirror him. And meanwhile, with full knowledge of the case (I will add a note), translate "jelly" with my own word, derived from another set of associations: *cendre* ("ash"). . . . Locally, the translation fails. But the act of translating has begun and will be concluded later elsewhere—that is, still *here*.

And now back to Yeats again, to "The Sorrow of Love," where he says of the girl with "red mournful lips" that she is "doomed like Odysseus and the labouring ships." "Labouring": the word conjures up long, difficult sea crossings and the rolling of the ship, but also emotional distress and grief—not to mention "to be in labor," that is, the process of giving birth. Not to mention, either, that the archaic sense of *laborer*—that is virtually *ensemencer* ("to sow")—is still current. All these senses have weight here, so what is to be done? But this time I wasn't even able to ask myself the question; irresistibly I translated "labouring" with *qui boitent / au loin*, thereby immediately rejecting some of the senses in my translation. And I would be equally able to justify or criticize these words: Odysseus did not flee, the children of Priam did—in quest of another Troy—and the death of Priam occurs in the next line.

---

1. Jean-François Duçis (1733–1816) was a dramatist who adapted five Shakespeare tragedies for the French stage. According to the *Oxford Companion to French Literature,* the adaptations were "feeble": "To suit French taste he introduced confidants in the classical manner, and provided *Othello* with an alternative ending in which Othello discovers his mistake in time and does not murder Desdemona."

But that's not the point here. For these words did not come to me
by the short circuiting that people think of as running from text to
translation by way of the translator. They came by a more round-
about route that took in my own past. I've often thought about the
limping of a ship. . . . Once even, coming back from Greece in
1961, with my heart full of the memory of the Sphinx of Naxos,
whose smile expresses ataraxy, that music, I imagined that the
boat—laboring in just this way, by night, off the coast of Italy—
was itself fleeing and searching. With Verlaine at the back of my
mind, I sketched out a kind of poem, in which the ever-rolling sea
also played its part, "comme du fer, dans une caisse close" ("like
iron in a closed chest"): a poem I've never since completed—and
which, twelve years later, on an impulse, I tore up to give life to
my translation. The relationship between what was there feeling its
way and my concern with the poetry of Yeats became the most
important, the true development. It was the English-speaking poet
who explained me to myself, and my own personal experience that
imposed the translation upon me. It is in the sympathy of destiny
for destiny, in short, and not of an English phrase for a French one,
that translations unfold, with lasting consequences one cannot
foresee (the boat and its limping appeared in my last book).

*

Following the logic of these remarks, I ought now to ask myself how my translations have fed back into my own poetry; and
how the poetry of other languages has contributed to the development of ours.

For want of time, I will do no more than raise another prelim-
inary question. Under what circumstances is this type of translation, the translation of poetry, not completely mad? "Translate
poets who are close to you," I once suggested. But what poet can
be close enough?

The irony of Donne, the luminous melancholy of Eliot—or
Baudelairean spleen, or Rimbaud's *mauvaiseté* (and always, too, his
hope)—are they not impenetrable worlds? And as for Yeats—the
aspiration toward the Idea, toward Byzantium, on the one hand,
but on the other "blood and mire," both mud and ecstasy, even the
fury of passion, and Adonis as well as Christ—can that be shared?

But in poetry, necessity is the mother of invention. What one has not tried is sometimes repressed, and translation, when a great poet speaks to us, can bypass censorship—this is part of the feedback which, as I was saying, the translated work may generate. An energy is released. So let us follow where it leads. But let us follow only this. If a work does not compel us, it is untranslatable.

EIGHTEEN
HENRY SCHOGT
Semantic Theory and Translation Theory

Although there is an undeniable and very important link between semantics and translation, the one dealing with meaning, the other with transfer of meaning, semantic theory and translation theory are not closely connected, and often translation specialists are even bothered rather than helped by the tenets of semantic theory. It is interesting to examine the two domains of semantics and translation in order to find out whether explanations can be given for this state of affairs where there is little positive interaction between the two.

Saying that semantic theory is concerned with meaning does not tell us more than a concise dictionary would do. So it is necessary to list some of the major questions semantics investigates. Without any claim to being exhaustive or to establishing a hierarchical order of importance, we can mention the following points: (1) the philosophical, epistemological problems of the relation between language, thought and the outside world; (2) the relation between a meaningful element of a language and the other elements of the same level of analysis one finds in that language; (3) the communication between individuals who speak the same language, the communication being either oral or written.

1. The first problem, although of a general character and not tied to any specific language, has important implications for the translator. If there is a link between language, thought and reality (*Language, Thought and Reality* is the title of a volume of selected essays by Benjamin Lee Whorf),[1] different realities engender dif-

Reprinted by permission from *Texte: Revue de critique et de théorie* 4 (1985).

1. B. L. Whorf, *Language, Thought and Reality: Selected Writings,* edited and with an introduction by J. B. Carroll (Cambridge, Mass.: MIT Press, 1956).

ferent languages, but also different languages shape different realities. In its most extreme form the so-called Sapir-Whorf hypothesis leads to the view that communication between two people who do not share the same native language is impossible, even if one of them has learned the language of the other. Even those who think they have learned a foreign language remain prisoners of their mother tongue's value system, and are therefore incapable of truly communicating with those whose language they think they have mastered.

This is a typical example of a clash between theory and practice: nobody accepts the Sapir-Whorf hypothesis completely and yet it is difficult to deny that the language one speaks focuses on elements of the outside world and creates abstract notions that other languages may leave either unnoticed or, in the case of abstract notions, unconceptualized. Verbal systems may differ in that one puts great emphasis on temporality and the anterior/posterior scale, whereas another has an overt marking of aspect, a category that does not have the deictic character of temporality.[2] Even if the first language is able to express aspect and the second language temporality, these categories do not have a prominent position, so that there is no real equivalence between the two languages as to temporality and aspect.

2. This leads to the second question of semantics concerning the immanent analysis by which each element is defined with respect to the other elements of the same level and thanks to them.

This principle of structuring linguistic elements and describing them from a functional point of view, rather than referring to any physical features they may have in isolation is best known from phonology/phonemics as presented by Prague structuralists, in the first place by Trubetzkoj.[3] Attempts to structure meaningful units in the same way as phonemes have been only partially successful until now.

When discussing the verbs *craindre* and *redouter* and the verbal expression *avoir peur* Saussure already pointed out that the value of each of the three units was determined by the existence of the two others.[4] Unfortunately Saussure does not specify in what respect

---

2. Cf. B. Comrie, *Aspect* (Cambridge: Cambridge University Press, 1976).

3. N. S. Trubetzkoj, *Grundzüge der Phonologie*. Travaux du Cercle Linguistique de Prague [TCLP], no. 7 (Prague, 1939).

4. F. de Saussure, *Cours de linguistique générale* (Paris: Payot, 5th ed. 1962 [1916]), p. 160.

they differ and whether the differences are part of the intellectual content or not. This opens up the question of connotation and denotation and the division into noncognitive and cognitive elements of meaning that plays such an important role in translation discussions.

Semantic or notional field studies illustrate more clearly than the example given by Saussure the possibilities and the limitations of the structural method as applied to the lexicon. The field idea is partly to be seen as an answer to the problem of structuring units belonging to an open, unlimited inventory. Contrary to phonemes, that are for each language a restricted, closed category with a number of units rarely exceeding 75—and mostly much lower than that—lexical units are so numerous that the principle according to which each unit influences all the other units at the same level is invalid for the lexicon as a whole, or if one wants to maintain it, without any verifiable significance. In the much smaller and more homogeneous lexical field, however, one can observe a situation similar to that prevailing in a phonological system. There are, however, some differences in spite of the similarity:

a. Phonemes are discrete units, whereas the signified of lexemes is often much fuzzier. It is difficult to give general rules: while in some instances the meaning is discrete (e.g., kinship terminology), in most cases there is no clear delimitation of the different meaning-areas, but rather fuzzy edges and overlap. (Saussure's *craindre, avoir peur* and *redouter* fall into this category).

b. Within a speech community there are only slight variations in the phonological system. Those variations are a group phenomenon, age, sex, social class, and regional origin being determining factors. Lexical field structure knows much wider deviations, and whereas the number of units in the phonological systems of a speech community is for all variations very close to the average (in other words, the difference between maximum, average and minimum is small), the number of lexical units in a given field may vary greatly from one individual to the next. This has important implications for the precise, lexical meaning of each item: the fewer terms there are, the less specific their meaning becomes. It should be noticed that grammatical categories such as person, number, case, tense, mood, and aspect come much closer to the phonological model.

c. Outside reality, social structure, way-of-life vary from one speech community to the other. Semantic fields reflect these differences (sometimes no longer pertinent in contemporary society).[5] A unit may belong to different fields in different languages. For a Dutchman potatoes belong to the same field as noodles and rice (starch component of the meal), whereas in France they are listed with vegetables. If the fields provide generic terms, those terms will be different in cases such as the potato one.

   d. Immanent analysis has to be complemented by knowledge of reference. As reference brings in the outside world as well as the mental constructs that are without material denotation, the experience of each individual speaker colors his or her frame of reference in a special way, even within one and the same speech community.

   If, as is very often the case, the semantic or lexical field study deals with one language, individual variations are not taken into account and the field that is constructed is supposed to be representative for common usage. Comparisons between fields in two or more languages are based on the same assumption of general validity of each field within its own speech community. By adhering to the principle of abstraction and generalization of the linguistic sign, the semantic field studies stay in the realm of *langue,* or competence. However, translators work with texts, and operate at the level of *parole,* or performance.

   3. Whether they are called speaker and hearer, sender and receiver, or encoder and decoder, the communication model postulates someone who forms a message and someone who receives that message and interprets it.

   If both persons follow the same grammatical rules, and have the same lexical inventory, the message gets across without change, and the communication is successful. This rosy picture does not take into account all the complexities that have been investigated by speech act descriptions and pragmatics.

   A simple example will suffice to illustrate the problems one may encounter. When I needed some crucial information for a paper I was writing, I phoned a friend for help. His three-year-old

   5. Russian kinship terminology offers a good example. The intricate system, still functional in rural society, lost its pertinence elsewhere in the nineteenth century. Tolstoy's unexpected shift from brother-in-law (brother of the wife): *šurin* to brother-in-law (husband of the sister): *zjat'* in section 3 of *The Death of Ivan Ilič* may be a result of terminological confusion. In *Besy* (*The Possessed,* pt. 2, chap. 1, sec. 5) Dostoyevsky makes one of his characters confuse the terms for mother-in-law (mother of the husband): *svekrov'* and daughter-in-law: *snoxa.*

son answered the phone, as he loved to do. To my question, "Is your father home?" he answered "Yes," and left the phone dangling, without calling his father. The semantic interpretation of my question was correct, but the communication was not really successful.

Semantic theory focuses on cognitive meaning and leaves the complexities of intention and innuendo to other disciplines. It should be mentioned that John Lyons in his book on semantics deals extensively with the problems of illocutionary acts, paralinguistic phenomena, and multiple interpretation levels.[6] He seems to use "semantics" as a generic term, and then use the same signifier as a hyponym for the branch dealing with cognitive meaning, thus falling in line with traditional usage.

The Geneva school, with Charles Bally and Albert Sechehaye and the Dutch author of a French syntax, Cornelis de Boer,[7] puts emphasis on the distinction between old and new information in the *thème* and *rhème* or *thème* and *propos* theory. This theory foreshadows the notion of "foregrounding" that was introduced as a refinement of transformational description. Although the constituent elements are the same, different word order, different stress, or different construction result in a shift of focus, thus signaling different elements to the special attention of the listener/reader. When source language and target language do not have the same devices to create these special effects, the translator may find himself at a loss. Studies such as the one by Claude Hagège on the typology of languages show the extent of this problem.[8]

Before discussing any further the connections between semantics and translation, a few words should be said about the models presented by Klaus Heger[9] and Luis Prieto.[10] Both make an attempt to go beyond the *langue/parole* dichotomy. That dichotomy has proven to be a major stumbling block when the paradigmatic linguistic sign has to be integrated into a syntagmatic message.

For Heger the Saussurean sign is what he calls a *signème*, stress-

6. J. Lyons, *Semantics* (Cambridge: Cambridge University Press, 1977).

7. C. de Boer's *Syntaxe du français moderne* (Leiden: Universitaire Pers Leiden, 2d ed. 1954 [1946]) gives a good summary of the Geneva School views on this quotation.

8. C. Hagège, *La Structure des langues* (Paris: P.U.F., 1982).

9. K. Heger, "L'Analyse sémantique de signe linguistique," *Langue française* 1, no. 4 (1969): 44–66.

10. L. Prieto, *Principes de Noologie* (The Hague: Mouton, 1964).

ing by the choice of this term the -emic character of the unit. Its signified contains all the elements (*sèmes* and *noèmes*, the difference between which is explained by Heger, but is not relevant for his purpose) that may become pertinent in any instance of actual use of the term in question. Only part of the inventory is pertinent in each separate instance of actual use, depending on context and situation. Heger calls *sémème* this actualized part of the *signème*. One could also call it, according to his theory, the signified of the *signème monosémisé*. Heger does not indicate any procedure for establishing the inventory of all the *sèmes* (and *noèmes*) of a given *signème*. He may have Bernard Pottier's method[11] in mind or some other kind of componential analysis, it does not matter which one, the problem with all methods being that no formal means of verification can be given. (One should remember in this respect the criticisms made of Katz and Fodor and their *bachelor* example.)[12]

Luis Prieto stays, as does Heger, within the Saussurean structuralist tradition, but his approach is different. His sign is not the isolated lexical unit of which Saussure gave "arbor" as an illustration, but rather what Prieto calls a complete message. Linguistically the message may not be a complete sentence if circumstances allow one to leave out elements. Prieto starts from the signified, assuming somewhat optimistically that people want to say something before they start to speak. How they say what they want to convey depends on a number of factors, the first and most obvious one being the language that is used. Furthermore context and extralinguistic situation are taken into account. Prieto's originality lies in the way he interprets the notion of extralinguistic circumstances. For him not only the physical environment, but also the personality of the speaker, his assessment of knowledge and personality of his interlocutor and cultural traditions are part of the extralinguistic setting of the linguistic act. So, depending on context and extralinguistic circumstances (or, in North American terminology, linguistic and nonlinguistic context) the same message may take different forms, be expressed by way of a different signifier. As for the interpretation Prieto follows the same method. Interpretation depends on the same factors and will vary according

---

11. B. Pottier, *Linguistique générale* (Paris: Klincksieck, 1974).

12. J. Katz and J. Fodor, "The Structure of a Semantic Theory," *Language* 39:170–216. For a discussion of the article see H. G. Schogt, *Sémantique synchronique: Synonymie, homonymie, polysémie* (Toronto: University of Toronto Press, 1976), pp. 38–39.

to context and extralinguistic circumstances. The same signifier, then, may correspond to different signifieds. Prieto thus builds a framework in which he can accommodate sentence and utterance. He operates as a true Saussurean within the limits of one language and, although the flexible circumstances allow for the incorporation of generation differences, the description is basically synchronic.

Prieto's starting point, the desire to say something, is reminiscent of the transformational semanticists who put the semantic component in the deep structure, contrary to what the interpretative school is used to doing.

Prieto does not go into detail about the relationship between syntax and semantics. The most exhaustive study on that topic is undoubtedly by the Dutch linguist and slavicist Carl Ebeling.[13] Ebeling adheres to the principle of intentionality, including word order and stress, but leaving out sociolinguistic and regional involuntary indices. The intricate system of interrelationships and the abstract form in which the more than two hundred rules of the discovery procedure are presented form, however, a major stumbling block for those who want to apply Ebeling's important theory to solve practical problems.[14]

*

The picture one gets from this rapid and incomplete survey—the Saussurean principle of arbitrariness of the sign and the objections raised by others against that principle were not even mentioned—is not very encouraging for the translator for the following reasons:

1. immanent analysis yields for each language a unique set of components and there is never a one-to-one relationship between components belonging to different languages;

2. no method can guarantee the obtention of an exhaustive inventory (smallest meaningful elements not necessarily formally expressed in the signifier);

3. even within one speech community there are considerable differences of interpretation as well as of formulation (Prieto);

13. C. L. Ebeling, *Syntax and Semantics: A Taxonomic Approach* (Leiden: E. J. Brill, 1978).

14. See X. Mignot's review of Ebeling's book in *Bulletin de la Société de linguistique de Paris* 75(2):49–52.

4. expressive, emotive, and social elements, though very important in the communication process, are often not included in semantic description because they are of doubtful intentionality;

5. being of a synchronic character, analyses are only valid for a certain point in time; being linked to a—sometimes idealized—form of speech of a given speech community, they are also geographically determined;

6. and then, there is the Sapir-Whorf hypothesis to deal a final blow to the translator.

It is interesting to see how those who are not only translators, but also theoreticians of translation, cope with this mass of negative views on the possibility of interlanguage communication and translation, and how they incorporate some elements of semantic theory in their work, while discarding others.

To begin with the point just mentioned: as we said before, no translator accepts the Sapir-Whorf hypothesis in its most extreme form. The mere fact that interlanguage communication and translation have been going on for thousands of years is considered sufficient proof that Sapir and Whorf were wrong. Sometimes universals of language are used as a counterargument. However, apart from some basic principles (André Martinet's double articulation, the conventional character of language, the fact that all languages express actors and actions and can qualify those elements) most universals are of a relative type. If a language expresses A, then it is (almost) certain that it also expresses B. For the translator this sort of universal is not so helpful, because he may have to deal with two languages, one of which has A and B, while the other has only B or even neither B nor A.[15]

So even when the Sapir-Whorf view is rejected, the translator has to deal with differences in structure and of means of expression. Most translation manuals stress the fact that, in spite of differences in value in the immanent analyses, there may be equivalence in actual signification at the level of utterance. In other words, even if the total inventories of semes of the -emic signs are different, the pertinent semes (Heger's *sémème du signe monosémisé*) may be identical. If some semes are lost, they may be added in other parts of the sentence by way of compensation.

15. For a more detailed description of the limitations of universals see Claude Hagège, cited in n. 8.

A special case arises when a distinction that is optional in the source language and compulsory in the target language is not expressed in the source text. Roman Jakobson, who pointed out this problem where the translator has to add information not provided by the source text, believes that the passage from compulsory to not compulsory can always be made, and that lacunae can always be filled by circumscriptions or neologisms.[16] Whether or not, in the case of literature, the aesthetic value of the source text is destroyed by such solutions is a moot point. The translator has to decide whether to maintain the cumbersome element, to replace it, or to leave it out. His choice will often depend on the public he is translating for. His role as encoder in the target language after decoding the source language puts him in the position that Prieto describes, where the precise form of the message is adapted to presumed knowledge and background of the receiver and, one might add, in some instances to his expectations.

Do all these comments form a sound basis, or at least a starting point for a theory of translation? If existing work by linguists is any indication, the answer to this question turns out to be either a qualified "yes" or a qualified "no," depending on the kind of translations one has in mind. For texts where cognitive meaning prevails and formal expression of that meaning has no other function than expressing that meaning, the semantic theories are helpful, and are adequate for describing the double process of encoding and decoding. For literary texts, it is precisely the literariness that falls outside the domain of semantics. That fact reduces the importance of semantics considerably, although it keeps its significance for the denotative element of the text.

So it is not surprising that a linguistic theory of translation of general applicability does not exist. In most instances the authors of theoretical linguistic studies on translation do not give a general theory, but make a series of theoretical observations often in connection with specific types of translation. Sometimes this approach is reflected in the title: *Problèmes théoriques de la traduction;*[17] *Traduire: Théorèmes pour la traduction.*[18] In other cases such as *A Lin-*

---

16. R. Jakobson, "On Linguistic Aspects of Translation," in *On Translation,* ed. Reuben A. Brower (New York: Oxford University Press, 1966 [1959]), pp. 232–39. Reprinted in this volume.

17. G. Mounin, *Problèmes théoriques de la traduction* (Paris: Gallimard, 1963).

18. J.-R. Ladmiral, *Traduire: Théorèmes pour la traduction* (Paris: Payot, 1979).

guistic Theory of Translation,[19] the title does not give away the fact
that the book contains more or less independent chapters dealing
with various problems without tying them together. Nida[20] and
Nida and Taber[21] give a much more coherent and comprehensive
analysis of translation problems, but the authors are able to do so
by limiting themselves to one specific text, the Bible, seen not as a
work of art, but as a text written to educate and instruct, to con-
vince and convert. Therefore some of the choices that the translator
has to make do not cause any problems. They do not maintain what
Antoine Berman calls *l'étrangeté du texte*,[22] but adapt their translations to the system of the target language, and replace idiomatic
expressions and metaphors by more or less equivalent ones or circumscriptions. The clarity of the message prevails: level of speech
and accessibility should be adapted to the audience the message is
intended for, regardless of whatever the level of the original passage
may be.

So with Nida and Taber we are already entering the area of
specific texts and specific audiences (hearers or readers), and have
left behind the general level on which linguistics operates. And that
is precisely the reason why semantic theory and translation of literary texts have so little common ground. Whereas semantic description looks for what is generally valid and systematic, literary
translation requires the analysis of the idiolect of the source text,
not only from a semantic point of view but also with respect to all
the intentional and nonintentional indices that are deemed important in that text. It is obvious that Brian Fitch's megatype, where
more than one language is involved, falls outside what can be described in linguistic terms.[23] There is no general linguistic theory
either for François Péraldi's *r érectil*,[24] for Michael Riffaterre's *purée
septembrale*,[25] or, as Solange Vouvé has so clearly demonstrated, for

19. J. C. Catford, *A Linguistic Theory of Translation* (London: Oxford University
Press, 1965).
20. E. Nida, *Towards a Science of Translation* (Leiden: E. J. Brill, 1964).
21. E. Nida and Ch. Taber, *The Theory and Practice of Translation* (Leiden: E. J.
Brill, 1969).
22. See A. Berman, "La Traduction comme épreuve de l'étranger," *Texte: Revue
de critique et de théorie* 4 (1985).
23. See Brian T. Fitch, "The Status of Self-Translation," *Texte: Revue de critique et
de théorie* 4 (1985).
24. See François Péraldi, "Corps du texte et corps érotique," *Texte: Revue de critique et de théorie* 4 (1985).
25. See Michael Riffaterre, "Transposing Presuppositions: On the Semiotics of
Literary Translation," in this volume.

translating *Finnegans Wake*.[26] There are, of course, other translation theories, but they deal most of the time with specific types of literary texts, and put much emphasis on the aesthetic, the psychological, the subconscious. Very often they take almost for granted the semantic denotative component of translation.

One has to admit that linguists dealing with semantic theory do not have the same preoccupations as literary analysts and translators of literary texts. This does not mean, however, that it is not useful and even important that linguists and literary specialists listen to each other and try to understand each other's point of view.

26. See Solange Vouvé, "Aux limites du langage, aux limites de la traduction: *Finnegans Wake*," *Texte: Revue de critique et de théorie* 4 (1985).

NINETEEN
MICHAEL RIFFATERRE
Transposing Presuppositions on the Semiotics of Literary Translation

Literary translation is different from translation in general for the same reasons that literature is different from nonliterary uses of language. Literature is distinguished from them, first by the semioticization of discursive features (for instance lexical selection is made morphophonemically as well as or more than semantically). Second, by the substitution of semiosis for mimesis (this covers the consequences of the indirection of meaning that is the pivot on which literariness turns). And third, by textuality that integrates semantic components of the verbal sequence (the ones accessible to linear decoding)—a theoretically open-ended sequence—into one closed finite semiotic system, the very existence of which is not manifest until readers become aware of the connection between the text and an intertext. It is only then, in the light of that intertext, that the discrete meanings of the words, phrases, and sentences composing the text assume new functions in its general scheme. Only then do these discrete meanings yield to an overall significance resulting from their implication of or opposition to the intertext.

Literary translation must reflect or imitate these differences. First, it must semioticize forms and sounds like the original, although in a different system (which is easy: equivalent alliterations, for example, demand only a repetition of sounds, but not necessarily the same sounds as in the source text). This aspect, I will lay aside. Second, literary translation must render both meaning and significance. The literary text requires a double decoding, at the levels of both systemic structure and of its component parts. This

Reprinted by permission from *Texte: Revue de critique et de théorie* 4 (1985).

decoding too must be translated in a way that will induce the reader of that translation to perform likewise a double decoding. The signals guiding readers in such a decoding in the original must be reproduced in the translation.

Literary translation must also reproduce those features of the original text that are the traces left by its production. That is, the translation, like the original but not necessarily in the same way, must be visibly derivable from the formal or semantic given that determined that production. Other forms that we empirically sense to be signs of literariness also must be rendered, even though they do not directly or primarily carry meaning: for example, the signs indicating the genre the text belongs to, the signs making obvious that it is artifact rather than a plain representation of reality.

A simple way to rephrase these problems and define their constraints is to express them in terms of presuppositions—the implicit and requisite conditions of the text. A translation presupposes a source text. Within the source, its literary features in turn presuppose, and they function because of what they presuppose. The text's artifice, its being an artifact, presupposes an author. Whether implied or represented, this author is translatable, as style if implied, or as mimesis if represented. Style and topic presuppose a genre. Indirection of meaning (the subordination of word and sentence meanings to textual significance, and that of literality to figurativeness or symbolism) presupposes the sociolect and the intertext, the first because it contains the rule and the norms indirection violated, the second because it represents the substitute authority presupposed by the means used to violate the sociolect's authority.

No literary translation therefore can ever be successful unless it finds equivalencies for these literariness-inducing presuppositions. Some equivalencies however may not be found in the target language at the same level as in the source language: equivalencies to lexical features of the original may have to be found at the syntactical level in translation, and the reverse is true as well.

I will concern myself with these only, and propose the view that in order to palliate the fact that words translated term for term only rarely exhibit the same presuppositions as in the original, the translator must transpose presuppositions.

He will do so either by taking them up directly, or by shifting the burden of presupposing to another segment of the text. In the first instance, the presupposed word is translated, rather than the presupposing one. This, certainly, is the practice of successful translators.

In Milton's translation of Horace (*Odes*, I, V), than which one more perfect is hard to imagine, his only two departures from the source text illustrate the point:

Quis multa gracilis te puer in rosa
perfusus *liquidis* urget *odoribus*
       grato, Pyrrha, *sub antro?*
    cui flauam *religas comam,*

simplex munditiis? heu quotiens fidem
mutatosque deos flebit et aspera
       nigris aequora uentis
    emirabitur insolens,

qui nuc te fruitur credulus aurea,
qui semper uacuam, semper amabilem
       sperat [. . .]

What slender Youth bedew'd *with liquid* odours
Courts thee on Roses in some pleasant Cave,
       Pyrrha *for whom bind'st thou*
    In wreaths thy golden Hair,

Plain in thy neatness; O how oft shall he
On Faith and changed Gods complain: and Seas
       Rough with black winds and storms
    Unwonted shall admire:

Who now enjoyes thee credulous, all gold,
Who alwayes vacant, alwayes amiable
       Hopes thee [. . .]

Milton uses "golden" both for *flauam* "blonde" (l.4) and for *aurea* (l.9), "golden" the first for the hair, the second for the girl. This one rendering of two different words, I believe, is due to the pressure of semantic overdetermination: we have one physical and one moral representation, but the significance stems from the first symbolizing the second. Milton, of course, is aware that *Pyrrha* means "redhead, she of the flaming hair," so that the female protagonist is less a person than an embodiment of deceptively pleasant appearances. It cannot be by chance that "credulous" and "all Gold" should be linked together—Cupid's treachery teaches us that all that glitters is not gold.

The second departure is *bedew'd,* instead of "bathed in scents."
Clearly it transposes to the lover the features of a flower that is
presupposed by *odours,* thus avoiding in the target language the
effeminate connotations that being drenched in perfume would
suggest to the British. The power of implication (the latency of the
repressed *flower*) is such that a modern translator makes a telling
mistake: instead of liquid odours, he writes *liquid flowers.*

Transposing presuppositions will mean either making the implicit explicit or a lateral displacement whereby the semiotic detour,
a figurative turn of phrase for instance, will be replaced by a metonym of the representation that was blocking the way. I am not
suggesting that we replace translation with paraphrase, for the paraphrase would still be linear. Nor am I suggesting a commentary
which would mean separating the linear reading from the intertextual decoding of significance, keeping the first (not literary *per se*)
in the text and relegating the latter (the essence of literariness) to a
footnote. I am suggesting a limited periphrasis built around the
matrix word of which the periphrasis is the transform.

Whereas a normal periphrasis represses a lexeme (which remains present to the reader's mind as a referent, as the latent matrix
of the ambages he is forced to follow) by transforming it into a
syntagm, the translator's periphrasis will retain the lexeme's literal
meaning and will develop the significance, the implications of the
presupposed, in the syntagmatic derivation proper.

Nowhere can we find a better example of the role played by
presuppositions than in the case of specific, detailed literary descriptions. Their function, insofar as they are specific, runs the ga-
mut from creating the illusion of reality to creating an unacceptable
representation. In the former instance, such descriptions make for
verisimilitude. In the latter, the subverted mimesis generates an idiolect which, besides representing (however abnormally), gives its
visible, unique shape to the text's significance. In both cases, however opposed they may seem to be, accuracy in depicting and in
naming is equally essential in establishing the given from which
every pertinent, significant aspect of the source text is derived.
Translators are here faced with the peculiar difficulty of imitating
or duplicating text production in the target language: the translation of that part of the original that is derivative, which is to say,
generated from the given by a series of variants (these being literally translations of synonym into synonym, albeit within one language, as I pointed out earlier), must be as derivative as it is in the

original. Otherwise the unity of the text, its function as a semiotic agent of transformation, as one unit of significance, will be lost. The difficulty is not just that the translator must find a generator with a productivity equal to that of the original, but that he must define precisely what is at work in the original and which semes of the matrix word are activated. My point is that it is not the visible, explicit features of the matrix that make it functional, that makes it the motor of text production, the starting point of rhetorical amplification, but its presuppositions. The pressure that these bring to bear on the text's future development results from their being repressed by the very act of naming the word that refers to them, thus placing the burden of imagining them on the reader. The derivation from this starting point will be constituted by that which the matrix's explicit features entail, but these entailments themselves are none other than the lexical and syntactical surfacing of the repressed presuppositions.

Thus is generated a celebrated tableau of Latin poetry: the Ocean nymphs in the opening scene of Catullus's poem 64, the "Epithalamion of Peleus and Thetis," the parents of Achilles. The entire main stream of epic poetry flows symbolically from Thetis' bosom, leaving no doubt that the poem's thrust is to be a tale of beginnings, to be a type of splendid after-the-fact preface to Homer, the *Oresteia* and Virgil. Every detail thus is charged with the symbolism of the world of myths that the reader will be able retrospectively to connect with it.

This river of images rises from the very first scene, in which the Argonauts sailing to the conquest of the Golden Fleece are sighted by Nereids. One of them spots Peleus, falls in love with him and thus Achilles will be born.

The motif itself includes a double transgression. First, the symbolic and dramatic crossing of a frontier: a goddess marries a mortal. Then, a creature from the sea, she has to overcome yet another barrier, which separates the submarine world from the human, the fantastic from the natural. The power of this miracle (and its demonstration that Eros conquers all) can be verified in modern tales, since it still endures, from the mermaid of Hans Christian Andersen to Lois Lemaris, the siren-like temptress in *Superman,* to the amphibious maiden of the 1984 movie, *Splash.* From the depths, therefore, rise the Nereids, among them Thetis: "the ship's ram had hardly furrowed the windy plains, the waves torn open by the oars were just turning white with foam, when the Nereids emerged from the boiling abyss to marvel at this monster." And now the detail that I think begets the rest:

> hac, illa atqae alia uiderunt luce marinas
> mortales oculis nudato corpore Nymphas
> nutricum tenus extantis e gurgite cano (16–8)

[on that day, on the next and then once more, mortal eyes were able to see the sea Nymphs, standing out from the white abyss with their bodies exposed as far as the breasts][1]

No sailor could resist such an impudent come-on: "Then is Peleus said to have caught fire with love of Thetis, then did Thetis not disdain mortal espousals." This is the F. W. Cornish translation (Loeb Classical Library). Its lofty tone makes up for the graphic depiction of scenes of exhibitionism, for a glimpse at the power of raw sex, from which so many woes issue: Helen willingly ravished, and the fall of Troy, Agamemnon felled by Clytemnestra's axe and the Eumenides unleashed, Dido seduced and the rise of Rome and Carthage's ruin, etc. All this derives ultimately from the one detail translators refuse to come to terms with: the nymphs are shown upthrust above the waves baring their bodies naked as far as the breasts—"*nutricum tenus.*"

Every translation I have seen is inaccurate even when it dares to be specific. Lefevere: "as far as the nipples," and on second thought, "as far as the breasts," treading lightly as it were.[2] Burton averts his gaze and concentrates on the missing bra: "exposed bodies denuded of raiment Bare to the breast." Hart-Davies resorts to neutral commonplaces of ekphrasis: "fair naked forms with white breasts glistening." Sisson, on the contrary, more perceptive or cynical, sees the nymphs as women natives spotting Captain Cook's sailors, and he calls a spade a spade: "naked sea-nymphs sticking out of the water showing their tits." Despite, or rather because of the vulgarity of "sticking out" and of "tits," Sisson's female flashers do suggest accurately the frenzy of mutual hot pursuit, in which Peleus's lust matches his future bride's. But Sisson's explicitness and the others' evasions equally miss the other implications of Thetis's

---

1. From now on translations are mine unless otherwise indicated.
2. André Lefevere's *Translating Poetry* (Assen: Van Gorcum, 1975) conveniently lists the English versions discussed here (cf. pp. 40, 109, 115–16).

exhibition, of "nutricum tenus," for it is, I think, this phrase that gives the whole scene its significance.

Tenus, the preposition, *up to* or indifferently *down to,* in such a context is the very mechanism of sexual implication. It does not matter whether undressing starts from the top or from below the waist, unbuttoned blouses or lifted skirts, in any erotic text the indication of a limit to the baring of flesh is a presupposition of something more to come and more to expose. This is the suspense of striptease itself, the first step of voyeurism, the anticipation of desire. Furthermore, in the semiotic system of the body, the feminine breast is not bare, it is not shining forth erogenous unless the nipples stand out. Passing this point is the difference between a mere *décolleté,* however promising the cleavage may appear, and aggressive desire.

But what is it that you see? The word used by Catullus to speak of desirable breasts, of erotic symbols, is, to say the least, peculiar. So peculiar that not a single translator heeds it. Instead of speaking of breasts, or of nipples as in an equally hot passage fifty lines below (Ariadne panting for Theseus), Catullus uses *nutrices,* and *nutrix* emphatically and precisely designates she who suckles an infant, a *nurse,* not a synecdoche for *nurse,* not a milk-filled breast, but the whole person. These mermaids are naked to their nurses inclusive. It would be hard to find a worse letdown, at least in most Western sociolects, for they tend to separate sex from motherhood, and most readers therefore keep them apart in their fantasies. Probably also for Catullus's contemporaries, since this seems to be a once-only boldness of expression, and other literary uses of the word, figurative or literal, refer to the whole nurse from head to foot, and a professional one to boot. Translators seem to assume that by identifying *nutrices* as a metonymy, they are free to ignore it, since a literal translation would be grotesque, and free to substitute the generic word, *breast,* to which the metonym refers indirectly. The trouble is, indirection is precisely what points to the presupposition. It does so the more powerfully because *nutrix* is so inseparable from a vast descriptive system of words all very visibly its cognates (*nutricatus, nutricium,* breast feeding and also the nurse's fee, *nutricula,* the little mother etc. down the paradigm of compounds of *nutrio* "to feed"). So nothing can blunt the oxymoron, or get us acclimatized to the audacity of the image.

The whole weight of presupposition is that this lusting sea-goddess will not just be a wife to the hero, a development that is never more than anecdotal in mythology, but a mother. She therefore will be the source for one of those genealogies of heroes that *are* significant in mythology. They are semiotic rather than narrative, for they correspond to the impulse in mythopoesis to multiply characters that are exemplary in some way. They become the means of revealing the continued agency of Fate. Thetis will generate a line of terrifying goddesses, demi-goddesses and illustrious women sinners whose sexuality will change the face of the world, from generation to generation, and destroy empires. It cannot be by chance that towards the end of the epithalamium, on the morning after the wedding night, the task of verifying that the bride is no longer a virgin should be entrusted to her nurse (the same word *nutrix* is used again, now literally), nor is it by chance that the poem, on the whole cheerful and festive, should end on a pessimistic tableau of mankind as imperial Rome has corrupted it. It cannot be by chance that at the clausula, unexpectedly and seemingly gratuitously, we should have the image of an incestuous mother "mater substernens se impia gnato," this could not be more graphic—the mother lying supine under the body of the son of her womb.

There is a passage in Trollope (*The Duke's Children,* chap. 72) where not dissimilar anxieties are made explicit, evidently because a narrative always deploys what poetry implies, and because psychological analysis, that fiction favours, bare the character's inmost fears. This passage suggests that I am not reading too much into Catullus's two words:

> But this girl, this American girl, was to be the mother and grandmother of future Dukes of Omnium,—the ancestress it was to be hoped, of all future Dukes of Omnium! By what she might be, by what she might have in her of mental fibre, of high or low quality, of true or untrue womanliness, were to be fashioned those who in days to come might be amongst the strongest and most faithful bulwarks of the constitution.

Presupposition thus organizes the whole poem, regulating a derivation that pervades everything and the end of which dictates the clausula and affirms textuality. It seems to me that no translation that would be true can neglect it, and that it is revealing that translators should have recoiled from such a total experience. It is precisely the locus of originality, the source of all poetic power in a text that otherwise would be a mere epyllion, a graceful exercise on a literary genre. The poem is much more than that because a presupposition has been substituted for the only one the sociolect proposed as a metonym of sexuality—the ultimate ungrammaticality triggers the semiosis. Little wonder a literal translation should here be twice unbearable, first because the image is ludicrous, and second because the only way to be blind to its ridicule is to subordinate it to an even more troubling semiosis—that sex is the hereditary form of fate. Little wonder; but it is only more imperative that such a translation should be attempted: the only way, I suppose, would be a periphrasis suggesting that these jutting breasts are also a promise or threat of a harvest of heroes.

Some may still regard periphrasis as a translator's cop-out, a facile way out of a difficulty. No doubt a more elegant solution would be to maintain in the target language an implicitation matching the original's clever pointing to the presupposed. But such striving must be in vain, and indeed lead to the loss of the original's connotation, if the presupposed is intertextual. In such instances, the translator cannot hope to avoid providing an explicit equivalent, within the text, of what the original merely alluded to by its implicit reference to an intertext. In most cases it is not possible to find a comparable intertext in the target language, in which the literary canon is bound to be totally different from that in which the original text is immersed.

Take the following lines from a Maurice Fombeure poem entitled "Présence des Automnes" ("Presence of the Fall Season," or better, "Presence of Autumns") in which the plural refers to a recurrence, the natural cycle that enables us in the Fall to remember other autumns as well and experience anew their melancholy:

Le brouillard noie les cathédrales
[. . .]
Je songe aux brumes septembrales
Dessus les vignes de chez nous.

Fog is drowning the cathedrals
[. . .]
I dream of the mists of the vintage-season
Upon our village's vineyards.

One may wonder why I do not simply say "September mist" and why I invent a village instead of "the vineyards back home." Indeed, had I been more timid, the more obvious version I have just proposed as an alternative would still have translated accurately the surface of the text or its linearity. A literary text, however, cannot be cut off from its intertext, and a literary reading of it in an intertextual reading. An intertextual overdetermination takes charge, eliminating any chance that the adjective *septembre* might only refer to September, or that *chez nous* might only refer to home, that plain referentiality be a defensible interpretation. Intertextual overdetermination links together two representations of homely values: *chez nous*, "at home" or "back home" ("back home" is preferable because the first line, and the intervening lines make it clear that the speaker is in Paris and therefore harks back to the country, that is, to a nostalgic topos); *chez nous* is on a par with the preposition *dessus*, "upon". The reader expects *sur*.

"Expects" or rather "expected" would be more accurate, for the reader discovers a frustrated expectation *a posteriori*, after the text has given him a turn of phrase that in retrospect he might have expressed otherwise or more naturally. More precisely still, since the reader is unlikely to stop and ponder, what occurs is that he notices the relative ungrammaticality of *dessus*, of an adverb used where a preposition should be, and he therefore recognises it as the equivalent of *sur (sur les vignes)*, which is what one would naturally say. The reader intuitively performs this translation within his own language (such "translations" are our mode of perception of stylistic registers, of figurative discourse, and generally, of textual idiolects). He performs also an interpretation, because *dessus* used as a preposition is an archaism, and one known to him from folk songs. *Dessus* and *chez nous* connote traditional, quaint values, the values of life in the provinces, sheltered from the corrupt influence of the big city. The proper strategy for the translation is to shift the homely, comfortable connotations of the archaic preposition to "back home," and to make "back home" the village of our innocence, like Proust's Combray, the place where grandparents waited for the young ones raised in the city to come back to a bath of purity, etc., etc. I am thus transposing the presuppositions of an obsolete grammatical connective to a location symbolic of one's youth or roots. This harking back to an effective past is confirmed by the appearance in the next stanza of a shepherd wrapped in his cape—a character representing rustic simplicity, for the name of his cape or great-coat, *houppelande*, is another archaism and one that is used virtually only for folklore tableaux. It is perceived as designating metonymically a rustic character, whose silhouette merely translates a favourable, eulogistic idea of the past into a *human being* code.

What about *septembrale*? The adjective is not just an adjective corresponding to the noun *septembre*. For one thing, no other month-name has ever produced an adjective in French, so that *septembral* stands out as an exception, one that its ending underscores. No French reader is likely to pass it by without noticing it. Most will recognize it for what it is, that is, a quotation from Rabelais, who apparently coined the word. It is therefore a purely conventional sign, an index pointing to artificiality as a component of literariness, much more than just a word referring to a season of the year. Nor is this all. Rabelais uses it only once, in connection with the word *purée*, "a mash": *purée septembrale*. The two words are so inseparable that they function as a playful compound, a funny periphrasis for *wine* (*purée* then is the stuff that has been crushed and pressed in the wine press, a synecdoche for the wine that it will produce after fermenting). The periphrasis is the better known because it is a euphemism, and a playful one used by one of Rabelais' high-living monks to speak of a drunk while seeming to mince words, with a mock respect for propriety: he is drunk not because he drank too much, but because he sniffed the fragrance of a certain delicious purée. The fortune of the quotation has been enormous, since in any society overindulgence is the occasion for euphemism.

To summarize, Fombeure is using the code of the wine harvest to speak of the Fall, as Keats had used the code of winnowing to describe the hair of his allegorical Autumn lifted by the breeze.

In making my decision, as a translator, to spell out the wine harvest, to extract it from the adjective, I may still appear to read too much into Rabelais' coinage. Why could Fombeure not borrow a valorized and unique adjective, cleanse it from its winery connotations, and fit it to a new, serious purpose? This nonce-word would then be only a literary word, and presuppose a literary, exemplary autumn, a theme, with its attendant precise imagistic connotations, and its precise melancholy mood, rather than a season that would have to be for all men? Why can I not accept an author's choice to separate *septembrale* from its *purée*?

My first answer is that this September fog spreads over vineyards. This, however, would not suffice, and the text needed stronger associations to produce its final, fully motivated form that we will not be tempted to tamper with. Overdetermination does the trick, and it is provided here by the echo from another verbal joke. The stanza evokes an autumn of fog and mist. It functions as a description first of all because it unfolds a vaporous paradigm that continues in the next stanza with *le ciel fumeux,* "a sky as if smoky." And it so happens that there exists a word jokingly used to designate a thick fog, a borrowing from the colloquial English *peasouper,* a borrowing as intertextual and as conspicuous as the one from Rabelais. This word is *purée* in *purée de pois,* "pea soup." *Septembrale* as well as *brouillard* presuppose the same noun, the relatively rare word *purée*—rare, that is, in literature, unless it is used as a quotation and a humorous device. *Purée,* the silent, repressed link, steeps in Gallic tradition the image of a nostalgic autumn. *Purée,* equally pertinent to "fog," to the "wine-harvest," and to Gallic wit, represents now not just a presupposition but an interpretant, that links the metonyms, fog, vines, countryside, with the kernel word of the title—Autumn—an interpretant that replaces a reference from words to things with the presuppositions of an object that is itself a system of signs. Again, as with Keats, the season is represented through its atmospheric features and its seasonal business.

Since all this is achieved through the twist of an intertextuality that is not available in the target language, the only solution is to make the presupposed tableau explicit and complete, which I did.

Fombeure's next stanza corroborates this interpretation. It goes on representing autumn by further developing the paradigm of a metonym of it. This time, the metonym is the southward flight of migratory birds: the geese are leaving. Here again the text proposes the image indirectly, through an intertext, but one organized by virtue of a structure so generally known and whose variants are so widespread in Western culture that the translator will have no trouble finding equivalents.

Dans le ciel fumeux et léger
Crient les migrateurs isocèles.

[Through a sky of light smoke the isosceles migrators go trumpeting. *Or,* Through the light smoky sky the call is heard of the isosceles migrators.]

I am afraid that my variation will not prevent "isosceles" from sounding contrived. And yet I cannot and must not avoid it. It has the power of catachresis, turning as it does periphrastically around the familiar motif of the geese flying in triangle. It is only with the last lines that the image is retranslated into its ordinary version— repeated, but with a variation, which device elegantly serves as a clausula. The clausula makes it clear that the whole poem is centred on the nostalgia for an elsewhere. This is the theme for the whole collection the title of which (*À dos d'oiseau* [Riding on bird-back]) is now referred to by the clausula.

At this point, Fombeure's choice of a geometrical technicism, so strikingly at odds with the rustic, colloquial, homely context, appears compelling. For "isosceles" is now identified with two pre-suppositions so widely exemplified that they effortlessly transcend linguistic borders. What the image presupposes here is first that earthbound observers can tell migratory birds from their flying in triangle formation (a spectacle that in turn entails or completes the conventional tableau of autumn). Second, the flight formation it-self presupposes an aesthetic and ethical view of nature. In this view, an ordinary, natural spectacle is perceived and celebrated as an extraordinary, natural wonder. The presupposition is that these birds have by instinct an ideal navigation system. Hence an anthropomorphic praise of their natural ingenuity: they are to be admired insofar as they observe a regularity that should be the privilege of man. These birds twice qualify as a literary motif: because they stand for nostalgia, and because they act in a human manner. This causes a structural transformation whereby the theme of *animals equating man* is interpreted as *animals superior to man*. This trans-formation we recognize as subsidiary to an even more generally applicable structure, the paradoxical equation *natural is preterna-tural,* which is also basic to didactic poetry.

This being a fundamental structure of the imagination, trans-lation will raise no difficulty. To be sure "isosceles migrators" may always look artificial in English, but if so it remains faithful to the artifice of the French original. In both languages, however, this artifice is balanced, corrected, and given a perverse appropriateness by the fact that a geometrical term for birds in the air happens to be also a variation on spatial geometry, *géométrie dans l'espace.*

Textual overdetermination enabling readers to interpret (that is, to translate into simpler or more accepted phraseology) obscure or unusual images within their own language, and to find legiti-macy in bizarre metaphors, is the translator's surest guide. Diffi-cult, almost untranslatable passages bespeak the need for a gloss.

Not a gloss in the guise of a Nabokovian footnote *à la* Pnin, but a periphrasis. The near untranslatable simply demands that we replace the lexeme-for-lexeme substitution with a syntagm-for-lexeme substitution.

Presupposition lends itself naturally to this strategy, since presupposing requires a syntagm anyway. Descriptive systems stand by ready to supply such syntagms. Already with the source language, presupposition is actualized just as naturally in the mind of the reader as it is in the text, a parallel development made possible by the common model of the descriptive system. The translator's solution therefore should be to actualize the relevant parts of a system.

Perhaps the simplest way to state the difference between literary and non-literary translation is to say that the latter translates what is in the text, whereas the former must translate what the text only implies.

TWENTY
Jacques Derrida
From Des Tours de Babel
Translated by Joseph F. Graham

"Babel": first a proper name, granted. But when we say "Babel" today, do we know what we are naming? Do we know whom? If we consider the sur-vival of a text that is a legacy, the narrative or the myth of the tower of Babel, it does not constitute just one figure among others. Telling at least of the inadequation of one tongue to another, of one place in the encyclopedia to another, of language to itself and to meaning, and so forth, it also tells of the need for figuration, for myth, for tropes, for twists and turns, for translation inadequate to compensate for that which multiplicity denies us. In this sense it would be the myth of the origin of myth, the metaphor of metaphor, the narrative of narrative, the translation of translation, and so on. It would not be the only structure hollowing itself out like that, but it would do so in its own way (itself *almost* untranslatable, like a proper name), and its idiom would have to be saved.

The "tower of Babel" does not merely figure the irreducible multiplicity of tongues; it exhibits an incompletion, the impossibility of finishing, of totalizing, of saturating, of completing something on the order of edification, architectural construction, system and architectonics. What the multiplicity of idioms actually limits is not only a "true" translation, a transparent and adequate inter-expression, it is also a structural order, a coherence of construct. There is then (let us translate) something like an internal limit to formalization, an incompleteness of the constructure. It would be

Reprinted from Jacques Derrida, "Des Tours de Babel," translated by Joseph F. Graham, in *Difference in Translation,* edited by Joseph F. Graham. Copyright © 1985 by Cornell University. Used by permission of the publisher, Cornell University Press.

easy and up to a certain point justified to see there the translation of a system in deconstruction.

One should never pass over in silence the question of the tongue in which the question of the tongue is raised and into which a discourse on translation is translated.

First: in what tongue was the tower of Babel constructed and deconstructed? In a tongue within which the proper name of Babel could also, by confusion, be translated by "confusion." The proper name Babel, as a proper name, should remain untranslatable, but, by a kind of associative confusion that a unique tongue rendered possible, one thought it translated in that very tongue, by a common noun signifying what *we* translate as confusion. Voltaire showed his astonishment in his *Dictionnaire philosophique,* at the Babel article:

> I do not know why it is said in *Genesis* that Babel signifies confusion, for *Ba* signifies father in the Oriental tongues, and *Bel* signifies God; Babel signifies the city of God, the holy city. The Ancients gave this name to all their capitals. But it is incontestable that Babel means confusion, either because the architects were confounded after having raised their work up to eighty-one thousand Jewish feet, or because the tongues were then confounded; and it is obviously from that time on that the Germans no longer understand the Chinese; for it is clear, according to the scholar Bochart, that Chinese is originally the same tongue as High German.

The calm irony of Voltaire means that Babel means: it is not only a proper name, the reference of a pure signifier to a single being—and for this reason untranslatable—but a common noun related to the generality of a meaning. This common noun means, and means not only confusion, even though "confusion" has at least two meanings, as Voltaire is aware, the confusion of tongues, but also the state of confusion in which the architects find themselves with the structure interrupted, so that a certain confusion has already begun to affect the two meanings of the word "confusion." The signification of "confusion" is confused, at least double. But Voltaire suggests something else again: Babel means not only confusion in the double sense of the word, but also the name of the father, more precisely and more commonly, the name of God as name of father. The city would bear the name of God the father and of the father of the city that is called confusion. God, the God, would have marked with his patronym a communal space, that city where understanding is no longer possible. And understanding is no longer possible when there are only proper names, and understanding is no longer possible when there are no longer proper names. In giving his name, a name of his choice, in giving all names, the father would be at the origin of language, and that power would belong by right to God the father. And the name of God the father would be the name of that origin of tongues. But it is also that God who, in the action of his anger (like the God of Böhme or of Hegel, he who leaves himself, determines himself in his finitude and thus produces history), annuls the gift of tongues, or at least embroils it, sows confusion among his sons, and poisons the present (*Gift*-gift). This is also the origin of tongues, of the multiplicity of idioms, of what in other words are usually called mother tongues. For this entire history deploys filiations, generations and genealogies: all Semitic. Before the deconstruction of Babel, the great Semitic family was establishing its empire, which it wanted universal, and its tongue, which it also attempts to impose on the universe. The moment of this project immediately precedes the deconstruction of the tower. I cite two French translations. The first translator stays away from what one would want to call "literality," in other words, from the Hebrew figure of speech for "tongue," where the second, more concerned about literality (metaphoric, or rather metonymic), says "lip," since in Hebrew "lip" designates what we call, in another metonymy, "tongue." One will have to say multiplicity of lips and not of tongues to name the Babelian confusion. The first translator, then, Louis Segond, author of the Segond Bible, published in 1910, writes this:

> Those are the sons of Sem, according to their families, their tongues, their countries, their nations. Such are the families of the sons of Noah, according to their generations, their nations. And it is from them that emerged the nations which spread over the earth after the flood. All the earth had a single tongue and the same words. As they had left the origin they found a plain in the country of Schinear, and they dwelt there. They said to one another: Come! Let us make bricks, and bake them in the fire. And brick served them as stone, and tar served as cement. Again they said: Come! Let us build ourselves a city and a tower whose summit touches the heavens, and let us make ourselves a name, so that we not be scattered over the face of all the earth.

I do not know just how to interpret this allusion to the substitution

or the transmutation of materials, brick becoming stone and tar
serving as mortar. That already resembles a translation, a translation of translation. But let us leave it and substitute a second translation for the first. It is that of Chouraqui. It is recent and wants to
be more literal, almost verbum pro verbo, as Cicero said should
not be done in one of those first recommendations to the translator
which can be read in his *Libellus de Optimo Genera Oratorum*. Here
it is:

> Here are the sons of Shem
> for their clans, for their tongues,
> in their lands, for their peoples.
> Here are the clans of the sons of Noah for their exploits,
> in their peoples:
> from the latter divide the peoples on earth, after the flood.
>
> And it is all the earth: a single lip, one speech.
> And it is at their departure from the Orient: they find a canyon,
> in the land of Shine'ar.
> They settle there.
> They say, each to his like:
> "Come, let us brick some bricks.
>
> Let us fire them in the fire."
> The brick becomes for them stone, the tar, mortar.
> They say:
> "Come, let us build ourselves a city and a tower.
> Its head: in the heavens.
> Let us make ourselves a name,
> that we not be scattered over the face of all the earth."

What happens to them? In other words, for what does God
punish them in giving his name, or rather, since he gives it to nothing and to no one, in proclaiming his name, the proper name of
"confusion" which will be his mark and his seal? Does he punish
them for having wanted to build as high as the heavens? For having
wanted to accede to the highest, up to the Most High? Perhaps for
that too, no doubt, but incontestably for having wanted thus to
make a name for themselves, to give themselves the name, to construct for and by themselves their own name, to gather themselves
there ("that we no longer be scattered"), as in the unity of a place
which is at once a tongue and a tower, the one as well as the other,
the one as the other. He punishes them for having thus wanted to

assure themselves, by themselves, a unique and universal genealogy. For the text of Genesis proceeds immediately, as if it were all a matter of the same design: raising a tower, constructing a city, making a name for oneself in a universal tongue which would also be an idiom, and gathering a filiation:

> They say:
> "Come, let us build ourselves a city and a tower.
> Its head: in the heavens.
> Let us make ourselves a name,
> that we not be scattered over the face of all the earth."
>
> YHWH descends to see the city and the tower
> that the sons of man have built.
> YHWH says:
> "Yes! A single people, a single lip for all:
> that is what they begin to do! . . .
> Come! Let us descend! Let us confound their lips,
> man will no longer understand the lip of his neighbor."

Then he disseminates the Sem, and dissemination is here deconstruction:

> YHWH disperses them from here over the face of all the earth.
> They cease to build the city.
> Over which he proclaims his name: Bavel, Confusion,
> for there, YHWH confounds the lip of all the earth,
> and from there YHWH disperses them over the face of all the earth.

Can we not, then, speak of God's jealousy? Out of resentment against that unique name and lip of men, he imposes his name, his name of father; and with this violent imposition he opens the deconstruction of the tower, as of the universal language; he scatters the genealogical filiation. He breaks the lineage. He *at the same time* imposes and forbids translation. He imposes it and forbids it, constrains, but as if to failure, the children who henceforth *will bear* his name, the name that *he* gives to the city. It is from a proper name of God, come from God, descended from God or from the father (and it is indeed said that YHWH, an unpronounceable name, *descends* toward the tower) and by him that tongues are scattered, confounded or multiplied, according to a descendance that in its very dispersion remains sealed by the only name that will have been the strongest, by the only idiom that will have triumphed. Now, this idiom bears within itself the mark of confusion, it improperly means the improper, to wit: Bavel, confusion. Translation then becomes necessary and impossible, like the effect of a struggle for the appropriation of the name, necessary and forbidden in the interval between two absolutely proper names. And the proper name of God (given by God) is divided enough in the tongue, already, to signify also, confusedly, "confusion." And the war that he declares has first raged within his name: divided, bifid, ambivalent, polysemic: God deconstructing. "And he war," one reads in *Finnegans Wake*, and we could follow this whole story from the side of Shem and Shaun. The "he war" does not only, in this place, tie together an incalculable number of phonic and semantic threads, in the immediate context and throughout this Babelian book; it says the declaration of war (in English) of the One who says I am the one who am, and who thus was *(war)*; it renders itself untranslatable in its very performance, *at least in the fact* that it is enunciated in more than one language at a time, at least English and German. If even an infinite translation exhausted its semantic stock, it would still translate into *one* language and would lose the multiplicity of "he war." Let us leave for another time a less hastily interrupted reading of this "he war," and let us note one of the limits of theories of translation: all too often they treat the passing from one language to another and do not sufficiently consider the possibility for languages to be implicated *more than two* in a text. How is a text written in several languages at a time to be translated? How is the effect of plurality to be "rendered"? And what of translating with several languages at a time, will that be called translating?

Babel: today we take it as a proper name. Indeed, but the proper name of what and of whom? At times that of a narrative text recounting a story (mythical, symbolic, allegorical; it matters little for the moment), a story in which the proper name, which is then no longer the title of the narrative, names a tower or a city but a tower or a city that receives its name from an event during which YHWH "proclaims his name." Now, this proper name, which already names at least three times and three different things, also has, this is the whole point, as proper name the function of a common noun. This story recounts, among other things, the origin of the confusion of tongues, the irreducible multiplicity of idioms, the necessary and impossible task of translation, its necessity *as* impossibility. Now, in general one pays little attention to this fact: it is in translation that we most often read this narrative. And in this translation, the proper name retains a singular destiny, since it is not translated in its appearance as proper name. Now, a proper name as such remains forever untranslatable, a fact that may lead one to conclude that it does not strictly belong, for the same reason as the other words, to the language, to the system of the language, be it translated or translating. And yet "Babel," an event in a single tongue, the one in which it appears so as to form a "text," also has a common meaning, a conceptual generality. That it be by way of a pun or a confused association matters little: "Babel" could be understood in one language as meaning "confusion." And from then on, just as Babel is at once proper name and common noun, confusion also becomes proper name and common noun, the one as the homonym of the other, the synonym as well, but not the equivalent, because there could be no question of confusing them in their value. It has for the translator no satisfactory solution. Recourse to apposition and capitalization ("Over which he proclaims his name: Bavel, Confusion") is not translating from one tongue into another. It comments, explains, paraphrases, but does not translate. At best it reproduces approximately and by dividing the equivocation into two words there where confusion gathered in potential, in all its potential, in the internal translation, if one can say that, which works the word in the so-called original tongue. For in the very tongue of the original narrative there is a translation, a sort of transfer, that gives immediately (by some confusion) the semantic equivalent of the proper name which, by itself, as a pure proper name, it would not have. As a matter of fact, this intralinguistic translation operates immediately; it is not even an operation in the strict sense. Nevertheless, someone who speaks the language of Genesis could be attentive to the effect of the proper name in effacing the conceptual equivalent (like *pierre* [rock] in *Pierre* [Peter], and these are two absolutely heterogeneous values or functions); one would then be tempted to say *first* that a proper name, in the proper sense, does not properly belong to the language; it does not belong there, *although and because* its call makes the language possible (what would a language be without the possibility of calling by a proper name?); consequently it can properly inscribe itself in a language only by allowing itself to be translated therein, in other words, *interpreted* by its semantic equivalent: from this moment it can no longer be taken as proper name. The noun *pierre* belongs to the French language, and its translation into a foreign language should in principle transport its meaning. This is not the case with *Pierre,* whose inclusion in the French language is not assured and is in any case not of the same type. "Peter" in this sense is not a *translation* of *Pierre,* any more than *Londres* is a translation of "London," and so forth. And *second,* anyone whose so-called mother tongue was the tongue of Genesis could indeed understand Babel as "confusion"; that person then effects a *confused* translation of the proper name by its common equivalent without having need for another word. It is as if there were two words there, two homonyms one of which has the value of proper name and the other that of common noun: between the two, a translation which one can evaluate quite diversely. Does it belong to the kind that Jakobson calls intralingual translation or rewording? I do not think so: "rewording" concerns the relations of transformation between common nouns and ordinary phrases. The essay *On Translation* (1959) distinguishes three forms of translation. *Intralingual* translation interprets linguistic signs by means of other signs of the *same* language. This obviously presupposes that one can know in the final analysis how to determine rigorously the unity and identity of a language, the decidable form of its limits. There would then be what Jakobson neatly calls translation "proper," *interlingual* translation, which interprets linguistic signs by means of some other language—this appeals to the same presupposition as intralingual translation. Finally there would be intersemiotic translation or transmutation, which interprets linguistic signs by means of systems of nonlinguistic signs. For the two forms of translation which would not be translations "proper," Jakobson proposes a definitional equivalent and another word. The first he translates, so to speak, by another word: intralingual translation or *rewording.* The third likewise: *intersemiotic* translation or *transmutation.* In these two cases, the translation of "translation" is a definitional interpretation. But in the case of translation "proper," translation in the ordinary sense, interlinguistic and post-Babelian, Jakobson does not translate; he repeats the same word: "interlingual translation or translation proper." He supposes that it is not necessary to translate; everyone understands what that means because everyone has experienced it, everyone is expected to know what is a language, the relation of one language to another and especially identity or difference in fact of language. If there is a transparency that Babel would not have impaired, this is surely it, the experience of the multiplicity of tongues and the "proper" sense of the word "translation." In relation to this word, when it is a question of translation "proper," the other uses of the word "translation" would be in a position of intralingual and inadequate translation, like metaphors, in short, like twists or turns of translation in the proper sense. There would thus be a translation in the proper sense and a translation in the figurative sense. And in order to translate the one into the other, within the same tongue or from one tongue to another, in the figurative or in the proper sense, one would engage upon a course that would quickly reveal how this reassuring tripartition can be problematic. Very quickly: at the very moment when pronouncing "Babel" we sense the impossibility of deciding whether this name belongs, properly and simply, to *one* tongue. And it matters that this undecidability is at work in a struggle for the proper name within a scene of genealogical indebtedness. In seeking to "make a name for themselves," to found at the same time a universal tongue and a unique genealogy, the Semites want to bring the world to reason, and this reason can signify simultaneously a colonial violence (since they would thus universalize their idiom) and a peaceful transparency of the human community. Inversely, when God imposes and opposes his name, he ruptures the rational transparency but interrupts also the colonial violence or the linguistic imperialism. He destines them to translation, he subjects them to the law of a translation both necessary and impossible; in a stroke with his translatable-untranslatable name he delivers a universal reason (it will no longer be subject to the rule of a particular nation), but he simultaneously limits its very universality: forbidden transparency, impossible univocity. Translation becomes law, duty, and debt, but the debt one can no longer discharge. Such insolvency is found marked in the very name of Babel: which at once translates and does not translate itself, belongs without belonging to a language and indebts itself to itself for an insolvent debt, to itself as if other. Such would be the Babelian performance.

This singular example, at once archetypical and allegorical, could serve as an introduction to all the so-called theoretical problems of translation. But no theorization, inasmuch as it is produced in a language, will be able to dominate the Babelian performance.

∗

. . . I do not wish only or essentially to reduce my role to that of a passer or passerby. Nothing is more serious than a translation. I rather wished to mark the fact that every translator is in a position to speak *about* translation, in a place which is more than any not second or secondary. For if the structure of the original is marked by the requirement to be translated, it is that in laying down the law the original begins by indebting itself *as well* with regard to the translator. The original is the first debtor, the first petitioner; it begins by lacking and by pleading for translation. This demand is not only on the side of the constructors of the tower who want to make a name for themselves and to found a universal tongue translating itself by itself; it also constrains the deconstructor of the tower: in giving his name, God also appealed to translation, not only between the tongues that had suddenly become multiple and confused, but first *of his name,* of the name he had proclaimed, given, and which should be translated as confusion to be understood, hence to let it be understood that it is difficult to translate and so to understand. At the moment when he imposes and opposes his law to that of the tribe, he is also a petitioner for translation. He is also indebted. He has not finished pleading for the translation of his name even though he forbids it. For Babel is untranslatable. God weeps over his name. His text is the most sacred, the most poetic, the most originary, since he creates a name and gives it to himself, but he is left no less destitute in his force and even in his wealth; he pleads for a translator. . . .

TWENTY–ONE

HANS ERICH NOSSACK
Translating and Being Translated
Translated by Sharon Sloan

It is a great honor for me as an amateur to be allowed to speak to experts, for me as a writer to speak to translators. In order to justify choosing me as a keynote speaker, the organizers of this conference could use the argument that every writer is in fact a translator, since his occupation is to transfer facts, experiences, thoughts into another reality—that of language. A nice argument, and certainly accurate, but one that does not concern us here. What concerns us at this conference is limited to translation from language to language, or rather the costume change of a given character on a stage—and the stage in this case is reality.

I call myself a nonspecialist, although it so happens that I have translated a few books from English into German and am very proud of two of them, actually prouder of them than I am of the books I have written myself. I translated these books, however, not as a translator but as someone who loved them. And if I should ever translate again, it would be for the same reason. At the time it just seemed more important to me to translate a foreign book than to write one myself. My identification with this particular book was so complete, that I imagined myself the only person capable of translating it properly. Or to put it another way, perhaps a bit more emphatically: I had heard another's voice and was convinced that I could never say what he said as well as he did—at most it would have led to an unnecessary repetition.

This is also an interesting phenomenon, and one that both lit-

From a speech, "Übersetzen und übersetzt werden," given at the International Congress of Literary Translators in Hamburg. © Hans Erich Nossack 1965. All rights reserved by Suhrkamp Verlag, Frankfurt am Main.

erary scholarship and sociology, which live on such phenomena, should be aware of. There is, for each individual writer, something that seems to exist that could only be called a feeling of national solidarity with other members of the literary community, a feeling of citizenship in literature as a supranational and antinational and, one might add, ahistorical community. In certain moments this feeling of solidarity intensifies—most often as a defense against the recurring historical tendency to be dominated and controlled by one single ideology. It then becomes more important for the individual writer to advocate literature as a whole than to offer his own individual contribution to literature. Without this instinctive feeling of belonging, how can we explain that we often receive—across all temporal and linguistic barriers, from a single sentence of an author, even occasionally from an insignificant comment about the author—the message: aha! that's one of us speaking. Or to put it more sentimentally: that's a brother speaking. There is then still a language or a means of expression that can be understood without translation—even today in a highly bureaucratic world—and therein lies a great hope for humankind.

But being an aficionado of something does not guarantee quality. May heaven preserve us from such an idea, because that would only result in a dreadful, pretentious piece of work. It would be ideal, however, if every translator were in a position to love what he translates, if he had to translate only what appealed to him. We writers, who want to be translated, greatly depend upon this emotional, human element of translation. We assume that through this mode of translation more of ourselves and the intentions of our books will be communicated to the foreign reader than through a philologically exact translation. Indeed, the writing of a book is not only an intellectual process but also borders on a biological necessity for the author, and it is crucial that this be apparent in a vivid translation. No actor would normally be expected to attempt a role that is in opposition to his character, physical appearance, or age. Memorizing the part is not enough: what fascinates the audience and makes the role believable is the barely perceptible tension that comes from the attempt, always to no avail, to assimilate oneself into the role, that is, to give oneself over completely to the role and to be totally in love with it. Of course, considering the current economic conditions of the literary marketplace, I know that the ideals I demand from a translator are utopian. But can a person exist without utopias?

To repeat once more: a translated book that is merely gram-
matically correct is hardly more than a mannequin draped in the
colors of the foreign country. There is no breath of life. I know of
a recent German novel that has been translated into classical
French. The novel was strangled by this translation; it was neither
written nor conceived in classical German, but in a clean, contemporary, colloquial German that any one of us might use on the
street without sounding strange or appearing affected. Nobody
could believe any German today who tried to explain his problems
to us in the language of Kleist. One would prefer to interrupt him
impatiently and say: "Could you please make sense!" We are, of
course, very much aware that the French language has not
changed—or, as the purists maintain, deteriorated—to the same
extent as, for instance, English or German. We are envious of the
power of that French tradition, which prevents language from de-
teriorating to the purely utilitarian. However, a translator is in no
way forced to resort to Franglais or military slang, since there has
been a written nonclassical French language at least since Céline.

How did the transformation into such a classical costume
come about for the above-mentioned book? A professor emeritus
of German studies was engaged to produce the translation; his German proficiency was certainly better than the average German's but
was also very much a textbook German. The professor lacked a
certain instinct for the rhythm and atmosphere of the language,
and above all for its current pulse. Reality or, let's say, truth is today
no longer directly expressed either in life or in novels; a sense of
shame and an instinct for self-preservation has driven it into the
spaces between unimaginative and noncommittal sentences, into a
realm that cannot be explored with grammar alone. Unfortunately,
critics often make a great fuss when they discover three or four
mistakes in a book of five hundred pages, causing the entire translation to be seen by the casual reader as an immediate failure. This
is a gross injustice, and to put it bluntly, an unseemly pomposity
with respect to their own language proficiency. Mistakes should by
no means be defended, but let us not forget that often so-called
mistakes in translation are matters of interpretation that could be
debated for years. In the transferral of unusual metaphors, this is
almost always the case. I admit quite openly that as a reader I
would much prefer to accept a couple of insignificant mistakes,
which I possibly might not even notice, than a falsification of the
entire atmosphere of a book, which I cannot help but notice, even

if only because the book is a lifeless jumble and bores me. Thus I know today, for example—because I was enlightened by the philologists fifty years after my first reading of *Hamlet*—that the word "nunnery" in the English text was no longer used in its original sense even during Shakespeare's time and that the famous line "Ophelia, get thee to a nunnery," correctly translated into German, would have to read: "Ophelia, geh in ein Bordell" ["Ophelia, get thee to a bordello"]. In spite of this piece of scholarly information, Schlegel's translation, through which Hamlet has become a living character for the German public over the last one hundred and fifty years, survives. Nothing against philology, but a philologist who is not prepared to discard the results of his cumulative research for the sake of another living being is like the attorney who considers his marriage perfect because he strictly follows the relevant paragraphs of the law.

When I was young, no one told me that, more than anything else, translating would require being able to speak and write in one's native language. Evidently this is considered an obvious statement; however, that assumption is unfortunate and, as everyone knows, misleading. Again and again one comes across translations considered to be authoritative simply because they were done by language experts who can actually prove that they know all the nuances of the other language and speak it as fluently as a native since they have lived and worked in the country for twenty or thirty years. But to master a foreign language at the level of a certified simultaneous translator by no means indicates the ability to properly serve the native tongue. One can destroy a work of art from a foreign language much more decisively with awkward and incorrect English—or whichever other target language might be appropriate—than with one or the other translation error. The task is to put a readable book in the hands of the reader, not an amateurish rough draft in which one stumbles at every turn over Anglicisms, Germanisms and other "isms" from Romance languages in participial phrases and other similar syntactical constructions. It is sometimes so bad that while reading one experiences the involuntary urge to go to the trouble of retranslating a translated passage back into the original source language in order to get closer to the sense of it. Just to mention a small, rather absurd example of this: dialogues translated from English into German—and not only from detective novels—are consistently translated using the phrase "ich schätze" for "I guess." No German would ever say "ich schätze" in such conversations; he would be considered extremely odd. Depending on the pace of the dialogue, a German would probably say "ich nehme an" or "vermutlich." Detective novels in particular have a pace that is incredibly fast, so it becomes especially important that the pace not be broken by unwieldy idioms. However, in the dictionary one finds "I guess" for "ich schätze," so the expression is technically correct. Unfortunately though, the dictionaries and lexicons are never sufficient when one attempts to render a dynamic situation.

I have gained a valuable insight from the few translations I have done, and I always try to pass it on to younger writers. I advise them—most probably in vain, who pays attention to advice, anyway?—that they should try translating at least once, without any intentions of becoming a professional translator, just for the discipline it requires. One does not necessarily learn more about the foreign language but rather learns to use one's native language more precisely. In order to find an equivalent in one's own language for a foreign metaphor or to communicate a foreign linguistic gesture with a corresponding expression, one is forced to use words that do not belong to his normal vocabulary. The translator's working vocabulary exceeds his personal vocabulary by more than double. Seen in this way, translation is practical training for every writer in the use of available material; he learns to recognize the riches of his own language and to make use of its flexibility. As I have mentioned before, writing in itself is, after all, already translation.

But you are aware of all these things—excuse me for even bringing them up. I only do it in order to satisfy my obligation to the title given my remarks in the program, "Translating and Being Translated." A great many relevant comments have been made about the splendor and the misery of translation, and whatever needs to be said again about translation—in order not to have the art of translation degenerate—does not belong in a speech such as this, but to commissions and committees of experts. Nevertheless, I would like to draw your attention to the relatively new appearance of a very objectionable practice related to the misery of translation—the tendency of foreign publishers to seek to exploit the success of a book that has just become a "bestseller" in the original language by insisting on an all too hasty translation. There have been a few cases in recent years in which the translations were so horrible that the original writers felt compelled to file legal suits to prevent a second printing of these thrown-together translations of their works. We should all be on guard against such practices that discredit literature as a whole. As much as we all like to earn money, we should remember that literature is not practiced to produce consumer articles. For that we have more profitable industries, including unfortunately the military.

Yet even this topic falls within the purview of commissions. Please allow me then to present my own translation of the title, "Translating and Being Translated," in order to transfer it from the level of professional translating onto a much more important level where translating is a moral activity or, in case that adjective is suspect, where translating is a human activity that has wide-reaching effects outside the narrow realm of literature.

It is said that the Germans translate a great deal, much more than other peoples. I do not know the exact statistics, but I tend to think the claim is accurate based on the fact that, when I was young, my education consisted more of foreign literature in translation than of that of my own country. This fact can be seen as both an advantage and a disadvantage. It is an advantage to the extent that interest in foreign literatures indicates an open-mindedness and can result in a continuous revision of one's own literature, preventing a lapse into a self-complacent nationalism or stagnating provincialism. It is a disadvantage to the extent that a one-sided, snobbish admiration of foreign literature reflects an inherent weakness: an insecure society and oppressive, overcompensatory feelings of inferiority. The image in the mirror is unsatisfying, so one primps and preens in foreign feathers. As a result, in current discussions of German books, for example, pedantic judgments such as "Not as good as Camus" or "Huxley said that much better" or "This author doesn't live up to Faulkner" can often be read. What a nonsensical standard! Maybe the writer had no intention of living up to Faulkner. Besides, it is just cheap name-dropping. The reading public learns how widely read the critic is, which was not even in question, but learns nothing at all about the book, the writer, the writer's intentions and whether or not they have been realized to some or any degree. A French attorney in Bordeaux asked me once, as we were discussing Europe and de Gaulle, "Would you please explain to me why it is that the Germans are always either Marxists or Americans? Why can't you just be yourselves?" An extremely sensitive and painful question, which touches on our historical ambivalence. However, this might be considered a purely

German affair, which we must cope with alone. Being German is not always easy and is everything but a recommendation.

However, what matters here is that in today's world the act of translating carries out a mission—a mission that is erroneously considered unproductive by the established communication media and censored or even completely repressed as undesirable by the presumptuous world of politics. It is probably vanity that makes it impossible even to admit that there could be other needs besides political or economic ones. For this reason translation represents a means of exchanging news between one human being and another, a kind of underground radio station used by partisans of humanity throughout the world to send news of their endangered existence, almost without hope of being heard because the jamming signals are so much stronger. The retreat into the life of the partisan is not a political act—that would only be seeing the situation superficially. Quite frankly, politics has not been humanity's main enemy for a long time now. Political and ideological differences are interchangeable pretensions that mask a much more dangerous tendency. The real enemy of humanity today, all over the world, is an all-consuming abstraction, which is a product of something called the system: the system is a means to its own end, independent of political affiliation, and reduces the human being to a well-oiled cog of the system in his every waking moment. It was once possible to revolt against social orders or dictatorships; even if the revolution itself failed, it still made sense. Rebellion in this historical sense is not possible against the dictatorship of the system, however; revolutions are a planned part of the system and are simply diverted into demonstrations of manageable proportions. A methodical and calculated change in the machinery is accomplished, yet the system remains the system. In this inhuman situation, which has only recently become so absolutely inhuman, there is just one thing left for a person to do if he wants to preserve the fiber of his being and escape the reach of the machinery—to wear the cloak of compliance with the system: that is, outwardly follow the system's prescribed behavior in each situation and inwardly retreat into the exile of silence. Just satisfy the system, give it what it wants, and everyone will leave you alone! People all over the world instinctively act according to this principle in the hope that, through the total separation of humans and system, the machine will run itself into nothingness, overheat out of its sense of futility, and in some absurd way destroy itself. An incredible risk, but since when has humanity not been a risk?

It is the task of all who attempt to create literature, whether they be writers or translators, to make this silence perceptible. Let's consider for a moment exactly what it is that appeals to us about a book written in another country, in another language—even in another time. It is not the folklore or the exotic elements. That is all at best interesting, and like everything interesting, magazines and travel agencies will jump at the chance to make a profit from it. It is not the foreign way of dressing that we simply accept as a costume. It is not the foreign living habits that differ from our own. It is not the foreign religions, foreign ideologies, foreign institutions. As I said before, that is all very interesting and informative material for comparative studies. But, like everything that is merely interesting, it is subject to fashionable trends and is quite transitory. However, we as readers immediately understand something over and above these superficialities: to use a hackneyed phrase, we recognize that things are no different anywhere else, which relieves us momentarily of our sense of isolation as human individuals. We recognize that human conflicts are the same everywhere, however perfect or however strange the façades of our institutions are. We recognize that behind the polished platitudes of the megaphones, which we obediently respect in order not to stand out in the crowd, there is another means of communication, one much more realistic than the "realism" of the system. In other words, another language does exist beyond that of official jargon—one that alone remains human. It is the great chance of today's translators to transfer this language and thereby preserve and strengthen the supranational and supraideological community of human beings.

In order to avoid being abstract myself about such a passionate appeal, let me demonstrate what I mean with two short and concrete examples. Examples should always be as simple as possible if they are to be valid. There are a few cases (the actual number is irrelevant, thank goodness) in which former prisoners of war have corresponded with their captors, in which these so-called enemies have exchanged invitations and visited one another, even become godfathers of each other's children. They do not visit only the country in which they were held prisoner, or the people or the nation that caused them so much suffering, but instead they visit a person, a human being, who was their enemy due to the circumstances at the time and, yet, whom they spontaneously recognized as a human being with exactly the same existential desires as their own. And it is important to point out that all of this happened without even understanding the foreign language, perhaps through just one single human gesture, which remains unnoticed in the political arena. Supposedly, if one can rely on the trial transcripts, there were even cases in the concentration camps where SS guards inconspicuously dropped cigarettes in front of a prisoner. This is not meant to minimize or sentimentalize the atrocities. However, these vestiges of human response in an inhuman situation are indications of a silent language whose significance cannot be overestimated, because it can be understood without translation and gives us the hope that a place does exist where resistance is possible, where the phraseology of the system is not a viable commodity in the market.

The second example has to do with a book that was written by a Japanese doctor, Dr. Nagai, and has the German title *Wir waren dabei in Nagasaki* [We Were There in Nagasaki]. When something catastrophic like the dropping of an atomic bomb happens, we read about it in our daily newspapers around the world, far away from the actual occurrence, and we feel alarmed and shocked. We ask a neighbor or a co-worker at the office, "Did you read about . . . ?" but his reaction at best is to babble something incoherent to hide his shock. Something has happened that words cannot convey. A few days later we see a news report showing us the extent of the destruction—it seems like a nightmare. We hear the death count and how many are wounded. The statistics swell with pride at their own exactness, and our registration of their cold-bloodedness increases our own feeling of impotence. Reports from doctors come, telling us about the new way of dying that radiation has brought with it and warning us about possible future genetic damage. All of this cannot simply become reality for us; it overtaxes our imagination and experience. The numbers are too large; what we hear about genetics is too abstract. The actual experience of having only one single personal acquaintance who died in the catastrophe would be sufficient to give us a better understanding of what happened than statistics and expert opinions could ever communicate.

That is the function of the Japanese doctor's book: he gives us a report from personal experience rather than a series of so-called facts. He lets ten of his relatives—simple people who by chance survived the catastrophe—tell their stories, among them his own five-year-old daughter. The child's story begins with the words, "Suddenly the crickets stopped singing," and concludes with the line, "In the afternoon the crickets began to sing again." There is hardly anything more moving than this naive observation. This is not literature, this is not a sensational report, this is the message of a helpless human being. What is characteristic of these ten people, or rather what it is that they have in common, is that they have no words to describe the facts; they have no idea what to do with the accident of their survival, so they simply blame themselves for it. Their narratives are like a porcelain cup with a crack so that it no longer rings when it is tapped. Each of us who has seen a large city after it has been totally destroyed—like the one in which we are guests today—understands this type of toneless language immediately. We understand the absolute helplessness and the guilt of having failed, which cannot be comforted by conventional means. The experience does not consist of the number of dead or the destruction of cities, but of the completely new fact that in a matter of seconds all of our habits and securities can prove insufficient to survive this experience. No religion, no ideology, no previous truth up to now, not to mention governments or police, are capable of helping a person in the face of a suicidal experience of absolute destruction; if it happens that he does survive in spite of it all, then it is more than likely because of a careful kind of sleepwalking. And no reconstruction is capable of erasing the complete meaninglessness of the reality of the experience. Humans the world over seem to have developed a new form of *Résistance* against the negative reality. Respect for humanity requires literature to be silent about it yet convey the silence perceptibly between the lines.

But how would I have ever known about this Japanese book if it had not been translated? I mentioned earlier that I was brought up with literature in translation, with Strindberg, Stendhal, and, of course, Dostoyevsky, who influenced my entire generation. These masters were long deceased when they taught me; I have never been able to thank them personally. However, I owe the fact that they could influence me so vitally to their translators, who were still living as I was growing up. Yet, I never thanked them either. I was too young and just took it for granted that books would be translated.

I know now that translating is more than just a way to earn a living, that translating is a demanding occupation, which benefits some person out there who is lost in the labyrinth of the system. Above all it benefits those persons who are as young as I was then and searching for their own way.

Today I would like to make up at last for my earlier omission by publicly extending my gratitude to all translators.

BIOGRAPHIES OF ESSAYISTS

WALTER BENJAMIN (1892–1940). Benjamin was a German philosopher, essayist, and critic who received his Ph.D. at Bern. He worked as a freelance writer and translator in Berlin before he emigrated to Paris in 1933. He took his own life in 1940. Selections of Benjamin's writings in English translation can be found in *Illuminations*, edited by Hannah Arendt and translated by Harry Zohn (1955) and *Reflections: Essays, Aphorisms, Autobiographical Writings*, edited by Peter Demetz (1978).

YVES BONNEFOY (b. 1923). Bonnefoy is a poet, essayist, educator, and translator. Since the appearance of his first volume of poetry, *Du Mouvement et de l'immobilité de Douve*, in 1953, Bonnefoy has been widely declared the most important French poet since Valéry. Among his poetic works available in English translation are *On the Motion and Immobility of Douve, Written Stone, The Lure of the Threshold*, and *In the Shadow's Light*. Also renowned as a translator, Bonnefoy's translations into French include several plays by Shakespeare and the poetry of Yeats. *Quarante-cinq poèmes de W. B. Yeats* was published in 1989. The University of Chicago Press published *The Act and the Place of Poetry* (1989), a collection of Bonnefoy's essays in English translation. Currently, Bonnefoy holds the Valéry Chair for poetry at the Collège de France.

JACQUES DERRIDA (b. 1930). Derrida is a philosopher, literary theorist, and translator. He is best known as the father of the deconstructionist school of literary theory and criticism. He is a professor of philosophy at the École des Études en Sciences Sociales in Paris. Among his best-known works are *Of Grammatology*, published by Johns Hopkins University Press in 1976, and *Writing and Difference* (1978), published by the University of Chicago Press.

JOHN DRYDEN (1631–1700). Dryden was a poet, playwright, and translator. He served as poet laureate under Charles II and James II, but lost this position when Protestant William III assumed the throne in 1688. At that time, Dryden turned seriously to translating. His most notable efforts include the following works: the *Satires of Juvenal and Persius* (1692), the *Works of Virgil* (1697), and the *Fables*, which consists of a collection of works by Ovid, Boccaccio, and Chaucer.

HUGO FRIEDRICH (1904–79). Friedrich has distinguished himself as one of the outstanding scholars of Romance languages and literatures. His book *Die Struktur der modernen Lyrik* (*The Structure of Modern Poetry*) is without doubt one of the most illuminating studies written on the interpretation and understanding of modern poetry. He has also written studies on Montaigne, Flaubert, Balzac, and Calderón. From 1937 until his retirement, he was Professor of Romance Languages at the University of Freiburg in Germany.

JOHANN WOLFGANG VON GOETHE (1749–1832). As one of the strongest promoters of world literature in the nineteenth century, Goethe was naturally very much interested in translation. The comments reprinted in this collection from the *East-West Divan* are considered a major contribution to the history of translation theory.

WILHELM VON HUMBOLDT (1767–1835). Humboldt was a statesman, humanist, and linguistic scholar in Potsdam, Germany. His younger brother was the scientist and explorer Alexander von Humboldt. He studied Greek, philosophy, natural sciences, and political economy. Through his friendship with Friedrich Schiller and Johann Wolfgang von Goethe, he came into contact with contemporary aesthetic problems. From 1802 to 1807 he served as Prussian Ambassador to the Vatican. In 1808 he was appointed to the ministry of religion and educational affairs in Berlin, where he was chiefly responsible for the founding of the University of Berlin. Humboldt wrote several important essays on the study of Greek antiquity, the comparative study of anthropology, and the task of the historian. Humboldt's language studies represent his chief legacy to posterity and, as Ernst Cassirer said, marked a new epoch in the history of the philosophy of language.

ROMAN JAKOBSON (1896–1982). Jakobson was born in Moscow and was educated at the renowned Lazarev Institute of Oriental Languages and Moscow University. He linked the study of language with that of literature and folklore. He was also associated with avant-garde painters and poets, such as V. V. Mayakovsky. Jakobson came to the United States in 1941. He taught at Harvard and MIT. He received honorary degrees from twenty-six universities and was an honorary member of nearly thirty learned societies. The best examples of his writing are contained in the seven-volume *Works: Selected Writings.*

VLADIMIR NABOKOV (1899–1977). Nabokov was a Russian and American novelist, short-story writer, poet, essayist, and translator. His family emigrated from Russia in 1919, and he attended Cambridge University, where he received a degree in Slavic and Romance literatures. He arrived in the United States in 1940 and went on to teach at Cornell. After publishing *Lolita* in 1958 he moved to Switzerland. There his Russian novels were translated under his close supervision, making Nabokov one of the most widely read contemporary Russian authors. His *Lectures on Russian Literature* was published in 1981 to great critical acclaim.

FRIEDRICH NIETZSCHE (1844–1900). Nietzsche was a German philosopher and poet. He received an excellent classical education, and studied theology and classical philology. As a student at Leipzig, Nietzsche discovered Schopenhauer and Richard Wagner, the two greatest influences on his early thought. At the age of twenty-four he was appointed associate professor of Classical Philology at the University of Basel. Among Nietzsche's best-known works are *The Birth of Tragedy* (1872) and *Thus Spake Zarathustra* (1891).

HANS ERICH NOSSACK (1901–77). Nossack was a German short-story writer, novelist, playwright, critic, and translator. During the Nazi period in Germany he was not allowed to publish his work because of his collaboration with the Resistance. When Hamburg suffered almost total destruction in 1943, he lost all of his accumulated manuscripts, notes and diaries, as well as his home and personal belongings. He was a Georg-Büchner Prize winner in 1961 for his own fiction, and he translated Joyce Cary and Sherwood Anderson into German. He returned to Hamburg in 1969 and died there in 1977.

JOSÉ ORTEGA Y GASSET (1883–1955). Ortega y Gasset was a Spanish philosopher, essayist, and cultural critic who received his Ph.D. from the University of Madrid, where he was Professor of Metaphysics until 1936. In 1923 he founded the *Revista de Occidente,* one of the most influential journals in the Spanish-speaking world. He died in Madrid in 1955. His most famous books include *The Revolt of the Masses* (tr. 1932), *The Dehumanization of Art* (tr. 1948), and *Meditations on Quixote* (tr. 1961).

OCTAVIO PAZ (b. 1914). Paz is Mexico's outstanding man of letters and winner of the Nobel Prize for Literature in 1990. His writings include poetry, literary criticism, philosophy, anthropology, art history, and cultural, social, and political commentary. From 1932 to 1937 Paz studied at the National University of Mexico. In 1944 he received a Guggenheim Fellowship, which allowed him to spend a year in the United States. At that time he encountered the works of T. S. Eliot, Ezra Pound, William Carlos Williams, Wallace Stevens, and e.e. cummings. In 1946 he joined the Mexican diplomatic service and was sent to Paris where he met Jean-Paul Sartre, Albert Camus, Jules Supervielle, and many others. He stayed in the diplomatic service for the next twenty years. In 1962 he was appointed ambassador to India, a post from which he resigned in 1968 in protest against the Mexican government's overreaction to student riots. In 1971 he founded the journal *Plural*, published until 1976, when he founded his current literary and cultural periodical, *Vuelta*. Paz has published numerous collections of essays and poetry and has translated a number of British and American poets into Spanish.

Ezra Pound (1885–1972). Pound, although well-known as a poet, was also a translator and critic of great significance in the development of twentieth-century thinking. His translations are collected in the volume, *Ezra Pound: Translations*. T. S. Eliot selected and introduced a volume of his literary essays, entitled *Literary Essays of Ezra Pound*, which was published by New Directions in 1954 and reprinted in paperback in 1968.

Michael Riffaterre (b. 1924). Riffaterre received degrees from the University of Lyons and the University of Paris, and a Ph.D. from Columbia University where he served as professor and chair of the French Department. The editor of the *Romanic Review* since 1971, Riffaterre is currently Director of Dartmouth College's School of Criticism and Theory. His books in English include *Semiotics of Poetry* (1980), *Text Production* (1983), and *Fictional Truth* (1989).

Dante Gabriel Rossetti (1828–82). Rossetti was a poet, painter, and translator. His contributions to nineteenth-century aesthetics include not only his own paintings, poems, and his founding of the Pre-Raphaelite Brotherhood, but also his translation and dissemination of many early Italian poets published as *Dante and His Circle*. Included in this collection are poems by Dante, Cavalcanti, and Degli Uberti.

Friedrich Schleiermacher (1768–1834). Schleiermacher studied theology and became Professor of Theology at the University of Berlin in 1810, where for the remainder of his life he taught dogmatic theology, new testament theology and criticism, hermeneutics, practical theology, history of philosophy, ethics, and dialectics. He was particularly interested in building a philosophy of culture, and in the role of language in culture.

Henry Gilius Schogt (b. 1927). Schogt was born in Amsterdam. He received his M.A. in French and Russian and his Ph.D. in French from the University of Utrecht. Currently, he is professor of French and Linguistics at the University of Toronto. To date, his only book translated into English is *Linguistics, Literary Analysis, and Literary Translation*, published by the University of Toronto Press in 1988.

ARTHUR SCHOPENHAUER (1788–1860). Schopenhauer was a German philosopher. His mother was a novelist who established a salon in Weimar, which allowed him to come in contact with a number of literary figures, including Goethe. Schopenhauer entered the University of Göttingen as a medical student studying, among other subjects, physics, chemistry, and botany. In 1811 he left Göttingen for Berlin, at that time the philosophical center of Germany, where he attended lectures by Fichte and Schleiermacher. His principal work is *The World as Will and Idea* (1818).

PETER SZONDI (1929–71). Szondi was the head of the Institute for General and Comparative Literature at the Free University of Berlin at the time of his death in 1971. A collection of his essays, *On Textual Understanding* (1986), and his study of drama entitled *Theory of the Modern Drama* (1987) were published by the University of Minnesota Press.

PAUL VALÉRY (1871–1945). Valéry was a poet, philosopher, essayist, critic, dramatist, and translator. He is widely acclaimed as the most important French poet of the twentieth century. His *Collected Works* in English translation comprise fifteen volumes. As a translator, Valéry brought out *Les Bucoliques de Virgile* in classical French verse. He also translated selections of Poe's *Marginalia* which he published as *Fragments des Marginalia* together with his own commentary. He served as Professor of Poetry at the Collège de France from 1937 until his death in 1945.

SELECT BIBLIOGRAPHY

1680–1711

Dryden, John. Preface to his translation of *Ovid's Epistles*. 1680.

———. Preface to *Sylvae: or, the Second Part of Poetical Miscellanies*. 1685.

———. Dedication to his translation of the *Aeneis*. 1697.

———. Preface to his translation of the *Fables*. 1700.

———. "The Life of Lucian." 1711.

1715

Pope, Alexander. Preface to his translation of the *Iliad*.

1763

D'Alembert, J. L. "Essai de traduction de quelques morceaux de Tacite." In *Mélanges de littérature III*. Paris.

1751–65

D'Alembert, J. L., and Diderot, Denis. "La traduction." In *Encyclopédie ou dictionnaire raisonné des sciences, des arts, et des métiers*, 16:510–12. Paris and Neufchatel.

1790

Tytler, Alexander Fraser. *Essay on the Principles of Translation*. Edinburgh. Repr. Edinburgh: Neill & Co., 1813.

1791

Cowper, William. Preface to his translation of *The Iliad of Homer*.

1800

Schopenhauer, Arthur. "Über Sprache und Worte." In *Parerga und Paralipomena*. Reprinted in *Sämmtliche Werke*, ed. Julius Frauenstädt, vol. 6, chap. 25, sec. 309, pp. 601–7. Leipzig: Brockhaus, 1891.

1813

Schleiermacher, Friedrich. "Über die verschiedenen Methoden des Übersetzens." Berlin. Reprinted in *Schleiermachers Sämtliche Werke, III. Zur Philosophie*. Berlin: Reimer, 1838.

1816

Humboldt, Wilhelm von. "Einleitung zu *Agamemnon*." In *Aeschylos Agamemnon metrisch übersetzt*. Leipzig.

Staël-Holstein, Anne Louise Germanie (Mme. de). "De l'esprit des traductions." Paris. Reprinted in *Oeuvres complètes*, 17: 387–97. Paris: Treuttel et Würtz Libraires, 1821.

1819

Goethe, Johann Wolfgang von. "Übersetzungen." In *Noten und Abhandlungen zum bessern Verständnis des west-östlichen Divans*. Stuttgart.

1826

Burnouf, J. L. *De la traduction*. Paris.

1827

Goethe, Johann Wolfgang von. "Letter to Carlyle, 20 July." Reprinted in *Goethe-Briefe*. Berlin: D. Eisner, 1902–5.

1861

Arnold, Matthew. "On Translating Homer." London. Reprinted in *Essays Literary and Critical*. Introduction and Notes by W. H. D. Rouse. London: John Murray, 1905.

Newman, Francis W. *Homeric Translation in Theory and Practice: A Reply to Matthew Arnold*. London: Williams and Northgate.

Rossetti, Dante Gabriel. Preface, in *The Early Italian Poets*.

1864

Hugo, Victor. "Préface pour la nouvelle traduction de Shakespeare." Reprinted in *Oeuvres complètes, Oeuvres critiques complètes,* ed. F. Bouvet. Paris, 1963.

1882

Nietzsche, Friedrich. "Übersetzungen." In *Die fröhliche Wissenschaft*. Leipzig. Reprinted in *Werke in drei Bänden (Band 2)*. Section 83, p. 91f. Munich: Hanser, 1962.

1886

Mommsen, Tycho. *Die Kunst des Übersetzens fremdsprachlicher Dichtungen ins Deutsche*. Frankfurt.

Nietzsche, Friedrich. "Zum Problem des Übersetzens." In *Jenseits von Gut und Böse*. Leipzig: C. G. Naumann. Reprinted in *Werke in drei Bänden (Band 2)*. Section 28, p. 593f. Munich: Hanser, 1962.

1892

Keller, J. *Die Grenzen der Übersetzungskunst*. Karlsruhe.

1893

Bellanger, Justin. *Histoire de la Traduction en France*. Paris. Reprinted by Alphonse Lemerre Editeur, 1903.

1896

Cauer, Paul. *Die Kunst des Übersetzens*. Berlin: Weidmann.

1914

Fränzel, Walter. *Geschichte des Übersetzens im 18. Jahrhundert*. Leipzig: R. Voigtlander Verlag. Special Issue of *Beiträge zur Kultur-Universalgeschichte* 25, ed. Karl Lamprecht.

1917–18

Pound, Ezra. "Notes on Elizabethan Classicists." In *Egoist* 4, nos. 8–11. Reprinted in *Literary Essays of Ezra Pound*, Ed. and with an introduction by T. S. Eliot. Norfolk, CN: New Directions, 1954. The original essay was serialized in the *Egoist* and appeared in vol. 4, nos. 8–11, 1917 and vol. V, no. 1, 1918.

1918

Ritchie, R. L. G., and Moore, J. M. *Translation from the French*. Cambridge: Cambridge University Press.

1919

Phillimore, J. S. "Some Remarks on Translation and Translators." *The English Association Pamphlet* 3, no. 42. Oxford: Oxford University Press.

1920

Amos, Flora Ross. *Early Theories of Translation*. New York: Columbia University Press.
Pound, Ezra. "Translators of Greek: Early Translators of Homer." In *Instigations*. Reprinted in *Literary Essays of Ezra Pound*. Ed. and with an introduction by T. S. Eliot. Norfolk, CN: New Directions, 1954. This essay was composed of parts of an earlier series that originally appeared in the *Egoist* 5(7–9), 1918, and 6(1–2), 1919.

1922

Postgate, J. P. *Translation and Translations: Theory and Practice*. London: G. Bell and Sons.

1923

Benjamin, Walter. "Die Aufgabe des Übersetzers." In *Baudelaire: Tableaux parisiens*. Heidelberg. Reprinted in *Schriften*, ed. Theodor Adorno et al., 1:40–54. Frankfurt: Suhrkamp Verlag, 1955.

1924

Belloc, Hilaire. "On Translation." In *London Mercury* 10: 150ff. London. Reprinted in *A Conversation with an Angel and other Essays* (London, 1929) and *On Translation: The Taylorian Lecture* (Oxford: Clarendon Press, 1931).

1925

Vossler, Karl. *Geist und Kultur der Sprache* [*The Spirit of Language in Civilization*]. Munich. Tr. Oscar Oeser. London: Kegan Paul, Trench, Trubner and Co., 1932.

1926

Rosenzweig, Franz. *Die Schrift und Luther*. Berlin: Lambert Schneider.

1927

Conley, C. H. *The First English Translators of the Classics*. New Haven: Yale University Press.
Schadewaldt, Wolfgang. "Das Problem des Übersetzens." In *Die Antike* 3.

1928

Lemonnier, Leon. *Les Traducteurs d'Edgar Poe en France de 1845 à 1875: Charles Baudelaire*. Paris: Presses Universitaires de France.

1930

Smith, F. Seymour. *The Classics in Translation: An Annotated Guide to the Best Translations of the Greek and Latin Classics into English*. London: Charles Scribner's Sons.

1931

Matthiessen, F. O. *Translation: An Elizabethan Art*. Cambridge: Harvard University Press. Repr. New York: Octagon Books, 1965.

1932

Richards, I. A. *Mencius on the Mind: Experiments in Multiple Definition*. New York: Harcourt, Brace and Company.

1933

Lathrop, H. B. *Translations from the Classics into English from Caxton to Chapman 1477–1620*. University of Wisconsin Press.

Newald, Richard. *Deutscher Horaz in Fünf Jahrhunderten*. Berlin: Junker und Dunnhaupt Verlag.

Petersen, Julius, and Erich Trunz. *Lyrische Weltdichtung in deutschen Übertragungen aus sieben Jahrhunderten*. Berlin: Junker und Dunnhaupt Verlag.

1934

Pound, Ezra. "Guido's Relations." From "Cavalcanti," in *Make It New*. London: Faber and Faber.

Yates, Frances A. *John Florio: The Life of an Italian in Shakespeare's England*. Cambridge: Cambridge University Press.

1936

Bates, E. Stuart. *Modern Translation*. London: Oxford University Press.

1937

Ortega y Gassett, José. "Miseria y Esplendor de la Traducción." In *Obras Completas*. Madrid.

1941

Nabokov, Vladimir. "The Art of Translation." *New Republic* 105.

1943

Bates, E. Stuart. *Intertraffic: Studies in Translation*. London: Jonathan Cape.

1946

Larbaud, Valéry. *Sous l'invocation de Saint Jérôme*. Paris: Gallimard.

1947

Nida, Eugene A. *Bible Translating: An Analysis of Principles and Procedures, with Special Reference to Aboriginal Languages.* New York: American Bible Society.

1951

Knight, Douglas. *Pope and the Heroic Tradition: A Critical Study of his Iliad.* New Haven: Yale University Press.

1953

Auden, W. H. "Translation and Tradition: A Review of Ezra Pound's *Translations.*" *Encounter* 1:75–78.

Barzun, Jacques. "Food for the N.R.F." In *Partisan Review* 20:660–74.

Valéry, Paul. "Variations sur Les Bucoliques." In *Traduction en vers des Bucoliques de Virgile.* Paris.

1955

Frost, William. *Dryden and the Art of Translation.* New Haven: Yale University Press.

Mounin, Georges. *Les Belles infidèles.* Paris: Cahiers du Sud.

Nabokov, Vladimir. "Problems of Translation: *Onegin* in English." *Partisan Review* 22.

1956

Austin, R. G. "Some English Translations of Virgil: An Inaugural Lecture." Liverpool.

Cary, Edmond. *La traduction dans le monde moderne.* Geneva: Librairie de L'Université George & Cie S.A.

Leishman, J. B. *Translating Horace: Thirty Odes translated into the original metres with the Latin text and an Introductory and Critical Essay.* Oxford: Bruno Cassirer.

Rosenberg, Justus. "Constant Factors in Translation." In *On Romanticism and the Art of Translation: Studies in Honor of Edwin Hermann Zeydel.* Princeton: Princeton University Press.

1957

Knox, R. A. *On English Translation: The Romanes Lecture delivered in the Sheldonian Theatre 11 June 1957.* Oxford: Clarendon Press.

Levy, Jiri. *Ceske Theorie Prekladu.* Prague: Statni Nakladatelstvi Krasne Literatury, Hudby a Umeni.

Savory, Theodore. *The Art of Translation.* London. Repr. Boston: The Writer, Inc., 1968.

1958

Booth, A. D. et al., eds. *Aspects of Translation: Studies in Communication 2.* London: Secker and Warburg.

Jacobsen, Eric. *Translation: A Traditional Craft.* Copenhagen: Nordisk Forlag.

1959

Brower, Reuben A., ed. *On Translation*. Cambridge, Mass.: Harvard University Press.

Jakobson, Roman. "On Linguistic Aspects of Translation." In *On Translation*. Cambridge, Mass.: Harvard University Press.

1961

Arrowsmith, William, and Shattuck, Roger, eds. *The Craft and Context of Translation*. Austin: University of Texas Press.

1963

Bonnerot, L. *Chemins de la Traduction*. Paris: Didier.

Borst, Arno. *Der Turmbau von Babel: Geschichte der Meinungen über Ursprung und Vielfalt der Sprachen und Völker. Band IV Schlüsse und Übersichten*. Stuttgart: Anton Hiersemann.

Cary, Edmond. *Les Grands Traducteurs Français*. Geneva: Librairie de L'Université George & Cᶦᵉ S.A.

Cary, Edmond, and R. W. Jumpfelt. *Quality in Translation: Proceedings of the IIIrd Congress of the International Federation of Translators, Bad Godesberg, 1959*. New York: Macmillan.

Güttinger, Fritz. *Zielsprache: Theorie und Technik des Übersetzens*. Zürich: Manesse Verlag.

Mounin, Georges. *Les problèmes théoriques de la traduction*. Paris: Gallimard.

Störig, Hans Joachim. *Das Problem des Übersetzens*. Darmstadt: Wissenschaftliche Buchgesellschaft.

1964

Mounin, Georges. *La Machine à Traduire: Histoire des Problèmes Linguistiques*. The Hague: Mouton & Co.

Nida, Eugene. *Toward a Science of Translating with Special Reference to Principles and Procedures Involved in Bible Translating*. Leiden: E. J. Brill.

1965

Catford, J. C. *A Linguistic Theory of Translation: An Essay in Applied Linguistics*. London: Oxford University Press.

Friedrich, Hugo. "Zur Frage der Übersetzungskunst." Heidelberg.

Italiaander, Rolf, ed. *Übersetzen: Vorträge und Beiträge vom Internationalen Kongress literarischer Übersetzer in Hamburg 1965*. Frankfurt am Main: Athenäum Verlag. The essay by Hans Erich Nossack, "Translating and Being Translated," was originally published in this collection.

Kemp, Friedhelm. *Kunst und Vergnügen des Übersetzens*. Stuttgart: Günther Neske Pfullingen.

1966

Selver, Paul. *The Art of Translating Poetry*. Boston: The Writer, Inc.

1967

Kloepfer, Rolf. *Die Theorie der literarischen Übersetzung: Romanisch-deutscher Sprachbereich*. Munich: Wilhelm Fink.

Levy, Jiri. "Translation as a Decision Process." In *To Honor Roman Jakobson: Essays on the Occasion of his Seventieth Birthday, 11 October 1966*. Paris: Mouton.

Sdun, Winfried. *Probleme und Theorien des Übersetzens (in Deutschland vom 18. bis zum 20. Jahrhundert)*. Munich: Max Hueber Verlag.

1969

Nida, Eugene A., and Taber, Charles R. *The Theory and Practice of Translation*. Leiden: E. J. Brill.

Waley, Arthur. "Notes on Translation." *Delos* 3:159–69.

Wandruszka, Mario. *Sprachen: Vergleichbar und Unvergleichlich*. Munich: R. Piper & Co.

Wuthenow, Ralph-Rainer. *Das Fremde Kunstwerk: Aspekte der literarischen Übersetzung*. Göttingen: Vandenhoeck & Ruprecht.

1970

Day-Lewis, C. *On Translating Poetry: The Jackson Knight Memorial Lecture, University of Exeter 1969*. Abingdon-on-Thames: Abbey Press.

Holmes, James, editor. *The Nature of Translation: Essays on the Theory and Practice of Literary Translation*. The Hague: Mouton.

Nims, John Frederick. "Poetry: Lost in Translation?" *Delos* 5:108–26.

1971

Paz, Octavio. *Traducción: Literatura y Literalidad*. Barcelona: Tusquets.

Proetz, Victor. *The Astonishment of Words: An Experiment in the Comparison of Languages*. Austin: University of Texas Press.

Raffel, Burton. *The Forked Tongue: A Study of the Translation Process*. The Hague: Mouton.

Reiss, Katharina. *Möglichkeiten und Grenzen der Übersetzungskritik: Kategorien und Kriterien für eine sachgerechte Beurteilung von Übersetzungen*. Munich: Max Heuber Verlag.

Senger, Anneliese. *Deutsche Übersetzungstheorie im 18. Jahrhundert (1734–1746)*. Bonn: Bouvier Verlag Herbert Grundmann.

The World of Translation (Papers delivered at the Conference on Literary Translation, New York City in May, 1970). New York: PEN American Center.

1972

Haugen, Einar. *The Ecology of Languages: Essays by Einar Haugen*, selected and introduced by Anwar S. Dil. Stanford: Stanford University Press.

Koller, Werner. *Grundprobleme der Übersetzungstheorie: Unter besonderer Berücksichtigung schwedisch-deutscher Übersetzungsfälle*. Bern: Francke Verlag.

Mason, H. A. *To Homer Through Pope: An Introduction to Homer's Iliad and Pope's Translation*. New York: Barnes and Noble.

Szondi, Peter. "Poetik der Beständigkeit: Celans Übertragung von Shakespeares Sonnett 105." In *Celan-Studien*. Frankfurt.

Tate, Allan. *The Translation of Poetry: A Lecture*. Washington, D.C.: Library of Congress.

1973

Adams, Robert M. *Proteus: His Lies, His Truth: Discussions of Literary Translation.* New York: W. W. Norton.

Partridge, A. C. *English Biblical Translation.* London: Andre Deutsch.

1974

Allen, Leslie C. *The Greek Chronicles: The Relation of the Septuagint of I and II Chronicles to the Massoretic Text.* Leiden: E. J. Brill.

Walsh, Donald D. "Poets Betrayed by Poets." In *Fact and Opinion*, pp. 140–44.

1975

Davie, Donald. *Poetry in Translation.* Walton Hall, Milton Keynes: The Open University Press.

Steiner, George. *After Babel: Aspects of Language and Translation.* London: Oxford University Press.

Steiner, T. R. *English Translation Theory: 1650–1800.* Amsterdam: Van Gorcum.

1976

Bonnefoy, Yves. "La Traduction de la poésie" (Translating Poetry). *Entretiens sur la poésie.* Tr. John Alexander and Clive Wilmer. *PN Review* 48, 1985.

Brislin, Richard W., ed. *Translation: Applications and Research.* New York: Gardner Press.

Levy, Jiri. "The Translation of Verbal Art." In *Semiotics of Art.* Cambridge, Mass.: MIT Press.

Mounin, Georges. *Linguistique et traduction.* Bruxelles: Dessart et Mardaga.

Reiss, Katharina. *Texttyp und Übersetzungsmethode: Der operative Text.* Kronberg: Scriptor Verlag.

1977

Lefèvere, André. *Translating Literature: The German Tradition from Luther to Rosenzweig.* Amsterdam: Van Gorcum.

Wilss, Wolfram. *Übersetzungswissenschaft: Probleme und Methoden.* Stuttgart: Ernst Klett.

1978

Barnstone, Willis. "ABC's of Translation." *Translation Review* 2:35–36.

Beaugrande, Robert de. *Factors in a Theory of Poetic Translating.* Amsterdam: Van Gorcum.

Bellitt, Ben. *Adam's Dream: A Preface to Translation.* New York: Grove Press.

Kelly, L. G. *The True Interpreter: A History of Translation Theory and Practice in the West.* Oxford: Blackwell.

1980

Bassnett-McGuire, Susan. *Translation Studies.* London: Methuen.

Cohen, Jonathan. "*Neruda in English: A Critical History of the Verse Trans-*

lations and their Impact on American Poetry." Ph.D. diss., State University of New York at Stony Brook.

Felstiner, John. *Translating Neruda: The Way of Macchu Picchu.* Stanford: Stanford University Press, 1980.

Hawkes, David. "The Translator, The Mirror and the Dream: Some Observations on a New Theory." *Renditions* 13:5–20.

Stein, Dieter. *Theoretische Grundlagen der Übersetzungswissenschaft.* Tübingen: Gunter Narr Verlag.

Toury, Gideon. *In Search of a Theory of Translation.* Tel Aviv: The Porter Institute for Poetics and Semiotics.

Zuber, Ortun, ed. *Languages of the Theater: Problems in the Translation and Transposition of Drama.* Oxford: Pergamon Press.

1981

Gaddis-Rose, Marilyn, ed. *Translation Spectrum: Essays in Theory and Practice.* Albany: State University of New York Press.

Horguelin, Paul A. *Anthologie de la manière de traduire. Domaine Français.* Montreal: Linguatech.

Jones, Frank. "Translation: Fun or Folly?" *Georgia Review* 35(3):557–70.

1982

Larson, Mildred L. "Translation and Semantic Structure." *Estudios Filologicos* 17: 7–21.

Newmark, Peter. *Approaches to Translation.* Oxford: Pergamon Press.

Stolze, Radegundis. *Grundlagen der Textübersetzung.* Heidelberg: Julius Groos Verlag.

1983

Apel, Friedmar. *Literarische Übersetzung.* Stuttgart: J. B. Metzlersche Verlagsbuchhandlung.

Clayton, J. Douglas. "The Theory and Practice of Poetic Translation in Pushkin and Nabokov." *Canadian Slavic Papers* 25:(1):90–100.

Koller, Werner. *Einführung in die Übersetzungswissenschaft.* Heidelberg: Quelle & Meyer.

1984

Ballard, Michel, ed. *La Traduction de la Théorie à la Didactique.* Paris: University of Lille 3.

Berman, Antoine. *L'Epreuve de l'étranger: Culture et traduction dans l'Allemagne romantique.* Paris: Editions Gallimard.

Frawley, William, ed. *Translation: Literary, Linguistic, and Philosophical Perspectives.* Newark: University of Delaware Press.

Reiss, Katharina, and Vermeer, Hans J. *Grundlegung einer allgemeinen Translationstheorie.* Tübingen: Max Niemeyer Verlag.

1985

Gibbons, Reginald. "Poetic Form and the Translator." *Critical Inquiry* 11(4):654–71.

Graham, Joseph, ed. *Difference in Translation.* Ithaca: Cornell University

Press. The essay by Jacques Derrida, "Des Tours de Babel," was orig-
inally published in this collection.
Honig, Edwin. *The Poet's Other Voice: Conversations on Literary Translation.*
Amherst: University of Massachusetts Press.
Riffaterre, Michael. "Transposing Presuppositions on the Semiotics of Lit-
erary Translation." *Texte: Revue de Critique et de Théorie Littéraire*
4:99–110.
Schogt, Henry. "Semantic Theory and Translation Theory." *Texte: Revue
de Critique et de Théorie Littéraire* 4:151–60.
Schulte, Rainer. "Transferral of Poetic Frontiers: Renovation and Inno-
vation." *World Literature Today* 59(4):525–30.
Schulte, Rainer. "Translation and Reading." *Translation Review* 18.

1987

Larose, Robert. *Théories contemporaines de la traduction.* Québec: Presses
de l'Université du Québec.
Radice, William, and Reynolds, Barbara. *The Translator's Art: Essays in
Honour of Betty Radice.* Middlesex: Penguin Books.
Reiner, Erwin. *Aspekte der Übersetzung.* Vienna: Wilhelm Braumüller
Universitäts-Verlagsbuchhandlung.

1988

Newmark, Peter. *A Textbook of Translation.* New York: Prentice Hall.
Raffel, Burton. *The Art of Translating Poetry.* University Park: University
of Pennsylvania Press.
Schulte, Rainer. "Multiple Translations: An Interpretive Perspective."
Translation Review 28.
Snell-Hornby, Mary. *Translation Studies: An Integrated Approach.* Philadel-
phia: John Benjamins Publishing Co.
Worth, Valerie. *Practising Translation in Renaissance France: The Example
of Étienne Dolet.* Oxford: Clarendon Press.

1989

Biguenet, John and Rainer Schulte, eds. *The Craft of Translation.* Chicago:
University of Chicago Press.
Schulte, Rainer. "The Study of Translation: Re-creative Dynamics in Lit-
erature and the Humanities." *Mid-American Review* 9(2):69–80.
Warren, Rosanna. *The Art of Translation: Voices from the Field.* Boston:
Northeastern University Press.
Weissbort, Daniel, ed. *Translating Poetry: The Double Labyrinth.* Iowa City:
University of Iowa Press.